YAMAMOTO

Other books by Edwin P. Hoyt

YAMAMOTO

THE MAN
WHO PLANNED
PEARL HARBOR

Edwin P. Hoyt

McGraw-Hill Publishing Company

New York   St. Louis   San Francisco   Auckland   Bogotá   Hamburg
London   Madrid   Mexico   Milan   Montreal   New Delhi
Paris   São Paulo   Singapore   Sydney   Tokyo   Toronto

1 2 3 4 5 6 7 8 9 DOC DOC 9 5 4 3 2 1 0

ISBN 0-07-030626-5

Library of Congress Cataloging-in-Publication Data

Hoyt, Edwin Palmer.
  Yamamoto : the man who planned Pearl Harbor / by Edwin P. Hoyt.
    p. cm.
  ISBN 0-07-030626-5
  1. Yamamoto, Isoroku, 1884–1943. 2. Admirals—Japan—Biography.
3. Japan. Kaigun—Biography. I. Title.
DS885.5.Y3H68 1990
952.03′3′092—dc20
[B]   89-13169
                                                                CIP

Book design by Eve Kirch

CONTENTS

Contents

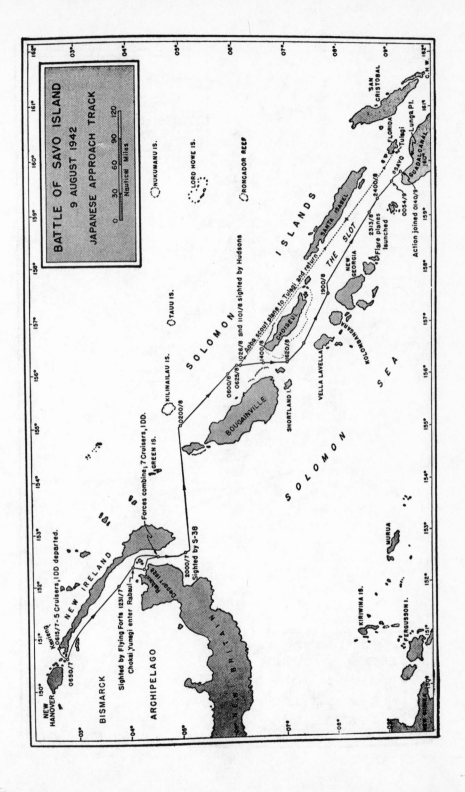

BATTLE OF SAVO ISLAND
9 AUGUST 1942
JAPANESE APPROACH TRACK

Nautical Miles
0   30   60   90   120

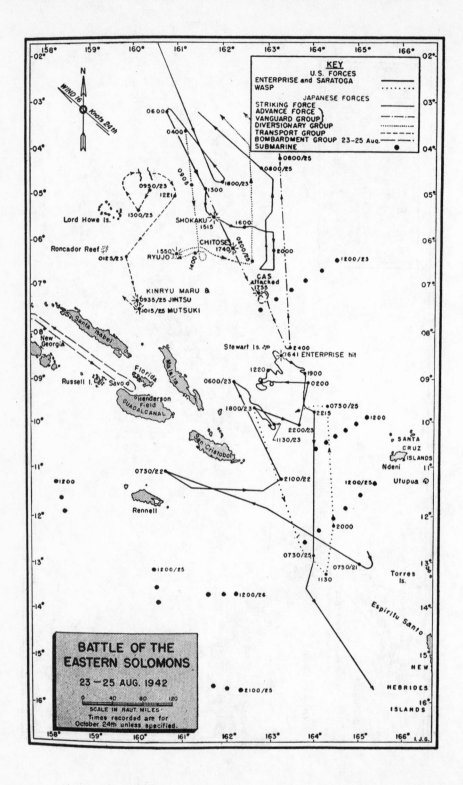

BATTLE OF THE
EASTERN SOLOMONS
23 – 25 AUG. 1942

SCALE IN NAUT. MILES

Times recorded are for
October 24th unless specified.

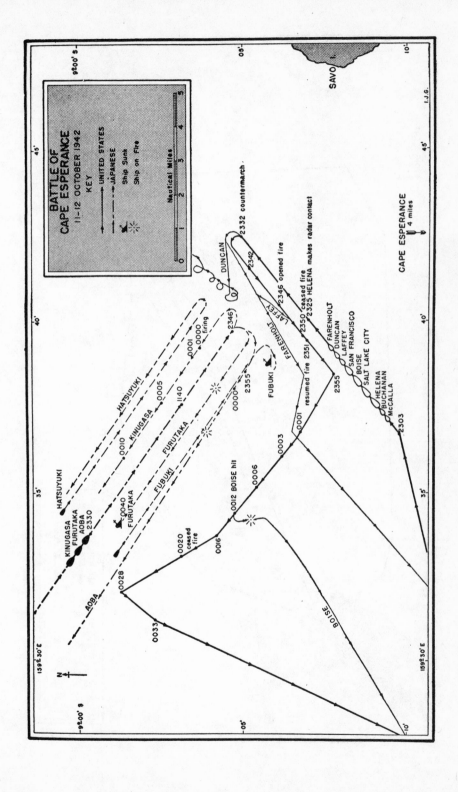

BATTLE OF
CAPE ESPERANCE
11–12 OCTOBER 1942
KEY

→ UNITED STATES
⟶ JAPANESE
Ship Sunk
Ship on Fire

Nautical Miles
0 1 2 3 4 5

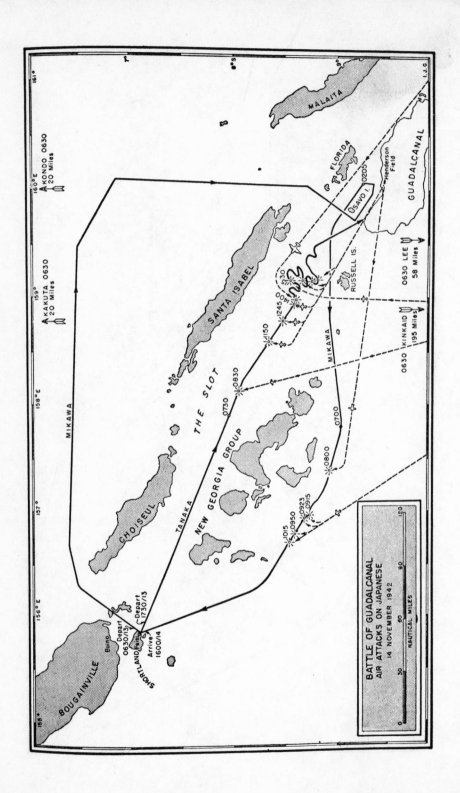

CROSSROADS

In the first six to twelve months of a war with the United States and Great Britain I will run wild and win victory upon victory. But then, if the war continues after that, I have no expectation of success.

—Admiral Yamamoto in an interview with Shigeharu Matsumoto, a member of the Japanese cabinet, 1940

1 Odd as it may seem, in the 1930s when Japan was arming furiously and seemed bent on the conquest of Asia, one of the most vigorous opponents of war was a young admiral who was generally regarded as the rising star of the Imperial Japanese Navy, Isoroku Yamamoto. He was a navy man through and through, and always a Japanese patriot. But he knew the United States and Great Britain as did few Japanese military or naval men, and far more than any others he recognized Japan's strategic inferiority to these great nations in terms of raw materials and financial staying power. For a dozen years—all the time that Admiral Yamamoto had been rising in the councils of the Empire—he had opposed any Japanese expansionism that would lead to war with the United States and Britain. Now, in August 1939, Yamamoto, who had been serving as vice minister of the navy, was appointed chief of the Combined Fleet, the operational head of Japan's fighting navy. The irony was that although Admiral Yonai, first as the navy minister and later Prime Minister, had been Yamamoto's mentor and was largely responsible for Yamamoto's views, these two men would be given the task of preparing Japan for just the war they hated.

In the past few years, the Imperial Japanese Army had been moving closer and closer to gaining absolute power over the Japanese govern-

1

ment. The Kwantung Army had first arranged the murder of Warlord Zhang Zoulin of Manchuria and then in 1931 had staged the "Mukden incident," a shooting along the South Manchurian railroad that had enabled the army to seize Manchuria. The army had continued its expansionism and had dragged the navy along with it. The war had begun with China. Admiral Yamamoto, as a principal advocate of naval air power, had found himself sending aircraft against China and deeply involved in the incident on the Yangtze River in 1938 when the American gunboat *Panay* had been sunk and two British gunboats had been attacked by Japanese air force planes.

Admiral Yamamoto had been aghast at the army's temerity, and his views had become very well known within the army and among that group of young naval officers who believed that it was Japan's destiny to rule Asia.

In the summer of 1939, a group of young naval officers began talking about Admiral Yamamoto and Admiral Yonai. Both of them, they said, ought to be eliminated as obstructionists. Since 1932, assassination had been a popular method of eliminating army and government officials who opposed the "young lions," so the threat was not to be taken lightly. Yamamoto was the most outspoken and thus the most likely target for assassination. A crisis arose when Germany and the Soviet Union signed a nonaggression treaty, which many in Japan thought was aimed at Japan. So the cabinet of Prime Minister Hiranuma collapsed (since Hiranuma favored close relations with Germany) and his cabinet members resigned with him. This meant that Admiral Yonai was out as minister of the navy. The admiral took the threat to Yamamoto's life so seriously that as Yonai's term came to an end he arranged for Yamamoto to head the Combined Fleet. This would take him out of a Tokyo government office and put him aboard the battleship *Nagato*, the Combined Fleet's flagship. Out of Tokyo he would be out of sight, and his views would no longer be heard in the streets.

And so on August 28, 1939, Admiral Yamamoto succeeded Admiral Zengo Yoshida as commander of the Combined Fleet. Commander Motoshige Fujita escorted Admiral Yoshida up to Tokyo from the fleet base at Kagashima.

On the morning of August 29, Admirals Yoshida and Yamamoto met at the home of Admiral Yonai, and on August 30 they were received at the Imperial Palace by Emperor Hirohito. The admirals came up to the palace gate in cars accompanied by men of the Kempeitai, or military police. These policemen were known to be spies of the army, which was on the verge of seizing total power over Japan. As Admiral Yamamoto emerged from the ceremonial greeting from the Emperor, he told his aide to get rid of the policemen. Since he was no longer vice minister of the navy, he pointed out, he was not entitled to a police escort. So the policemen were dismissed, and Admiral Yamamoto emerged from the scrutiny of the army into the safer hands of his own navy.

News of the appointment had spread through Tokyo, and as Admiral Yamamoto went to Tokyo station that day, hundreds of people came to see him off. He waited in the special room set aside for very important people and was escorted to the observation car of his train, where a red carpet had been laid out for him. At 1 P.M. the train pulled out of the station with Yamamoto on the observation platform giving a snappy salute to all his well-wishers and then waving his cap at them as the train gathered speed. Admiral Yamamoto, a handsome, athletic figure in his white uniform and medals, fifty-five years old and at the height of his powers, was off to a new adventure. There was no man in the Imperial Japanese Navy just then who was more suitable for command of the most modern naval fleet in the world, for from the beginning of the Japanese naval modernization program, Yamamoto had been deeply involved. Indeed, Yamamoto was responsible for Japan's emergence as the prime advocate of naval air power among the major fleets of the world.

Already Admiral Yamamoto was so well known in Japan that as the train headed for Osaka, crowds came out to the stations en route to have a look at him and, in Japanese fashion, to load him down with small gifts of cigarettes, sake, and food delicacies. He smiled and gestured his gratitude, and the train moved on: Yokohama, Shizuoka, Nagoya. At Nagoya the greetings ended, and the admiral changed from his formal uniform into a civilian suit. Reporters from the Nagoya *Chunichi Shimbun* and the Osaka *Mainichi Shimbun* boarded the train and sought interviews. The admiral, whose views were so well known, suddenly became shy and refused to comment. It would not be proper, he said, for an officer on active naval duty to mix in political matters. And from that point on, for the rest of his life, Admiral Yamamoto refused to discuss political affairs. His friends who had sought to save his life from assassination by getting him to sea had also silenced one of the most vigorous critics of a government that was moving headlong toward war.

From this point onward, too, Yamamoto confined his efforts to perfecting the Japanese carrier fleet as a first-strike weapon.

One of the problems all too apparent to Admiral Yamamoto in the summer of 1939 was the shortage of oil that dogged the fleet. Yamamoto had always been interested in oil; his childhood home, Nagaoka, was located in Niigata district, the major oil-producing area of Japan. When Yamamoto had gone abroad in the early 1920s to study at Harvard University, oil had been one of his major interests, and he had spent one long summer vacation touring the Mexican oilfields. Now, as commander in chief of the Combined Fleet, entrusted with the development and training of the Japanese navy as a fighting force, Yamamoto faced a perennial oil shortage so serious that it dominated the training schedule. The fleet seldom left the waters adjacent to Japan because there was not enough fuel to allow waste on a "show voyage" or anything like it.

For this reason, a great deal of the Imperial Navy's training was carried out ashore. The fleet practiced its gunnery at Cape Ashizuri, carrier landings in the Ise Bay, and torpedo firing in the Inland Sea. Yamamoto immediately toughened up the training program to the point that some of his forty thousand officers and sailors began to complain that the navy week had no weekends. But all Yamamoto's efforts were devoted to the creation of a completely efficient fighting machine. Thus the ships, when at sea, never stopped their training from the moment they upped anchor until the moment the anchor went down. Some ship captains really hated the moments of leaving and entering port, particularly at night because Yamamoto insisted that they become particularly efficient at after-dark operations, which—for four long weeks at a time—meant nightly travel along the shore without lights, catapulting and managing takeoffs and landings of aircraft from blacked out decks. One of the admirals of the fleet, Yuzuru Tayui, later recalled that when Yamamoto came to the fleet, the entire ambience immediately became geared to war. Of course, Japan was already engaged in a war, the "China incident" that had begun at Marco Polo bridge in the summer of 1937, but until this point, the naval forces not actually engaged off the China coast or in the rivers had lived on a peacetime schedule. No more.

In October of 1939, after his first month as commander in chief, Admiral Yamamoto held maneuvers in Hyuga Bay. The battle force, led by the flagship *Nagato*, sailed from Ariake Bay up the east coast of Kyushu Island. It was the job of the land-based naval air forces ashore to find and "destroy" the "invasion fleet." Lieutenant Commander Mitsuo Fuchida was the flight leader of the torpedo planes that came out to attack the fleet in the maneuvers.

In the night, while the flagship led the fleet up along the Japanese shore, Commander Fuchida's torpedo planes took off from their shore station. Twenty-seven torpedo bombers tailed the *Nagato* for miles and finally delivered their attack, scoring hits with all their twenty-seven torpedoes. They actually used live torpedoes, but these were set to pass beneath the ships. When they did so, the umpires scored hits, and in a real battle these would have been real explosions. It was as fine a training record as had ever been achieved. From the bridge of the *Nagato*, Admiral Yamamoto watched with satisfaction. For this method of attack, the torpedo planes were all products of his hard work over twenty years in the Japanese naval air service. He spoke about the results to his chief of staff: "It makes me wonder if they couldn't get Pearl Harbor," he said.

Two months later, as 1939 ended, the Combined Fleet was turned upside down at the behest of its new commander. Yamamoto did not have, and never would have, personal control over the posting of officers; this was the responsibility of the naval personnel service and was most closely guarded. But his word did have its effects, and so in the first week of 1940, the chief of staff, Rear Admiral Takahashi Ibo, was retired, and the senior staff officer under him, Captain Kono, also was retired. Rear Admiral Shigeru Fukudome became chief of staff, and a whole new crew of younger officers stepped forward.

And thus on New Year's Day 1940, Admiral Yamamoto looked up and saw the sun and composed a verse of haiku for the occasion:

> *Today as chief*
> *of the guardians of the seas*
> *of the land of the dawn,*
> *I gaze up in awe*
> *at the rising sun.*

Of course, the guardians of the seas were the navy, the land of the dawn was Japan, and the rising sun was the symbol of Japan from time immemorial. It was not great haiku—Admiral Yamamoto was much more a fighting man than a poet—but in the fashion of the Japanese, whenever Yamamoto was stirred by deep emotion, he unleashed it with poetry. He had been doing so for more than thirty-five years as a naval officer, and as a schoolboy in Nagaoka before that, and as Yamamoto very early in life showed himself to be a "comer," many of these poems were preserved.

The year 1940 was a worrisome one for Admiral Yamamoto, and it was well for him that he was at sea and out of the political sphere. The "fleet faction" of the navy was gaining power in the reflected glory of the young army officers who were pushing Japan toward war and alliance with Germany. General Hideki Tojo, who had been deputy war minister in 1938—holding the same position relative to the army that Yamamoto had held in the navy—had gone too far in a threatening speech to industrialists and was temporarily in disgrace. But not really. He and the activist element of the army were merely biding their time.

Just at the moment, however, Admiral Yamamoto could heave a sigh of relief because on January 19, 1940, his mentor, Admiral Yonai, had become Prime Minister. The idea of having Admiral Yonai in power appealed strongly to Emperor Hirohito, who was doing his best to stem the tide of army nationalism, as well as to the privy council, whose leaders mostly advocated a conservative policy. They knew how powerful the army had become, and they hoped that by inserting the navy into the political arena, they could counter the effect.

Admiral Yamamoto might have gotten back into politics then, but Yonai was too wise to move him. And so Yamamoto remained as commander in chief of the Combined Fleet, devoting his efforts to building up the Japanese navy and still hoping that the navy would not be used in war.

This attitude was increasingly unpopular among the "young Turks" of the army and the navy, and its unpopularity had spread into many areas of Japanese life. The industrial city of Osaka, which manufactured much for the army and the navy, was especially militant. Just after Yonai became Prime Minister, Admiral Yamamoto was scheduled to take the Combined Fleet into Osaka for rest and recreation, but when a staff officer who visited Osaka reported how unpopular Yamamoto was there because of his political views, the admiral abruptly switched gears and took the fleet to Nishinomiya instead.

* * *

Admiral Yonai's government was in trouble from the very beginning. The war between Germany and France and Britain had broken out in the fall of 1939, and by the summer of 1940, the "phoney war" had ended and the Germans were on the march. Yonai struggled against the force in Japan that wanted an alliance with Germany, but in the cabinet he was outnumbered by Admiral Suetsugu, General Iwane Matsui, and Foreign Minister Yosuke Matsuoka. The hard-liners finally resigned in protest against Yonai's soft policies, and that was the end of the Yonai cabinet. Yonai was very nearly assassinated that spring by the "young Turks," and by mid-July the forces of war were in power once again in Japan. This time there was no stopping them. Prince Konoye, more or less a moderate, but still acceptable to the army, became the new Prime Minister, and General Tojo came back from the hustings to the seat of power. Now it was only a matter of time before the army took over the government entirely. Admiral Yonai was out. The navy minister was Admiral Kashiro Oikawa, a very mild fellow who could be expected to do what the navy men around him said to do, and most of these in Tokyo just then were of the "fleet faction."

During the summer of 1940, Admiral Oikawa presided over the last gasp of the navy's peace advocates. Since Tojo and most of the cabinet members were moving toward an alliance with Germany, and Germany was at war with Britain, the odds were that the alliance would lead to war in the Pacific. Seeing this, Admiral Oikawa called a meeting of the admirals in Tokyo, because he knew as well as anyone that Yamamoto and some of the others had strong feelings against war with Britain and the United States.

The purpose of the meeting was to ascertain just how strong the opposition was to the tripartite pact with Germany and Italy that General Tojo and most of the cabinet favored. As they sat down at the big table in the Navy Ministry, Admiral Oikawa stated the position accepted by the cabinet of Prime Minister Konoye: that the alliance was essential to the well-being of Japan. Admiral Yamamoto had come bearing a sheaf of materials to buttress his arguments that war with Britain and the United States would be suicidal, but he had no real chance to make the case. Oikawa stated that the cabinet was bent on the treaty and that if the treaty was rejected by the navy, where the only real opposition in Japan was known to exist, then the cabinet would resign in a body.

Everyone around the table knew what that would mean: a military dictatorship. The army had already shown its power a few weeks earlier, when General Hata, the war minister, had told the Prime Minister that the army insisted on an end to political government in Japan and had resigned to prove the point. Thus had fallen the Yonai government and thus, Admiral Oikawa insisted, would fall the Konoye government if the admirals did not support the treaty with Germany and Italy. The power of the army was indicated in one of Konoye's first actions: He announced the end to political parties and the establishment of the Imperial Rule Assistance Association, a public group designed to give a rubber stamp to the cabinet.

On this day, Minister Oikawa did not say what would happen if the admirals did support the treaty, but everyone knew that that would mean open conflict with the army, which controlled the government. The timetable was already set: General Tojo was convinced that he could defeat Chiang Kai-shek's Republic of China government if he could cut off China's supplies from the West. The first step in this was to move into Indochina, a French colony. And the fact that France had fallen to German might and the French government at Vichy was now subordinate to the Third Reich was a major element in Tojo's insistence on support for the Japan-German-Italian alliance. Thus he would secure German support for the Japanese move into Indochina.

After this was all explained, Admiral Oikawa cut the ground completely from beneath Admiral Yamamoto by calling for the admirals to give their immediate assent to the plan. No discussion was wanted, and no arguments were asked for.

Like all the others around the table, Admiral Yamamoto remained silent, his five-foot three-inch frame immobile, his self-control masking his distress. Nor did the other admirals move, an indication that they too were wrestling with strong emotions.

Finally, Admiral Yamamoto stood up, but obviously this was not a sign of assent. He had a question, he said. He had no objections to any steps the minister had decided to take, he said, but when he had been vice minister in 1939 the cabinet's secretariat had produced a report on the material resources in hand and those needed by the Imperial Japanese Navy. As he recalled, the report showed that eighty percent of the resources needed by the navy to continue operations after the stockpiles were gone would have to come from British and American sources. If the government now allied itself with Germany and Italy, the Americans would cut off the flow of oils and steel, rubber and minerals. Where would those resources then come from?

Admiral Oikawa did not respond to the question, because it was apparent that there was only one possible answer: They would come from conquest of Southeast Asia. Instead, he repeated his request that the admirals all approve the tripartite pact, and one by one they did, including Admiral Yamamoto. He had promised, when he went to command the Combined Fleet, that he would remain out of politics, and he was living up to that promise. In that brief moment around the table, he had once again made his personal views crystal clear, but he also knew that there was nothing more to be done to prevent war. Admiral Yonai was retired. There was no one in the wings who could save the situation.

And so Admiral Oikawa went back to report to Prime Minister Konoye that there was no opposition within the navy to the tripartite pact.

But the fact was that within a matter of hours Konoye knew the real views of the "left" wing of the Imperial Navy. For he had asked Yamamoto to come by the Prime Minister's residence before returning to his flagship, and reluctantly Yamamoto came. Konoye then probed, and Yamamoto aired his own views privately. He made that same statement he had made before—that for six months or a year he could put up a strong fight and win, but if the war continued for two or three years, he expected that Japan would lose. He indicated that Konoye should do everything possible to avoid trouble with the United States. Konoye became petulant and suggested that Yamamoto had done a disservice by not standing up in the admirals' conference for his beliefs. This was the sheerest hypocrisy, for Konoye knew as well as anyone that had Yamamoto spoken up, he might well have been assassinated before he could get back to his flagship and the safety of the fleet. The atmosphere in Tokyo that September was deadly, with the "fleet faction" of the navy completely in control of the Navy Ministry.

After Yamamoto had left Tokyo, Konoye conferred further with Admiral Oikawa, Foreign Minister Matsuoka, and General Tojo, who was pressing hardest for the tripartite pact.

Foreign Minister Matsuoka began the moves that would align Japan with the Germans and the Italians.

On September 19, 1940, the Prime Minister asked for an imperial conference to be held at the Imperial Palace in Tokyo to discuss the tripartite pact. At that time, Naoki Hoshino, the director of the cabinet planning council, raised the issue of resources once again. If the Japanese got into trouble with the United States, he said, there would be extreme difficulty in securing the oil supply the navy must have.

General Tojo had an answer to that question. The movement of the army south into the Dutch East Indies would guarantee the Japanese the oil supplies of Java, Sumatra, and Borneo. These should be plenty for the needs of both the Japanese army and navy. Of course, the government would make every effort to secure these sources by diplomatic means, but, if necessary, force might have to be employed.

Foreign Minister Matsuoka suggested that all this was so much talk, because he did not believe that the United States would live up to its implied threats to cut off Japan's oil supplies if she did not stop her movements in China. Matsuoka was regarded as the cabinet expert on the United States, not just because he was foreign minister, but because he had been educated at the University of Oregon and was therefore presumed to know the American spirit. General Tojo, who did not read English and whose personal knowledge of the United States was limited to that gained on a single transcontinental train trip on his way home from Germany to Japan, leaned heavily on Matsuoka in such matters. The conferees agreed that the important matter was to settle the China question very soon, and then the whole issue would be moot and Japan could go on her way in absorbing China into the Greater East Asia Co-Prosperity Sphere, making Japan, as General Tojo said she should be, the leader of East Asia.

Having had his say at the admirals' conference in Tokyo, as well as privately to the Prime Minister, Admiral Yamamoto made no further efforts to sway the course of events. Instead, he concentrated on the buildup of the Combined Fleet. As he said,

> A navy man's place is, after all, on board a ship. There is still more than enough for me to do here at sea, and anyway I believe that a sailor's business is to be an expert on maritime affairs; it is a fatal mistake for him to meddle in unfamiliar political matters.

Of course, this was Yamamoto's rationalization of his own failure to change the course of events and his realization that the battle was lost.

Admiral Yonai was of the same mind. Japanese troops crossed the border into Indochina on September 22, 1940, and Admiral Yonai said nothing, although the press tried to get a statement from him, knowing his personal views against such a move. Nor would Admiral Yamamoto volunteer any comments. The tripartite pact was signed five days later, and neither Yonai nor Yamamoto had anything to say.

Not long after the deed was done, Yamamoto adopted a completely fatalistic view of the days ahead. He expected war with the United States, and he expected that Japan would lose: "I expect to die in battle aboard the *Nagato*," he said. "By that time I imagine, Tokyo will have been set on fire at least three times, and Japan reduced to a pitiful state . . . but there's no going back now. . . ."

Indeed, for Admiral Yamamoto there was not. Although he detested the concept of war with the United States, he had been chosen as the principal designer of that war, and now he proceeded to do his best.

Taking a note from the career of his personal hero, Admiral Heihachiro Togo, who had defeated the Russians in the naval war of 1904, Admiral Yamamoto began planning for a preemptive strike against the American navy. The American Asiatic Fleet was no problem; it consisted of a handful of superannuated ships, including the old carrier *Langley*, now of little use except as a plane transport. Its flagship was a cruiser. There was not a battleship in the fleet, and most of its modern ships were service ships and submarines. The American Pacific Fleet was another story; it consisted of ten battleships and several aircraft carriers (the number depending on Washington, which transferred ships back and forth through the Panama Canal from Pacific to Atlantic Fleets). If Admiral Yamamoto could knock out the Pacific Fleet's ability to fight for a year, then the Japanese army could move unopposed through the South Pacific, perhaps even to Australia, and might persuade the Americans to make peace in a hurry. This was the only possible way that Admiral Yamamoto could see of managing a victory in this war.

To accomplish this undertaking, several matters had to be resolved. One was communications: Unless the fleet could manage real security, its efforts would be jeopardized in the very beginning. Admiral Yamamoto had little faith in the Japanese naval codes of the past, so he asked for, and got, a new "admirals' code."

The second necessity for the attack was the immediate step-up of the navy's modernization program. This meant the completion of ships under construction within a year and an enormous increase in the number of aircraft available.

First, however, Admiral Yamamoto had to show the highest officials of the government that all this was vital to the navy. On October 11, 1940, he staged a review of the fleet off Yokohama, for the inspection of the Emperor. The whole fleet, its half-dozen new aircraft carriers and its scores of battleships and cruisers, destroyers, and submarines, was brought into Tokyo Bay and assembled in five lines. Emperor Hirohito boarded the battleship *Hiei* with Admiral Yamamoto, and the admiral showed him the fleet and spoke of the problems. Five hundred planes swept over the review, displaying Japan's massive naval air strength.

Two weeks after the review, Admiral Yamamoto took a delegation of high naval officers to Osaka, the big industrial city, to meet with a conference of Japanese bankers. There he outlined the immediate needs of the Japanese navy. For three days the naval delegation made its case for more money to build faster, and at the end of the conference, the navy had its way.

In November, Vice Admiral Yamamoto became full admiral, which helped increase his enormous prestige within the navy itself. That month, Admiral Yamamoto also prepared his plan for the preemptive strike on the U.S. Navy at Pearl Harbor and sent it to Tokyo. There it was examined in the plans department of the Navy Ministry and in the headquarters of the navy itself. Various experts were given copies of the proposal for study. One of these men was Commander Minoru Genda, a highly experienced air officer. Genda and others agreed that the Yamamoto proposal was dangerous, as Yamamoto had indicated, but that it had a fair chance of success. So by the end of 1940, the wheels were turning. Agents were sent to various listening posts in Mexico and the Pacific, including Hawaii, to learn about the movements of the U.S. Pacific Fleet and to keep track of that fleet. They learned the call numbers of the various ships and tracked them thereafter.

In the spring and summer of 1941, Admiral Yamamoto's planning continued. He was half inclined to retire from the service—he had been in the navy for thirty-six years and had served for two years as commander in chief, which was about as much as anyone ever did. But the international situation was so tense that the Emperor and the councillors did not want any such changes, so Yamamoto stayed on and continued to plan for the war he did not want.

In the second week of August, the senior government officials reviewed the navy's plans. The fleet's bomber pilots trained constantly over unfamiliar mountain territory to get ready for an attack on Pearl Harbor. In mid-August, the navy presented its timetable for an attack. At about this time, Lieutenant Commander Fuchida, who had come to Yamamoto's attention with his successful "air attack" on the fleet in the 1940 maneuvers, was selected to be flight commander of the *Akagi*, a job he thought was a demotion until he was told that it had come because he was to lead the raid on Hawaii. And a whole section of training was set up at Kagoshima on the Island of Kyushu, where mockups of the Hawaii scene were built and Japanese airmen began to train for an attack.

In early September, Admiral Yamamoto and other naval officers met at the naval staff college near Shiragane and showed a vast plan for simultaneous operations at Hawaii, Malaya, the Philippines, Guam, Wake Island, Borneo, and Java. Out of these meetings came a deadline of October 10, by which time the decision to move toward war or not had to be made. The fleet had to be prepared. There was some opposition within the naval establishment to the Pearl Harbor raid, but Yamamoto continued to insist that it was the only way.

In October, war games were held at the naval staff college, and the whole plan was aired. Many officers studied the feasibility of the Pearl Harbor attack. The umpires suggested that the Japanese navy might lose a third of its ships in the attack, but that it was worth this price to stop the American Pacific Fleet before it could get started. Among those consulted in these busy days was Count Hisaichi Terauchi, and on September 21, Admiral Yamamoto began work on Order Number One, a comprehensive naval war plan.

Prime Minister Konoye accepted October 15 as the cutoff date for meaningful negotiations with the Americans. But Konoye's government was already faltering, and a few days later it failed. General Tojo was asked to become Prime Minister. From this moment on, the fate of Asia was in the hands of the Japanese army.

The plans moved ahead. On November 3, Admiral Yamamoto staged more war games. The next day an attack force of planes from the Japanese carrier force struck the Japanese fleet in Saeki Bay and proved to Yamamoto's satisfaction that the Pearl Harbor raid was quite feasible. December 8, 1941 had been selected as the target date for the operation against Hawaii.

On November 5, Imperial General Headquarters ordered Admiral Yamamoto to prepare for war with the United States, Britain, and Holland in the first ten days of December 1941, and Yamamoto issued Combined Fleet Secret Operational Order Number One. Yamamoto went up to Tokyo and conferred with the senior army leaders. They put the seal on the plans to strike against Malaya, the Philippines, and the Dutch East Indies simultaneously.

On November 13, Yamamoto summoned his senior officers to the *Nagato*. It was agreed that the fleet would assemble in a few days at Hitokappu Bay in the Kuril Islands. From there, in late November, it would take the northern route to Hawaii.

On November 17, Admiral Yamamoto sailed down to Saeki and there gave a farewell party for Admiral Chuichi Nagumo and the other commanders who would lead the fleet to Pearl Harbor. Admiral Yamamoto was grim that day. He confined his words to one sentence. "I wish you Godspeed and pray for your success," he said as he lifted his sake cup in toast. If he was grim, it was in contemplation of the future, for in his heart he still opposed the war and had considered resigning in protest. Knowing that it would do no good at all, he had refrained, but he expected that Japan would lose the war and that he would be killed in battle.

That day, the Pearl Harbor Force flagship *Akagi* left Japan proper for Hitokappu Bay. The next destination would be Pearl Harbor. Admiral Chuichi Nagumo was on his way.

THE BOY FROM NAGAOKA

2 Nagaoka is a medium-size city in the Niigata Prefecture on the northern shore of Honshu Island whose major claim to fame was once its annual snowfall, which is the heaviest in Japan. It is not as cold in Nagaoka as in other areas of Honshu Island—Matsue, for example, is much more frigid in winter—but the snow stacks up in enormous drifts in the winter months, and were it not for modern snow removal equipment, it still would.

Nagaoka has other claims to fame, however, and two of them are interrelated; one is that it has developed an educational system that is enlightened and almost unique in Japan, and the other is that one of the products of that system became the area's first commander in chief of the Japanese Combined Fleet, thus rescuing from oblivion imposed after the Bosshin War Niigata's reputation as the home of naval fighting leaders. This leader was Isoroku Yamamoto, and after a distinguished naval career, he was appointed in 1939 commander in chief of the Combined Fleet, a post he held until his death. To the Western world and particularly to America, Admiral Yamamoto has come down in history as the perpetrator of what Americans called the most infamous surprise attack in the history of warfare. But Nagaoka is not responsible for that; in striking a preemptive blow at the American Pacific Fleet on December 7, 1941, Yamamoto was taking a page from the book of his

mentor, Admiral Togo, who had done precisely the same to the Imperial
Russian Fleet at Port Arthur in 1904.

For hundreds of years, Nagaoka was the home of seafaring men. The
Nagaoka clan produced strong fighting men, or samurai, and one family
of that clan, the Takano family, was particularly notable for the strength
and character of its samurai. In the 1860s, after Japan had been opened
to Western influence by Commodore Matthew Perry and his "black
ships," Japan was shaken by major differences in approach to the foreigners and to the new industrial era. The troubles that developed became
a civil war, with the forces of the Tokugawa shogun on one side and
an alliance of strong men dedicated to the restoration of Imperial power
under their guidance on the other. The Nagaoka clan allied itself with
the old shogun group. This was an unfortunate decision, because in so
doing the Nagaoka men pitted themselves against old rivals of the Satsuma clan, who lived in southern Kyushu Island around Kagoshima.
The civil war that followed in 1868—the Bosshin War—resulted in
complete victory for the Imperial forces and establishment of the modern
Japan. It was extremely hard on the men and women of Nagaoka, for
their leaders had chosen the wrong side in the war. When the war was
over, the seigneurial grants disappeared and were not replaced by other
forms of assistance. Prefectural governors and other officials were
brought in from the outside. The Nagaoka men who had fought against
the government were not given employment.

Among those who suffered severely was a former samurai named
Sadayoshi Takano, Isoruku Yamamoto's real father. The word "former" is important, for one of the reasons for the civil war, which lasted
until 1877, was the decision of the new Meiji government to destroy
the samurai system, or feudalism, and replace it with a modern army
based on the European scheme.

Among those who objected to the change were the Takano family,
who had adopted Sadayoshi, and whose name he had taken. The adop-
tion had come as a result of Sadayoshi's marriage to a Takano daughter,
a common manner in which important families ensured the longevity
of the family line. Sadayoshi and his wife had four sons. When the civil
war began, Takano and his two eldest sons fought and were wounded.
For the next few years the family drifted from one place to another in
northern Honshu, seeking such employment as they could get. They did

have some resources. They knew a lot about the manufacture of weapons, for such matters had been within the legitimate purview of the samurai. And they were scholars, for reading, writing, and poetry also were proper occupations for a samurai to while away the time between fights. So they made a living of sorts, but they never accumulated much. Ultimately, Sadayoshi Takano returned to Nagaoka, where he had a small house. There his wife died, whereupon he married her younger sister and had three more children with her. The eldest was a daughter, Kazuko, the second a son, Kihachi, and the third also a son, Isoroku, who was born in 1884.

So Isoroku grew up in the little wooden house in Nagaoka. It was a poor and uncertain life, for the Satsuma clan that had been victorious in the civil war was not inclined to forget its old enemies. But the old Nagaoka families stuck together, as they always had. Shortly after the civil war ended, when the people of Nagaoka were virtually starving under the harsh rule of their enemies, the government relented to the extent of sending 100 hyo (a little more than six tons) of rice. If this rice had been divided among the people, it would have provided about a bowl for everybody. So Torasaburo Kobayashi, one of the Nagaoka councillors, cautioned against this use of the grain. He proposed that the rice be sold to a dealer and that the money be used to build an educational fund for the children of Nagaoka.

"We are too hungry to think of education," said another councillor, and the crowd took up that response, demanding distribution of the rice. But Kobayashi stood firm.

"Yes," he said, "we cannot afford to eat to the full, and that is the very reason we resort to education. A handful or two of rice per head, when divided among so many people, will go in a day or so once we eat, and nothing will be left. But the rice turned into education will last long. It is more than that. It is more than that. Think of Nagaoka for tomorrow. Think of Japan for tomorrow."

Ultimately, Kobayashi's view prevailed, and the rice was sold to establish an Educational Institute for Japanese and Chinese Classics. Later, courses in "Things Occidental" and "Medical Sciences" were added. And from this, in time, came the establishment of the Nagaoka *chu gakko*, or Middle School, which young Isoroku Takano attended.

Isoroku had secured a part of his earlier education at the hands of Christian missionaries, although he never became a Christian. But he did have a Bible, which he read, and some exposure to American ways and the English language, through a missionary named Newall. Mr. Newall taught English at Nagaoka Middle School for six years, and Isoroku was one of the students who used to come to his place for coffee and practice English. This early experience set Isoroku on an unusual road for a Japanese of the nineteenth century—at this early age he began to have an appreciation of things English and American.

When Mr. Newall moved from Nagaoka to the larger city of Niigata, Isoroku attended the Sakanoue Primary School, where his education took a more pronounced Japanese trend. It was not long afterward that Isoroku began studies at the Nagaoka Middle School, one of the first and most progressive of the modern institutions brought into being in the early days of the Meiji Restoration. At Nagaoka, the emphasis was on catching up with Western science and technology. But with all this, the school was very Japanese in spirit. Okujiro Mishima, the school's founder, combined elements of Confucian philosophy, particularly those emphasizing individual responsibility and opportunity, with some ideas of his own. He regarded vigor and fortitude as essential elements of the Japanese spirit, and he combined these, too, with a strong urge toward cooperation. Thus from the beginning of his purely Japanese education, the boy who would be an admiral was exposed to a very strong spiritual factor.

By the time Isoroku took up his studies at the middle school, the pattern was set there for the "Cho-Chu spirit," which emphasized individual responsibility, and all his life Isoroku honored and furthered this spirit, almost unique among Japanese schools. (Indeed, in a country where the school uniform is ubiquitous, Nagaoka High School in the 1980s has no uniforms. The student body opted against uniforms as promoting uniformity of mind as well as clothing, and the levels of responsibility and conduct of the student body persuaded the school authorities to go along with this radical departure from the social structure of Japanese education. As of 1988, the program was working very well, and the headmaster of the school was extremely proud of his school and its records.)

The Takano family was very poor, and as a youngster Isoroku had few of the advantages that money can bring. But Nagaoka was a city of parks and open spaces, and there was plenty to interest a young boy. In the spring, after the snow melted, the cherry blossoms burst almost immediately into bloom and for a few days the Kaji River's banks were alive with what looked almost like snow.

Most of Isoroku's life was spent in hard work—work at home to help the family and work at school to win some sort of scholarship that would enable him to pursue the new education and escape from the poverty of the Takano family in Nagaoka. It was in 1894 that Isoroku went to the middle school. The school had been built on the ruins of the old Nagaoka castle near the old village called Yonhoga. In Isoroku's day it was a splendid building for its time, with a thatched roof and sturdy construction. It was not long before the playing fields were expanded, and they continued to be expanded into the rice paddy land around the school. There was always a heavy emphasis on athletics at the middle school, and it has persisted. (Even today Nagaoka High School has one of the largest campuses of any school in Japan, with baseball, football, tennis, and archery fields for the students.)

The playing fields around the school were Isoroku's delight. He and his family and friends would often take box lunches and go to the fields to watch the baseball games, for baseball was becoming a favorite Japanese sport then.

Isoroku's great love was gymnastics, and in this he was coached by a teacher named Haneda. The school had a limited gymnastics program, one set of parallel bars, a set of rings, and a horse for vaulting. Teacher Haneda aroused the boys' competitive spirit by staging the Bosshin War on the athletic field, and so Isoroku and most of his classmates lived with that war all over again. Isoroku was not very strong—his picture shows a slender young man with a protruding lower lip and a thoughtful expression—and he was often ill. His father kept a faithful diary, and recorded many of the young Isoroku's illnesses, especially influenza during Nagaoka's hard winters.

In those early days, Isoroku had a hard time keeping up in athletics, but he worked hard at gaining strength and ultimately succeeded. In later years when he felt like showing off, he would often do a handstand on the rail of a ship or a boat with a great air of insouciance.

All this lasted until 1901, when in the spring the young Isoroku won an appointment to the Imperial Naval Academy at the little island of Eta Jima, off the shore of Hiroshima. This appointment was a sign of the changing times of Japan. Although the enmities of the Bosshin War had not all died out, the government was making efforts to pull the new Japan together. The Japanese navy was still in the hands of the Satsuma

clan because these people had fought the Emperor's battle against the
supporters of the old shogunate, including the Nagaoka men. But in
recent years the navy had assumed a new, national shape guided by the
Emperor Meiji and his ambitions for Japan. The Emperor had ordered
the building of the navy along the lines of the British Royal Navy, and
many young officers had been sent to study in Britain. By the summer
of 1894, Japan was ready to make her first challenge in the international
sphere, to augment her possessions and begin building the sort of empire
she saw all around her in the hands of the British, the French, and the
Russians.

In Korean waters in July of 1896, a young captain named Heihachiro
Togo had fired the first shot of the Sino-Japanese War, and after a period
of indecision about his action, Japan soon made him the hero of the
Sino-Japanese War. Togo reappeared in the great battle of the Yalu, in
which five Chinese ships were sent down while the Japanese suffered
damage to the *Akagi*, the *Hiei*, and three other ships. So the Sino-
Japanese War was won, and Japan secured the basis of her empire in
the turnover of Taiwan by the Chinese. The Imperial Japanese Navy
gained enormous prestige in Japan. The peace treaty had been signed
on April 17, 1895, six years before Isoroku came to the naval academy.
Since that time, the officer training program had been greatly enhanced.
An advanced naval college was established, and Captain Togo became
its chief. Soon he was an admiral and then a vice admiral.

In 1900, Togo was appointed admiral of the fleet, and in June he
sailed for China waters again, this time to Taku Bar, off Tianjin. His
goal was to avenge the murder of the counselor of the Japanese legation
at Peking, who had been killed by a revolutionary group called "The
Boxers Society."

The Boxer Rebellion was put down by a consortium of Europe,
America, and Japan, and by the winter of 1901, Japan was eyeing
Russia's ambitions in the Far East with a cold eye. The Meiji Emperor
had ambitions of his own, and the Russians seemed bent on swallowing
northeast China and Korea. Japan was building naval bases and starting
her own program of naval construction that would lead to the building
of the most powerful fleet in Asian waters. By the time that Isoroku
entered the naval academy that summer of 1901, all these wheels were
in motion. The Japanese navy was on the move. The ambitious young
Isoroku was in the right place at the right time.

ETA JIMA

3 In the winter of 1901, Isoroku, the son and grandson of samurai from proud Niigata Prefecture, entered the new Imperial Japanese Naval Academy at Eta Jima. It was a proud day for the Takano family and an indication of the new healing of the old wounds left by the Bosshin War.

His was an odd name—Isoroku—which means "five, ten, six" in Japanese. But there was a very good reason for the name. The boy had been born when his father was fifty-six years old and his mother was forty-nine. This late child was very dear to both of them, as is indicated in the father's daily diary, kept all during Isoroku's formative years. The diary recorded the weather and the family activities, and virtually every entry had some mention of the last child of the Takano family, which had such high hopes for him and so many fears arising from the recent past.

Isoroku's success in entering the naval academy, however, was not a matter of politics but a matter of ability. He had taken a competitive entrance examination and had scored second from the top among the students of the entire nation. So young Isoroku had his appointment, along with two other youngsters from Nagaoka, Shichiro Tachikawa and Rokuhei Sato. Early in 1901, therefore, young Isoroku went off to the southern school. He went to Hiroshima and took the ferry across the bay to the little island where the academy had been built.

As a student, Isoroku was a leader from the first. He was a slender serious youth, with a protruding lower lip that belied his sense of fun and even a certain recklessness that would stand him in good stead as a naval officer. Most of the young men at Eta Jima did a certain amount of drinking, but Isoroku discovered very early in the game that he was not a drinker. His face would turn fiery red and he would usually get sick after drinking a few glasses of sake. So he almost always quit after one or two cups. He always insisted on sharing in the expenses of the sake parties, however, and he often contributed to the drinking fund even if he was not going to participate.

Moreover, while Isoroku did not drink, he did not find it hard to hold up his end of any argument or to deal with the more difficult members of his class. Most of them were very insular and antiforeign in their feelings. Very early on it was noted that Isoroku, alone among the cadets, had a Bible, which he sometimes read. One night during a weekend party, a few of the hardheads decided they would seek out Isoroku and find out why this otherwise sensible fellow was involving himself with such foreign ways and a foreign religion to boot.

Was he a Christian, they demanded. No, he said, he was not a Christian, but the Japanese had something to learn from the Westerners, and one way to learn was to study their beliefs.

The others began taunting him and threw a hail of questions at him. He fielded them all with considerable grace, never losing his temper, and in the end he threw the rowdies out of his room and resumed his reading.

Eta Jima was a cold-water school. The young men arose at dawn in the summer and earlier in the winter, washed their faces and took their showers in cold water, and then went to the mess hall for their morning rice. After that it was a combination of military drill, for the sake of discipline, military specialty training, to make them good officers in the modern Japanese navy, and academic training. Isoroku continued his study of English and decided that gunnery would be his military specialty. The airplane was in the process of development, but its military uses had not yet become obvious; no navy or army in the world had an air department other than for lighter-than-air craft, which was hardly an exciting prospect.

Isoroku got on well with his fellow cadets, who recognized him as a leader. He never forgot the cooperative spirit instilled in him at Nagaoka Middle School, but to this was now added the more aggressive spirit of the old samurai.

Isoroku was, however, suffering from what would later be termed an "identity crisis," created by Japan's familial system, in which the eldest son is heir apparent to the position of head of family. All four of Sadayoshi Takano's children by his first wife were sons, and, of course, they were grown men by the time their father married again and the second batch of three children began coming along. Isoroku barely knew his half-brothers Yuzuru, Noboru, Jozo, and Tomekichi. He was very close to his full elder brother Kihachi and his sister Kazuko.

As a small boy, Isoroku had not given a lot of thought to such matters as inheritance and family status, particularly since the family was poor and there was not much to inherit, but the matter was pushed rudely to his attention when he was fourteen years old. That year his oldest half-brother, Yuzuru, died. The whole family attended the funeral, and Sadayoshi took that occasion to tell Isoroku that his position as youngest son in the family meant that he could never expect anything at all.

For a young man with Isoroku's temperament, this was a terrible shock. All his life he showed himself to be a very emotional person, and even in the days when he was a high and mighty admiral, he would sometimes burst into tears at the contemplation of some wrong or the death of someone dear to him. Thus the enforced equality of life at Eta Jima was most impressive to him. Every morning his brigade would assemble on the athletic grounds, built around a big oval track, and they would run. And then their day began: lessons in the morning, athletics and military exercise in the afternoon. Isoroku continued his interest in gymnastics, at which he became very skilled—particularly on the parallel bars and the horse. He was also adept at kendo, a Japanese sport developed by the samurai to train young boys for fighting. The participants donned padded jackets and bird-cage helmets and took up large cudgels that represented the *naganaka*, or Japanese lance, which was a favorite fighting instrument of the old samurai foot soldiers. Then they stabbed, beat, and pummeled each other ferociously. But kendo was also a sport of technique. The required combination of physical skills and mental agility appealed enormously to Isoroku's competitive spirit.

During the first year of training at Eta Jima, Isoroku's class did little but slogging physical work and demanding mental exercises. In the second year they went to sea, aboard warships, but only as far as Kure. They learned seamanship thus, and thereafter they made several cruises.

During the last two years of Isoroku's training at the naval academy, the shadow of war hung over the Japanese navy, war with Russia. The two countries were approaching confrontation in two areas, Korea and Manchuria, which both coveted for purposes of exploitation. In 1903, Vice Admiral Heihachiro Togo was informed that war was approaching and that the Japanese governing council had decided that he would be the commander in chief of the fighting navy.

So the talk on the cruises made by the Eta Jima cadets was also of war and the roles they would play in it. Isoroku's specialty at the academy was gunnery, which meant that he would become a deck officer. And in 1904, on graduation with a commission as ensign in the Japanese Imperial Navy, Isoroku joined the new cruiser *Nisshin* as a deck officer and gunnery specialist.

THE YOUNG
WARRIOR

4   After the Boxer uprising in China, the Russians and the Japanese began competing for influence in the north. Both governments wanted to extend their empires, and for a time the Japanese seemed to be seeking a free hand in Korea while letting the Russians have a similar free hand in Manchuria. The diplomacy was illusory, however, because secretly the Japanese were building their navy feverishly, in preparation for a war with the Russians. The final diplomatic step was to sign an alliance with England at the end of January in 1902 that promised that if either party went to war with another, the second party would remain neutral. Thus Japan was sure that England would not make war on her. Moreover, the United States was preoccupied with its own problems in the Philippines, and France was busy in Indochina. Only Russia stood in Japan's way.

On April 8, 1902, the Russians and the Japanese had signed the Manchurian Convention, in which Russia pledged to evacuate all her troops within 18 months, in three stages, ending on October 8, 1903. The first stage was carried out, but the second, which was supposed to be done in April, was not. The Japanese public reacted very quickly and violently, and antiforeign sentiment coursed through Japan, with heavy emphasis on anti-Russian feeling. This feeling was, of course, stimulated by the oligarchy that ran Japan in the name of and with the consent of the Emperor Meiji.

Several leading newspapers demanded that Japan declare war on Russia, and the idea spread rapidly. When the Russians did not meet the October deadline for troop evacuation, the Japanese government decided it was time to go to war. On October 17, 1903, Admiral Gonnohyoe Yamamoto, the minister of the navy, a baron, and an active member of the Japanese oligarchy, summoned a bright young admiral named Heihachiro Togo to the Navy Ministry and informed him (1) that Japan would go to war and (2) that Togo was to command the Japanese fleet.

Thus the modern Japanese fleet was organized in a system that would still be used by another Admiral Yamamoto in the middle of the twentieth century. The fighting ships of the Imperial Japanese Navy were grouped in three squadrons. The first two squadrons were the main line, and that unit was called the Combined Squadron. Its flagship was the battleship *Mikasa*. Aboard that ship, Admiral Togo laid the plans for a war he must win, against the world's fourth largest naval power. All the resources the Japanese government could manage were given to him.

By January of 1904, a hundred warships lay at anchor in Saseboa Harbor, and the entire fleet was ready to sail on an hour's notice. Togo's task was to strike the Russians before they knew what hit them and then to prevent them from bringing their entire navy of 272 ships into play. It would not be enough to destroy the Russian Far Eastern Fleet, for there were even more ships in European and Crimean waters. If Japan lost her hundred ships, she lost everything and then would be at the mercy of the European powers just as China was. It was an enormous gamble, to be made in the search for empire, and Togo was expected to win.

On February 5, Togo was ready and Admiral Yamamoto gave him his orders: The fleet would sail at 9 A.M. on February 6. The enemy was Russia. The ships would sail across the Yellow Sea to attack the enemy squadrons at Port Arthur, Manchuria, and Chemulpo, Korea. Rear Admiral Uryu would take the Second Squadron to Chemulpo and cover the landings of army troops there after his initial attack. All other ships would follow Admiral Togo to Port Arthur, and Togo's torpedo boats would attack the Russian fleet under night conditions on February 8.

And so on February 6, Admiral Heihachiro Togo moved, and on the night of February 8 the torpedo boats of his fleet attacked the Russian fleet anchored at Port Arthur, seriously damaging three major Russian ships.

Thus the Russian fleet was crippled for a time. Meanwhile, the Chemulpo landings had succeeded, and Japanese troops had swarmed ashore in Korea.

The war continued through the winter and spring of 1904 on land and on the sea. The great Japanese fear was about that day when the Russians would move elements of their European Fleet around the world. Meanwhile, the Japanese blocked Port Arthur harbor with sunken blockships. The Japanese ran into a Russian minefield, and in short order eight ships were sunk, including a third of Japan's battleships. But since the outset of war, more ships had been joining the Japanese fleet, including the new heavy cruisers *Kasuga* and *Nisshin*. So the war went on.

Following a severe defeat of the Russian fleet in August off Port Arthur, Admiral Togo had a breathing spell, but he also knew that he would fight again because the Russians had just renamed their Baltic Fleet the Second Pacific Squadron and were dispatching it to the Far East. On October 14, 1904, that squadron sailed for Japan.

On November 14, 1904, Isoroku graduated from the Imperial Japanese Naval Academy at Eta Jima, along with Hori and his Nagaokan friend Ohta. Hori was first in the class, Ohta was fifth, and Isoroku was seventh in a class of more than 200 graduates. The three were assigned to the training ship *Kanki Maru*.

They cruised around the Liaotung Peninsula and Port Arthur during November, December, and January, learning how to man a warship in time of war. On January 3, 1905, Isoroku was transferred to the new cruiser *Nisshin* as a watch officer and gunnery officer. The *Nisshin* was part of the Japanese cruiser force of six cruisers, which also included the *Fuji*, the *Yashima*, the *Shikishima*, the *Asahi*, and the *Hatsuse*.

Just before Christmas the Russian Second Pacific Squadron rounded the Cape of Good Hope: forty ships. On April 14, it anchored in Indochina's Camranh Bay. On May 18, a Japanese agent reported that the Russian squadron had sailed, moving north. This was the last intelligence Admiral Togo received. Now he had to prepare himself for a new battle.

By this time, attrition had cut the Japanese fleet to four battleships and eight heavy cruisers, plus a number of light cruisers and torpedo boats. The Russians had eight battleships but only three heavy cruisers.

They also had about twice as many large-caliber guns as did Togo, but the Japanese guns were more modern and could fire faster.

On May 26, 1905, Admiral Togo moved up to a base at Masan on the Korean coast of Tsushima Strait. That night, Isoroku was on watch. His battle station was in the masthead, and from that vantage point he was to scan the horizon through glasses and report on anything at all that seemed unusual.

There was nothing. His watch ended at 4 A.M., and he went below to catch some sleep. The night was cloudless but misty. The moon was in its last quarter. Suddenly at 4:45 A.M. came a message to the flagship: "Enemy fleet sighted in square 203, appears to be steering from the Western passage past Tsushima."

Aboard the *Mikasa*, the watch officer awakened Admiral Togo. Aboard the *Nisshin*, a seaman shook Ensign Isoroku's shoulder. He woke up, washed his face, and changed into a clean uniform down to underwear, *bushido* fashion; then he went on deck.

The Russian squadron steamed on toward the rendezvous at twelve knots, and Admiral Togo planned to meet them off the Island of Oki at about two o'clock in the afternoon.

Aboard the cruiser *Nisshin*, everyone waited. At 11 A.M., lunch was served, and at noon the officers and men went to their battle stations. Someone broke into the patriotic song "Gunka." At 1 P.M., all was silent, and everyone was waiting, but this time purposefully. Isoroku's task now was to take notes on everything he saw and transmit these to the captain by runner.

At 1:45 P.M., Isoroku saw the enemy—eighteen ships steaming up from the southwest. Admiral Togo formed his battle line, the *Mikasa* at the head. Then he ordered a 180-degree turn, and the Japanese ships changed course. Russian fire fell all around them and did some damage, but the Russian gunners were not very good. In half an hour the Japanese had changed course and had the advantage. From that point on it was slaughter: Most of the Russian heavy ships were sunk and thousands of officers and men died.

During the climax of the battle, something happened aboard the *Nisshin*. One account has it that an enemy shell exploded just below Isoroku's battle station. Another report, and perhaps the most accurate one, said that one of the *Nisshin*'s own guns exploded. In any event, the air was full of shrapnel, and Isoroku was badly hurt. He lost a chunk of his thigh about the size of an orange. His body was peppered with small metal fragments, and when he looked down at his left hand, he saw that the index and second fingers were hanging, attached only by a shred of skin. He bound up his hand with his handkerchief and remained at his battle station until the fight was over.

Then he was taken below and treated for his wounds. His trousers, his sleeves, and his jacket were all soaked with blood.

Soon Isoroku was on his way to a hospital ship. His bloody clothes were stripped off, but he insisted on saving them. His father later preserved them in a wooden box and in his meticulous calligraphy told the story (the exploding shell version) of Isoroku's battle.

Back at Sasebo, Isoroku went into the naval hospital. His hand was sewn up, and his thigh wound and other wounds were treated. He spent the next few weeks in the hospital there.

On May 30, Isoroku received a message of congratulations for his performance from Admiral Togo. It was as important to his career as a medal. On June 8 he was moved by hospital ship to Yokosuka Naval Base hospital. There he spent another fifty days.

By this time the Russo-Japanese War was all but over. The Russian fleet had surrendered, and the day after Isoroku moved to Yokosuka, the American President Theodore Roosevelt offered to mediate; the offer was accepted by both sides.

On August 5, Isoroku was healed enough to return to duty. He was sent to gunnery school at Yokosuka Naval Base, and in September he was promoted to sublieutenant. In October he received a letter of commendation for his conduct in the Battle of Tsushima Strait, which meant his career was on the rise. He remained at Yokosuka until 1907, when he went to sea again, aboard the *Kagero*, and his career resumed that slow, normal pattern of a military man in peacetime.

But the Russo-Japanese War was to have a lasting effect on Isoroku's future, far beyond his wounds, commendation, or experience in battle. For when the Treaty of Portsmouth ended the war, the Japanese military leaders and many people were furious. Japan had impoverished herself to build the armed forces for the Russo-Japanese War and had expected to recoup through a large cash indemnity forced on the Czarist government. Japan effectively secured possession of Korea and got Port Arthur and an international license to move in Manchuria, as well as the southern half of the Island of Sakhalin. But she did not get the cash indemnity, largely because President Roosevelt, who feared the growing strength of Japan, prevented it. Many army and navy officers were so angry they vowed revenge, and thus were sown the seeds of factionalism in the Imperial Japanese Navy. One element held that Japan could trust no Western power and must always be prepared to go it alone in her drive for empire. In this sense, the Russo-Japanese War left an effect that would ultimately shape Isoroku's career.

YOUNG OFFICER

5 As a student of Americana, Sublieutenant Isoroku watched with growing dismay the rift that was developing between his own country and another that he admired. There were several areas of conflict. One, of course, was the resentment of many Japanese navy officers against the Americans for interfering in the Treaty of Portsmouth and preventing Japan from securing the money from Russia that was needed to build up the army and the navy. There is no doubt that a major reason for this American attitude was the feeling of President Theodore Roosevelt that Japan was potentially America's enemy in the Pacific. In fact, Roosevelt consulted his State Department experts specifically about Japan's war capabilities and was assured that since Japan had not secured her indemnity, it would be years before her armed forces could recover from the expenditures of the Russo-Japanese War.

But there was another basic cause of friction, and this was more economic than anything else. During the burgeoning of continental America and the building of the Pacific Railroad in the 1860s, American industrialists had welcomed Oriental labor because it was cheap and efficient. First the Chinese had come to California and Hawaii to build the railroad on the continent and to work in the cane fields of the islands.

But in America the Chinese had proved to be a mixed blessing, because they were such good workers that they put Caucasians to shame and often took their jobs. The resentments of organized and unorganized labor were very great indeed, and they were seized upon by such newspapers as William Randolph Hearst's *San Francisco Examiner* as a basis for building readership. The Chinese Exclusion Acts of the last years of the nineteenth century "solved" the Chinese problem by virtually pushing the Chinese back home. But the Japanese, the proud Japanese, posed another problem.

The Japanese had come to America seeking opportunity. Most of them did not join industries en masse, but became individual entrepreneurs and farmers. As such they prospered, and their hard work paid dividends. Their success was envied by the whites, and real enmities developed, urged on by jingoists in both countries.

So the Americans forced upon Japan the Gentlemen's Agreement of the early 1900s, by which the Japanese agreed not to encourage emigration to the United States. President Roosevelt sent the American fleet on a voyage around the world, during which they visited Japan and the Japanese fleet, and Sublieutenant Isoroko had a look at the Americans.

In 1908, the sublieutenant served aboard the *Maezuru*, out of Sasebo, spending most of his time in Manchurian waters. The next year he joined the *Aso*, which was part of a Japanese squadron paying a return visit to the American west coast. They went to Seattle and then down to the naval base at San Pedro. There the sublieutenant had a reunion with an old friend from Nagaoka Middle School days. That cruise lasted from March until July, and then the ship and the squadron returned to Hakodate.

The next move in Isoroku's career was the command of a division of men aboard his ship. The ship then cruised in Chinese waters for several months, and he gained experience at several levels of command. Within a year he was promoted to lieutenant.

His career then proceeded as did a hundred others, moving slowly up the ladders of experience and promotion in a peacetime navy whose aims were clouded by the aging of the Meiji Emperor.

Isoroku's father died on February 21, 1912, and his mother fell ill. He got leave and came home for several weeks, but he knew that he would have to return to duty and his mother knew that she would not survive the year. She was so weak that she found it difficult to eat. He saw her wasting away. He knew she loved ice cream, and so one day he dug a block of snow from the drifts around the house at Nagaoka, made ice cream for her, and then fed her with a spoon.

Just before Isoroku left for duty, he and his mother had a long talk, and she told him she would not see him again. He said perhaps he should resign from the navy to take care of her, and she told him to go back to his duty: "You are my child and you are Japan's child," she said. "I am going to die, but Japan will live. You must work on for Japan."

On the day before Isoroku left Nagaoka, he was asked to visit his old middle school. He put on his formal uniform with medals and appeared at the school to address an auditorium full of pupils. He spoke of the guiding spirit of the school and the great opportunity it offered them. His speech was inspirational and dedicated, for Isoroku loved his home town and the people and the proud traditions of Niigata.

Isoroku then returned to Sasebo and his ship. He did not get home again that spring or summer, and in August his mother died. He was upset, but he remembered what she had told him and the traditions of their samurai family. Duty was everything.

His career moved into high gear in 1913 with his appointment to the Naval Staff College at Tsukiji. Graduation from this course was a prerequisite for staff work in the Japanese navy. Every command had its staff, but in Japan staff officers had a status quite unlike that in other countries. They did the spadework, as did staff officers of the German, British, and American navies, for example, but they also had much more command responsibility, delegated by their superiors. It was a system that would live through World War II.

Isoroku did very well at Tsukiji. He had an inquiring mind and a forceful personality, as well as the ability to persuade his fellows to follow a course of action. He went through the war college brilliantly.

He was attending the college when the European war broke out. Japan, allied to England by the treaty that had been so useful in 1904, was now obligated to move away from Germany, but not necessarily to declare war. But even under the weak Taisho Emperor, Japan's military forces were strong and aggressive. They saw in the war an opportunity to secure a foothold in China by taking over the German colony of Kaiochao, which included the important port of Qingdao with its beautiful and spacious halfmoon bay. So the Japanese fleet and Japanese army assisted in the assault on Qingdao.

These movements were followed in the curriculum of the navy staff college, and young Lieutenant Isoroku packed away knowledge of the strategies and tactics involved. In 1916, by the time Isoroku had graduated from the staff college, the navy had expanded further, moving into the Pacific with the investment of other German colonies at Saipan and in the South Pacific. The navy had changed, and with the change had come the necessity for a better understanding of the Americans and the British. This appealed to the lieutenant, who had continued his studies of the Westerners' language and customs.

MOVING AHEAD

6   In 1912, Isoroku was sent to the advanced course at gunnery school, and the next year he was gunnery officer aboard the *Shintaku*, a battleship of the Third Battleship Squadron.

Two years later he was selected for the navy staff college training course, a must for any officer who wanted to advance in the naval service outside the specialty establishments. This was the route to advancement through staff to command.

As noted, Isoroku did very well at the Navy Staff College. His hard intellectual work and the fact that he was a nondrinker gave him an educational advantage over the average hard-drinking young naval officers of Japan. But again, although he did not get drunk with the others, he was always eager to attend the parties and pay his share. As he sometimes said, it was not a moral question. He liked the idea of drink as well as the next fellow, but his physical makeup, not unusual among Japanese, was such that liquor turned his face fiery red and affected him very swiftly. So he was wise enough to drink only a few glasses. His amusement at the geisha parties was to spend the evening, and often the night, with the ladies. He was also a ferocious gambler and could stay up half the night playing shoji or go, sometimes for high stakes. There was nothing of the prude about him; to the contrary, he was almost elfin in his amusements, and totally un-self-conscious. If he felt like standing on his hands in the middle of a party, he stood on his hands. He had a way of sincerity and simple good will that won him friends everywhere. He was one of the most popular of the young officers.

He was also recognized by superiors as a "comer," and in 1915, he made the big jump to lieutenant commander. In peacetime this was often the point at which officers dropped out of the service, but 1915 was a war year. Japan had just swallowed up the German colony of Kiaochao on the Shandong Peninsula of China, the Marianas Islands, (except Guam), the Carolines, and several other little dots in the great Pacific that would prove in later years to be very important places. The navy leaders were very pleased; in a rush they had obtained coaling stations all across the Central and South Pacific and what might become important naval bases if Japan wished to expand her empire in this direction.

One of these little dots in the Carolines, a sandspit called Truk, would later become the most important base in the South Pacific. "Japan's *cajones*," Admiral Chester W. Nimitz would call them, perhaps vulgarly but certainly accurately. That possession and the determination of the navy to build up its position in the Pacific guaranteed the future of all the bright young men who were willing to work to that end.

Isoroku, who had no money except his officer's pay and no family position or future, was one of the young men for whom a military career seemed designed. Thus, in a heavily structured society, he had a route to the top. It was for this reason that the navy and the army were so highly regarded as career opportunities in Japan. Had Isoroku not been appointed to the naval academy, he might have managed some sort of higher education on his family's limited resources, but his life would almost undoubtedly have been spent teaching English or perhaps gymnastics in a secondary school in Niigata Prefecture. As it was with thousands of other young Japanese, the military had given Isoroku a key to the world.

After graduation from the staff college in 1916, Isoroku was appointed to the staff of the Second Battle Squadron. And that year came a major change in his personal status that was to affect all the rest of his life. He discarded the name Takano and adopted the surname Yamamoto.

Such a change was not unusual in Japanese life, where the family is the basic unit of society and the individual gives way to it. Many families that were so unfortunate as to produce only daughters would marry at least one of them to an eligible prospect on the condition that the young man assume the girl's family name and the responsibilities of continuing and building up the family ties.

The name Yamamoto was an honorable and ancient one in the history of Japan. Several members of the family had risen high in the new naval service. As we have seen, one had been a member of the oligarchy at the time of the Russo-Japanese War and had handed Admiral Togo his commission to attack the Russian fleet at Port Arthur.

Another, Tatekawa Yamamoto, had fought against the forces of the Emperor and his followers at the Battle of Wakamatsu during the Bosshin War. Isoroku's father and his two eldest brothers had been on Yamamoto's side. They were wounded in that battle but escaped death. But Tatekawa Yamamoto was a big fish and one of the leaders of the rebellion. He was captured and his head was cut off at Wakamatsu, thus severing not only his life but the future of the Yamamoto clan, since he had no sons.

For several years the family had looked for a new leader, and Isoroku's performance had been so impressive that they asked him to take on the family name and the responsibility. Mother and father dead, his elder brothers standing between him and leadership, there was no conceivable reason for Isoroku to refuse this considerable honor and the emoluments it brought him from an important clan. So in 1916 he became Lieutenant Commander Isoroku Yamamoto of His Majesty's Imperial Japanese Navy, and the change was duly recorded in the Yamamoto clan records.

This new relationship brought very real responsibilities to Isoroku. For several years he had been sending part of his pay to relatives of the Takano clan, but now he had to look to the Yamamoto clan. In addition, if he was to carry on the line, he had to remember that he was thirty-four years old and it was high time for him to get married. Out of the old filial piety Isoroku consulted with his elder blood brother about marriage, and out of the new filial piety he consulted with the family of Count Makino, allied to the Nagaoka Yamamotos, and Admiral Suzuki, another relative. They all approved the idea and suggested several possible candidates, but for Isoroku's taste, the girls were all too high born and demanded too much of a husband. He wanted a different sort of young woman.

She was discovered by his naval academy friend Takeichi Hori. Her

name was Reiko, and she came from Wakamatsu, which had a symbolic
meaning to the Yamamoto clan. She had been educated at the Aizu
Girls' School there, and after leaving in her midteens, she had gone to
work in the family business as a housemaid. Yamamoto approved heartily of all this, as he indicated in a letter asking the approval of his elder
brother (Takano):

> She stands about five foot one or two and is extremely sturdy; it looks
> as though she could put up with most hardships, which is why I'm in
> favor of the match.

It was quite apparent that the reason for the marriage was not love,
but the necessity of carrying out his responsibilities to the Yamamoto
clan by producing sons. And this explains a great deal about Isoroku
Yamamoto.

(Long after his death, a serious critical biography of Yamamoto
would be published in Japan by Hiroyuki Agawa, a prominent postwar
writer. Previous biographies had all concentrated on Yamamoto the
national hero and had dutifully reported the facts as stated in his father's
diaries, the progress of advancement through the naval establishment,
and his many honors. These read very much like the American political
biographies written about presidential candidates in an election year.
But Agawa chose a more "Western" or "warts and all" approach, and
he dwelt heavily on Yamamoto's long association with several geishas,
at least two of whom he loved.

When the biography was published, the Yamamoto family was scan-
dalized. And not only the family. Yamamoto is a national hero in Japan,
along with Admiral Heihachiro Togo, a hero of the caliber of Lord
Nelson in Britain. Artifacts and even a lock of his hair are carefully
preserved in a special room in the naval academy museum at Eta Jima.
He is prominently featured in the war museum-dedicated-to-peace at
Tokyo's Yasukuni Shrine. But he is an especially revered figure in
Nagaoka and all of Niigata Prefecture. Twenty-five years after Yamamoto's death, the revelations about his extramarital life were so shocking
to the historical preservation committees of Nagaoka that Agawa, who
had done much of his research in the museums there, was forbidden
future access to one of them, and nearly twenty years later, when I
visited these places, the curators were still mumbling about Agawa-
san's indiscretions, and the Yamamoto family politely avoided dis-
cussing the admiral with me.)

The courtship was very brief. The families had given their permission, and on August 31, 1918, Yamamoto and Reiko were married at the Navy Club in Shiba, Tokyo. They would have four children: two boys, Yoshimasa (1922) and Tadao (1932), and two girls, Sumiko (1925) and Masako (1929). It would be a standard Japanese family, with mother Reiko in charge of the household and the bringing up of the children. Perhaps Yamamoto would spend even less time with the family than most navy husbands, but he never shirked his family responsibilities. The children grew up with real filial pride in their mysterious but amiable and considerate father.

AMERICAN YEAR

7   After the Treaty of Portsmouth in 1905, the Japanese military establishment was so infuriated by the U.S. interference that America was designated the primary potential enemy of Japan and the navy war plan was drawn on that premise.

Under the philosophy "know thine enemy," the Japanese naval establishment began to concentrate on sending selected officers to the Western countries to observe and learn, particularly to perfect their command of the English language. Lieutenant Commander Yamamoto was one of these, and in the spring of 1919 he was posted to the United States.

No thought was given to Lieutenant Commander Yamamoto's taking Reiko with him to America. She spoke no English, she had absolutely no understanding or interest in foreign ways, and the whole idea of uprooting, leaving Japan, and living among strange white people was abhorrent to her. (In the 1980s even, a Japanese family that accompanies the husband on a sojourn abroad loses greatly. The returning children are regarded as freaks and have difficulty in reentering the educational system; the wives often try to conceal the fact that they have lived abroad and "acquired gaijin ways." Half a century earlier the strictures were much stiffer, the Japanese-American communities were tiny, and altogether, such a posting as Yamamoto's was regarded as a hardship not to be undergone by a family or a wife.)

So Yamamoto went to America alone, sailing on the *Suwa Maru* on April 4, 1919. He traveled first class, as befited the station of a Japanese naval officer.

He went to Cambridge, Massachusetts, to study several matters. One was English, and he was enrolled in a special course for foreigners at Harvard University called English E. He also undertook a study of petroleum resources, a matter of great importance to the Imperial Navy, which had only a few oil wells in Yamamoto's native Niigata Prefecture and otherwise had to depend entirely on imports for the source of energy that was now replacing coal to drive the battleships.

Many Japanese came to America to learn in the 1920s. While Yamamoto was a student at Harvard, there were also some seventy other Japanese there, many of them in his English E class. In fact, in later years this association became one of his favorites.

Yamamoto developed something of a reputation during the Harvard period, mostly as a sort of refined scapegrace who was inclined to acrobatics and who loved the ladies. He also became known as a ferocious bridge opponent and a very lucky one. He had no apparent responsibilities. In America, Yamamoto had a great deal of leisure and opportunity to learn. American Rear Admiral Arthur McCollum, who, as head of the Office of Naval Intelligence Far East desk later made it a point to know all he could about Yamamoto, said that as far as he knew, Yamamoto spent most of his time in Cambridge at the bridge table, exercising his propensity for gambling.

But was it just gambling? For more than chance, bridge is a game of gambits like chess or go, the sort of game that appealed to Yamamoto's competitive and vital character. Much later, after the Pearl Harbor attack, when he was being congratulated by high and low in Japan, Yamamoto likened his victory at Pearl Harbor to a small bridge slam "barely made." This was a left-handed criticism of Admiral Chuichi Nagumo's timidity in not sticking around the Pearl Harbor scene for a second and decisive attack in which he could have wrecked the port facilities and perhaps caught the carrier *Enterprise*, which was just coming into port that December 7, 1941, as Nagumo pulled out nervously.

In any event, Yamamoto had plenty of leisure during his two years in America on this first visit. He found time to read Carl Sandburg's massive biography of Abraham Lincoln, which, thereafter, he recommended to anyone who wanted to learn anything about America and Americans. He found time to visit Washington and to indulge poetically in nostalgia and a sweet feeling of loneliness:

> *Tonight once more*
> *The moon is pure*
> *And clear.*
> *It calls to mind*
> *My distant home.*

He found time to visit the burgeoning industrial city of Chicago, and there he was very much impressed with the American productive capacity. He traveled to Detroit, where Irving Olds had established a modern factory to make his Oldsmobile and Henry Ford was pioneering the assembly-line process of making many cheap automobiles for the multitude of Americans. He saw the variety of automobiles and the enormous resources of the American middle west.

In December, Yamamoto was promoted to full commander in the Imperial Navy. The next year, Emperor Taisho, who had succeeded his father, the Meiji Emperor, in 1912, handed down a proclamation that dedicated Japan to seeking world peace. Although the Taisho Emperor was mentally deficient, his advisors were not, and the idea of world peace was then very strong in all the civilized countries, including Japan. The economy was flourishing, the army was still occupying Siberia and was thus not yet feeling any pain of retrenchment after the end of World War I, and Japan looked forward to continual growth and prosperity.

Commander Yamamoto continued his studies of things American. One thing that interested Yamamoto considerably was aviation. By 1919, aviation had progressed rapidly in Europe, with air service established between Paris and London in the year that Yamamoto came to America. America was not that far along in the development of aviation, and naval aviation certainly had a long way to go. The admirals at this point saw the airplane as possibly useful, but only for observation purposes. The idea that an airplane could sink a battleship by dropping bombs or torpedoes seemed completely preposterous to them.

General Billy Mitchell of the U.S. Army Air Service had come back from World War I in France with the idea that the airplane was the wave of the future. Even the generals jeered at his advanced ideas: that cities could be held hostage to air power and that airplanes could sink battleships. At the time that Yamamoto was visiting the United States, Billy Mitchell was trying to convince Congress, his peers, and his superiors of the validity of his arguments—without a great deal of success.

Mitchell raised the idea before Congress that airplanes could sink battleships, thus infuriating the admirals. Josephus Daniels, the Secretary of the Navy, offered before Congress to stand bareheaded at the wheel of any battleship that Mitchell proposed to bomb. (He was lucky no one took him up on it.)

Captain William D. Leahy, director of naval gunnery, scoffed at the idea that a bomb could sink a warship. After Mitchell made his statements, the navy performed its own test on the battleship *Indiana* and so rigged the test that it could not possibly succeed. Captain Leahy then reported that Billy Mitchell was all wrong, and the admirals subsided, satisfied that a threat to the status quo had been defeated.

But this hiatus in the struggle for air power was only temporary. The controversy over whether an airplane could sink a battleship caught the American imagination, and the Sunday supplements of the newspapers were filled with speculation. The debate continued in Congress and could not have been missed by anyone in America who read a newspaper or listened to the radio. The vituperation unleashed against Billy Mitchell in this period, mostly by navy supporters, was enormous.

"Mitchell's challenge to sea power provoked world-wide repercussions, but the violence of the indignation he aroused among admirals was equalled only by the steadiness of his purpose to stand by a new science," wrote Emile Henry Gauvreau, biographer of Mitchell.

On July 18, 1921, before the Atlantic Fleet assembled off the Virginia capes, six army bombers limited to 600-pound bombs sank the captured German cruiser *Frankfurt*, and she gurgled to the bottom of the sea in thirty-five minutes.

Commander Yamamoto was not privy to American military secrets or demonstrations. He was, after all, a representative of the navy deemed by the U.S. Navy most likely to be the enemy of the future. But the word of developments had a way of getting out through the American press, and so Yamamoto knew something of what was going on. He developed right then a lively interest in naval aviation that surpassed his gunnery specialty in his own mind.

But in 1921 this interest was no more than that. His real purpose in

America was to learn about things American, to learn English, and to study the Japanese navy's greatest single problem: petroleum and everything that pertained to this fuel.

During his 1920 summer vacation, Yamamoto decided to go to Mexico, partly at least to look over the Mexican oil fields. He applied to the navy for expenses for an official trip and was turned down. The admirals in Tokyo were no more prescient than those in Washington, and they claimed that the navy did not have sufficient resources to underwrite such a trip. So Yamamoto decided to go on his own. He was a successful as well as ardent gambler, and he had won a lot of money at the bridge table. It would mean straining his slender resources, since most of his money went home to support Reiko and the household, but he saw how he could manage by living "on the cheap." He set out, then, for Mexico City.

There he called on the Japanese naval attaché, Lieutenant Commander Kenzo Yamada, and discovered that Yamada also came from Niigata Prefecture. To Yamamoto, this origin always created a feeling of kinship. Further, Yamada had been aboard the same ship as Yamamoto's brother Kihachi, who had served in the navy during the Russo-Japanese War.

So Commander Yamamoto and Lieutenant Commander Yamada became fast friends and were soon sharing confidences. Yamamoto learned that, like himself, Yamada was a gambler, but unlike Yamamoto, he was not a good one. He had lost a lot of money in the period he was in Mexico and had actually had to pay out in gambling debts the money allocated for his return to Japan by the navy. What to do? If he could not pay the bill, then the navy would most certainly cashier him for malfeasance.

Yamamoto solved the problem for his new friend. He gave him a large percentage of the money he was carrying, and Yamada went home in peace.

Commander Yamamoto then traveled around Mexico so spartanly that he came to the attention of the provincial police in the Tampico area. They could not believe that this man who lived in cheap hotels and ate in the cheapest restaurants could be a commander in the Imperial Japanese Navy. The Mexican government sent a message to the Japanese Embassy in Washington:

A man who claims to be Isoroku Yamamoto, a commander in the Japanese navy, is traveling around the country, inspecting the oil fields.

He stays in the meanest attics in the third rate hotels and never eats the hotel food, subsisting instead on bread, water, and bananas. Please confirm his identity.

The Japanese embassy confirmed the fact that there was a Commander Isoroku Yamamoto in the Western Hemisphere at the moment, and the police seemed satisfied. Yamamoto continued his tour, impressed by the enormous oil resources of Mexico and the cheap price of oil.

In the fall of 1920 he was back in Cambridge, continuing his English studies. The next year he was slated to go home.

This was 1921, the year of the Washington Naval Conference that would play such an enormous role in the future of Isoroku Yamamoto, but he had nothing to do with it. He went home that summer and was appointed to be an instructor at the naval staff college in Tokyo. He and Reiko began to raise a family, and their first child, son Yoshimasa, was born in October of 1922. Yamamoto was on his way, his career going well, and one of his obligations to the Yamamoto clan was already discharged with the birth of a son.

KATO vs. KATO

8   Although Commander Yamamoto did not attend the Washington Naval Conference of 1921, this is not to say that he did not know much about it. One of the most active of the younger officers at the conference was Commander Takeichi Hori, Yamamoto's best friend from the naval academy who also had a Nagaoka background.

The conference came about as a result of a congressional resolution calling for a reduction in the naval armaments of the world, but it was really more than that. It was an attempt to sort out some sticky problems in Asia and the Pacific. These included the restoration to China of Kiaochao and the Shandong Peninsula, which were still occupied by the Japanese; the extension of the American "open door" principle in China, regarding equal opportunity for trade for all nations, the status of various Pacific islands, some of them seized by Japan and some by Australia during the late war; and various other matters concerning cable rights and communications guarantees.

The Japanese, of course, were not eager to give up the Shandong Peninsula, but there was really no way out in view of the demands by China and the "big" powers. So the Japanese put the best possible face on the matter and settled down to negotiate the naval treaty to their best advantage.

The officers of the Imperial Navy were divided into two camps on the subject of arms limitation. One faction, known as the "fleet faction," held that Japan should not be in any way bound to limit her naval armaments, at least no lower than that of the United States and Britain. But the British and the Americans claimed that they each had two major seas to police and the Japanese had but one. The Italians and the French accepted this principle and agreed to limit their armaments to a ratio of 1.7 to the 5 of Britain and America. Japan was asked to limit her navy to three-fifths of the British and American navies.

The officers who accepted this principle were known thereafter as the "treaty faction," and the division became an important matter in the whole ambience of the Japanese navy. For example, Yamamoto from the beginning was an advocate of the treaty, and Chuichi Nagumo, another young officer of about the same age, was of the "fleet faction," opposed to arms limitation. This difference created real enmities that would last for years. After 1921, Yamamoto had very little use for Chuichi Nagumo, although they were traveling very similar courses in the navy.

Navy Minister Tomosaburo Kato went to Washington to attend the conference, with the happy idea of accepting the sixty percent ratio for Japan. His reasoning was very simple: Japan had virtually bankrupted herself in the Russo-Japanese War and had not recovered yet from that expense. Based on the theory that the United States was the probable enemy in the Pacific, the Japanese navy was building eight new battleships and eight new cruisers. The cost was enormous: The naval expenditure of 1921 threatened to come to a third of the total national expenditure.

The Washington proposals for naval disarmament, with the Americans scrapping 845,000 tons of warships while Japan scrapped 480,000 tons, would allow the Japanese to cut back on their naval expenditure, and this seemed vital at the moment. Minister Kato had been the advocate of the eight-eight navy, but he had also seen the light about expenditure, and he went to Washington with the approval of Prime Minister Kei Hara. He did not, however, have the approval of a large segment of the navy, which was unwilling to scrap the idea that America was the basic enemy of Japan.

The central point of the Kato policy was this, as he enunciated it in a speech to the conference: War with the United States was unthinkable and must be avoided at all costs. The defense goal of Japan was to maintain a military strength proper for her resources and give no thought to war.

And why not? Even in his last days, Emperor Meiji had been satisfied with the Japanese empire as it existed in 1910: the home islands, half of Sakhalin Island, Korea, and Formosa. The empire had been further augmented by assumption of the League of Nations Mandates for several Pacific islands. Japan was prosperous, and she had no visible need for further territory.

So the navy split into two camps on this issue, with such men as Hori, Misumasa Yonai, and Katsunoshin Yamanashi accepting the Kato idea and ultimate civilian control of the navy (which hitherto had always been controlled by military men and had been responsible directly to the Emperor.)

The opposite view, that Japan needed a larger navy and, further, that Japan must not in any way be fettered and that the navy should remain in the hands of navy men, was offered by Admiral Kanji Kato. So Japan witnessed a Kato-Kato confrontation, and thus the two factions had no personal names to them, but were "fleet" and "treaty" in shorthand.

The treaties (nine in all) were signed and sealed, however, and the parties went home to live happily ever after. Not quite. The conference was scarcely over when it began to create repercussions in Japan. In 1923, Tomasaburo Kato died. The struggle between the "fleet faction" and the "treaty faction" then began. In 1925, the battleship *Tosa* was scuttled, and many Japanese people saw this as an enormous waste of money and effort on the part of the people.

Admiral Kanji Kato became vice chief of the Navy General Staff and promulgated his "fleet" theory, which won much acceptance among the younger officers, as well as among the army and civilians, particularly civilians allied with the growing *Zaibatsu*, or business cartels. Such firms as Mitsubishi and Mitsui blossomed out into myriad business ventures in a big way. If it was construction, they would own their own cement factories, their own truck factories, their own lumber yards and brick kilns. In other words, in each industry they entered, they maintained complete control. And they split up the markets of Japan and the world among themselves. Obviously, shipbuilding was an important business, and warships were an important part of shipbuilding; therefore, the cartels were almost unanimous in favor of the "fleet" theory.

Taking his cue from Tekeichi Hori, Commander Yamamoto came

out on the side of the "treaty faction." He had seen enough of America to know that she had an enormous industrial potential, and he saw no reason for Japan ever to challenge that. No matter what differences might arise, these could be settled by compromises.

Actually, at this point Commander Yamamoto was not giving much serious consideration to such weighty matters as treaties and high naval policy. He was appointed to teach at the navy staff school, and here he exhibited two fields of interest. One was oil resources, and the other was aviation. In these early years, Yamamoto saw that aviation was going to be the wave of the future for the navy. At that time, the concentration for navy fliers was on float planes. New cruisers and battleships being built were to be equipped with this sort of plane, which could be launched from a spring platform and recovered by a crane alongside the ship. These aircraft would be the "eyes of the fleet." Yamamoto also was not unmindful of the Billy Mitchell controversy and the British development of the aircraft carrier.

In August of 1922, Commander Yamamoto left the teaching post and went back to sea as executive officer of the cruiser *Kitakami*. At the end of the year, he went to the navy command school. But the next year he was preempted from sea duty because of his knowledge of English and was sent with Admiral Kenji Ide on a study tour that took them to half a dozen countries in Europe. It was during this tour that Yamamoto first visited Monaco and the gambling casino there. He was enormously impressed and at one point indicated that he would not mind at all if something happened to his service career. Then he would become a gambler and live in Monte Carlo.

But the workaday world called, and he found himself on official visits to England, France, Italy, Austria, Germany, and finally once more the United States. The tour was instructive to Admiral Ide as well as his interpreter, who by this time had a good understanding of the Western world, far better than most of his compatriots.

AIR POWER

9 While Yamamoto was on his long trip with Admiral Ide, he was promoted to captain in the Imperial Japanese Navy. He was thirty-nine years old and obviously one of the "bright young men" of the Imperial Navy whose career from this point could go anywhere. He had the bonafides for ship command, and he also had what could be called "diplomatic" experience through his trip with Admiral Ide. He had served as a line officer often enough to keep that side of his record alive, and he had attended the proper command and general staff schools to give him a good understanding of naval procedures.

From the glories of Europe, Captain Yamamoto returned to the mundane life of an officer at the Yokosuka Naval Base, but not for long. In June of 1923, he was appointed captain of the cruiser *Fuji*.

This appointment ought to have made Captain Yamamoto very happy indeed. It was the sort of assignment that many a navy man would do anything to get, but Yamamoto had other ideas. His trips abroad had kindled an interest in naval aviation that would not subside. Forgotten was his dream of becoming the leading gunnery expert of Japan. Now he thought in terms of air power, and he foresaw the day when the aircraft carrier would replace the battleship as the first line of the Japanese fleet.

In the fall of 1924, Yamamoto managed to wangle himself a job in this new field that appealed to him very much. He was appointed to the staff of the new Kasumigaura Aviation Corps (only three years old). The school was located on beautiful Lake Kasumigaura, where the young men trained in seaplanes built of wood and covered with fabric.

Yamamoto was not very popular with the young men of Kasumigaura. He was too old for their liking, and he was a "battleship man" to boot, knowing absolutely nothing about aviation. They wondered what this short, crew-cut figure with graying hair was doing in their midst.

Yamamoto did not enlighten them. He stuck to his business, which at the moment was learning everything possible about naval aviation in Japan. And most important, he learned to fly.

Fortunately, he did have one friend at Kasumigaura, Shosa Osaki, who was a member of the teaching staff. Osaki had the admiration of all the cadets because he was the first man to fly over a Japanese battlefield, the field being that of Qingdao, during the Japanese-English siege of this German colony in 1915. Yamamoto and Osaki were good friends of long standing; both were from Nagaoka City. Yamamoto had been four years ahead of Saki at the Eta Jima Naval Academy. But as for the cadets, they snickered at the sight of an "old man" learning to fly.

It was not easy for Yamamoto. He had a whole new technology to learn, and because he was a captain, he felt impelled to learn it perfectly. So the light burned late in his room as he studied long past midnight every night.

Then, at the end of 1924, Captain Yamamoto suddenly emerged from the obscurity of study at Kasumigaura to become executive officer and director of studies. The announcement fell like a bomb on the students, who had been laughing behind the back of this pudgy little man.

The first shock came at a school assembly. Captain Yamamoto stood up and announced who he was, and then he began to promulgate some new rules for the conduct of cadets at Kasumigaura. First off, he said, was the matter of dress regulations. The dress regulations for officer candidates to any division of the Imperial Navy provided that they should wear their hair short and neat in a military fashion.

When Captain Yamamoto had finished with his list of new regulations, the cadet corps gave one long groan. For months they had managed a system of their own, dressing more or less as they liked in uniform clothing, and wearing their hair long, dragged down below the collarline of their tunics.

But, protested the cadets, they were only following the British fashion. The cadets at Sandhurst (the British army academy) wore their hair long. Why not the cadets at Kasumigaura?

No more, said Captain Yamamoto. Each and every one of them was going to get his hair cut immediately, in the prescribed fashion.

And what was the prescribed fashion? asked one wit. Just how long could their hair be?

Yamamoto looked the cadet in the eye and touched his own short crew cut.

"Just like mine," he said. "Just like mine." They did not have to know any more. The barbers would know.

"When?" asked the ringleaders, stalling for time.

"One week," said Captain Yamamoto. "One week. That's all you get." And so long hair went out of fashion in a hurry at Kasumigaura.

That was not the end of it. Once the uniform regulations were in force, Captain Yamamoto began whipping the cadet corps into shape. Next came the matter of promptness in obeying orders. The Kasumigaura cadets were a sloppy bunch, secure in the belief that they were an elite crew—flying men!—who did not have to obey the usual rules of naval cadets. It was a part of their esprit de corps, they explained.

But Captain Yamamoto soon taught them that esprit de corps depended on discipline, not on license.

It was not easy. The ringleaders of the cadet corps had seriously gotten the idea that they were above the usual regulations, and when the discipline appeared, a number of them dropped out. They thought that if enough of them resigned, then Captain Yamamoto would be disgraced and they could reenter on their own terms.

But it did not work that way. Captain Yamamoto stood firm, and the commanding officer stood behind him. When the dropouts kept coming back to the base to incite others to create difficulties, Yamamoto ordered the officer of the day to make guard tours to be sure that none of the dropouts came back into camp. One of the young officers, Ensign Sanwa, was walking his rounds in the rain late one night when he saw a figure ahead of him, walking along, in raincoat and navy cap. Sanwa thought it might be one of the dropouts and ran to catch up with him.

"Stop!" he shouted. "Stop!" Sanwa ran to catch up and grasped the figure by the arm. Then he discovered that he had collared Captain Yamamoto. Ensign Sanwa was very much embarrassed, but Yamamoto laughed.

"You did a good job," he said. "Now, you have a flight tomorrow, don't you? Why don't you go back and get some sleep. I'll take your duty."

And he did.

This happened to several other cadets in that first month, and they were all very favorably impressed by a high and mighty navy captain who would take security duty.

Captain Yamamoto did not have a lot to say from day to day, but after a month of his disciplinary methods, the young men of Kasumigaura were no longer late to class, no longer went absent without leave, and stopped dropping out of the corps in hatred of discipline. The esprit de corps they wanted was established.

One thing all the cadets admired about Yamamoto was his even-handed discipline. He set the rules, and he obeyed them. If he was on the campus (which he did not have to be after hours), he followed the rulebook. He ate in their mess, and he was available to hear their problems. But he accepted no nonsense. Biographer Hiroyuki Agawa tells a story of one cadet who decided that he was too important to accept the role of officer of the deck, which meant supervising security and attending to a myriad of details. Admittedly it was not a glamorous assignment, but one essential to every naval organization.

This young man bragged to his fellows that he would not take the job. Someone who had had some experience with the captain told him that if this was the case, he had best go to see Captain Yamamoto and tell him, so the cadet went off jauntily to "tell off the executive officer."

When he arrived in Yamamoto's presence and was greeted with steely eye, however, the cadet suddenly lost all his arrogance. Not only did he fail to "tell off" the captain, but he came out of the interview as officer of the deck, having promised to do his utmost to do a good job.

And that's the way it was with the cadets. Within a month of his advent as executive officer, Captain Yamamoto had them eating out of his hand. Soon he began to change the curriculum.

When Captain Yamamoto announced that hereafter Japanese composition would be a major study, some cadets complained. But Yamamoto told them sternly that one of the greatest failures in the navy was the inability of officers to communicate. They must learn how to impart to others in writing what they knew, because once outside the Kasumigaura Kokotai they were not going to be able to take their troubles to their commanders in person all the time.

There was a note of command in his voice and a look in his eye that raised him above the ordinary level. Men knew that he would accept the same hardships that he expected them to undergo. One time, when a seaplane was lost in winter and several cadets were drowned, Captain Yamamoto spent many hours, day and night, at the scene, in snow and ice and sleety storm, supervising the rescue operations, and he did not quit until all the bodies were recovered. Another time, when the technicians of the new science of aviation were testing various means of prolonging the life of the wood-and-fabric airplanes, he offered personally to test the planes when they reached the critical fatigue point. That was one of the secrets of his command technique: He would never ask another man to do something, particularly something dangerous, that he had not done or would not do himself.

Visitors who came to Kasumigaura that spring were impressed with the hard-working cadet corps and said so.

"Yes," said one cadet, "we work under Captain Yamamoto because we want to. He works harder than anybody."

In the spring of 1925, Admiral Kanji Kato, the "fleet faction" leader, who was then commander of the Yokosuka Naval Base, came to Kasumigaura for an inspection tour. That sunny spring day, under the trees next to the lake, the commander of the base gave a sake party for the admiral. Some of the high-spirited cadets decided to crash the party, and when they had had a little too much sake, some of them also got rowdy and began breaking things. The party deteriorated into a brawl, and the base commander was enormously embarrassed. He threatened to court-martial every cadet involved in this disgraceful affair. But Captain Yamamoto stepped forward and said that as the commander of the cadet corps he was solely responsible, and if they wanted to court-martial someone, it would have to be himself.

The official rumblings died down, and soon the matter was forgotten. Thereafter, as long as he stayed, Captain Yamamoto could do no wrong at Kasumigaura.

ATTACHÉ

10

In 1925, the year that Yamamoto's first daughter, Sumiko, was born, he was posted once more to America, this time as Japanese naval attaché to the U.S. government in Washington. The appointment came on December 1, 1924, in what was known in Japan as the fourteenth year of the Taisho Emperor's reign. On January 21 he sailed for America aboard the *Tennyo Maru* from Yokohama, and his friends from the Kasumigaura Naval Station buzzed the steamer, in a "simulated bombing raid," while Captain Yamamoto stood on the bridge and watched happily. The buzzing was strictly against regulations, but the young pilots did not care. They were determined to do honor to Captain Yamamoto, who was one of their own.

When Yamamoto reached the Japanese Embassy on Massachusetts Avenue in Washington, he learned that his predecessor as naval attaché, Captain Kiyoshi Hasegawa, had decided to top off his American experience by a trip to Havana, the most licentious city in the Western Hemisphere. When Yamamoto learned that Hasegawa was going, he dropped everything and went along too. Whatever Hasegawa's reason, Yamamoto's was the gambling table. He loved roulette, which was legal in Havana but not in America, and he came back from the voyage with enough fine Havana cigars to last for visitors all during his tenure as naval attaché.

55

Captain Yamamoto was a favorite with the staff. His assistant was a young lieutenant named Chikao Yamamoto (no relation), who came to worship the captain. It was a difficult worship because Yamamoto did love to gamble and was forever taking his young assistants out bowling and then insisting on a wager. Sometimes it cost them real money, such as the day when Yamamoto took three of his assistants to lunch and a little game and proposed that if any of them won, he would buy all three of them a gold watch, but if he won, they would buy him one. Being athletic and intensely competitive, of course, Yamamoto won, and the three junior officers had to chip in and buy their superior a watch.

He liked every sort of gambling game, but he particularly enjoyed shogi, a sort of Japanese chess that is complicated enough for a naval strategist. Somewhere in his belongings there was always a shogi board. One night when he was invited by Ambassador Tsuneo Matsudaira to a big party at the Japanese Embassy, Yamamoto grew bored with the formality. He suggested a game of shogi to one of the other guests, Kota Hoketsu, a junior diplomat working at the Embassy.

Years later Hoketsu told the story to biographer Hiroyuki Agawa. He remembered that Yamamoto had come on like a dragon, wiping him out and winning the first game in virtually record time. But then Hoketsu had considered the manner of Yamamoto's play and had adjusted his defenses accordingly. When the naval attaché came charging out again, he was met with firmness, and in the end, Hoketsu won the game. And the next. And the next. Captain Yamamoto did not ask him to play shogi again.

Considering the matter in the light of World War II, Hoketsu, who was a corporate executive by that time, suggested that if the Americans had known Naval Attaché Yamamoto better, they would have expected the sort of blasting attack that was delivered at Pearl Harbor. But the fact was that a number of American naval officers did know Yamamoto very well indeed. He knew several American naval captains and played bridge with them frequently. In fact, he used to boast later about the large sum of unpaid bridge debt owed him by a certain American naval captain.

So Yamamoto's American counterparts knew him very well and respected him, and there was a dossier on him in the U.S. Naval Intelligence files. Furthermore, in 1941 the Americans did expect from Japan a Togo-type attack, and they did know that Admiral Yamamoto, as commander of the Combined Fleet, would be the one to deliver it. The American problem was that after many months of alert for just that sort of attack, the guard was down and the attackers slipped in under it.

Captain Yamamoto was responsible for observation of all the activities of the U.S. Navy, particularly adherence to the Naval Treaty of 1922, which called for the reduction of naval arms by destruction of warships. But his major interest was aviation and the carriers. Japan had already jumped into leadership in carrier building. In 1922, Japan had launched the carrier *Hosyo*, which was the first ship built from the keel up for the specific purpose of launching aircraft. The Americans had the *Langley*, also launched in 1922, but it was a converted collier. The *Hosyo* was a flush-deck carrier, with no "island," or bridge, and this was the path the Japanese followed in those early years, while the British and Americans went to the "island" structure.

The Washington Naval Treaty of 1922 caused all nations with navies to turn to the carrier, because there was an "escape" clause in the treaty that allowed any nation to convert a ship under 33,000 tons to an aircraft carrier without penalty. Thus several cruisers were converted, and this is how the Americans got the *Lexington* and the *Saratoga* as carriers.

All aviation was developing rapidly during Yamamoto's Washington years. The first transcontinental American air mail route had been established during his first tour of America. Now, with the continuation of the Billy Mitchell controversy, the Americans were slowly beginning to accept aviation as a part of naval strategy, although they continued to believe that the carrier would always be subordinate to the battleship.

The frontiers of aviation were extended enormously by Charles Lindbergh, who flew the Atlantic Ocean in a single-engine plane in 1927. What that did to the frontier!

But to Naval Attaché Yamamoto, much more important was the news on May 9, 1926, that Lieutenant Commander Richard E. Byrd, a retired naval officer, had flown over the North Pole using scientific navigation to guide him.

Until this point, most airmen flew "by the seat of their pants," using intuition and local landmarks to guide them. But on a vast stretch of ocean there are no local landmarks, and a pilot carrying out an attack from a carrier against another ship would be completely lost if he depended on intuition. So Captain Yamamoto immediately recognized that Byrd's flight was not just a feat, but one of the hallmarks of real progress in naval aviation. He told one of his junior assistants to write up a report, which the young man did. Yamamoto then took it, added some information of his own, and made strong recommendations to the operations department of the naval high command in Tokyo to adopt this principle of flight from carriers and adapt the instruments of celestial navigation for aeronautical use.

In Washington, Yamamoto worked like a horse. He never ate lunch unless he had to attend some official function or had a visitor who was hungry. He often worked straight through the lunch hour, and some visitors came away from meetings with very empty bellies. He had strong feelings on the subject: "A military officer should eat only two meals a day," he said. "A military officer should live very simply."

He read voraciously, almost always in English, while he was in America. When he had no visitors or pressing work, the staff would find him with his door closed, reading a book. Studying is probably a better word. He reread Sandburg's *Lincoln* and other books on Lincoln, whom he regarded as one of the great men of history. Obviously, one thing that attracted Yamamoto to Lincoln was the similarity of their own lives. Lincoln was born into poverty; so was Yamamoto. The house in which he was born and grew up in Nagaoka is not so far from Lincoln's simple Kentucky log cabin, in amenities at least.

Yamamoto saw Lincoln as the emancipator of the poor, of women, of humanity, and this appealed to Yamamoto enormously:

> A man of real purpose always puts his faith in himself. Sometimes he even refuses to trust the gods. Thus he falls into error from time to time. This was often true of Lincoln, but that does not detract from his greatness because a man is not a god. Making errors is part of the attractiveness of a human being; it inspires a feeling of warmth and arouses admiration and devotion. In this way Lincoln was a very human person. Without this quality, one cannot lead others. Only if people have this quality can they forgive each other's mistakes and assist each other.

So here was a big part of the Yamamoto philosophy, turned over in his mind in America in contemplation of an American hero. Obviously Yamamoto was searching for the key to the qualities of leadership, and he found them within himself.

His yen for gambling was very human, and so was his feeling for women. Once someone asked what he did about sex when he was in America those two times and in Europe for that long year so far away from home and family. The question was prompted by the fact that the Japanese communities in Boston and Washington were very small, and the antipathy to Orientals in America was just about at its apex. He answered that he never lacked for partners. And that must be true, because although he was short, he had a strong physical drawing power; both men and women were drawn to his smile and his presence. And in a day when, because they were so often taught English by other Japanese, most Japanese people had trouble with their *l*'s, Yamamoto's command of spoken English was very good.

The spring of 1928 was the time for Captain Yamamoto to go home. He traveled to Los Angeles, where a colony of people from his own Nagaoka had settled much earlier, and he stopped off to visit and encourage them. They told him about the new restrictions imposed by the American government, under which a child born of Japanese parents, who was an American child, was regarded as superior to his parents in every way. The parents could not even administer land that was owned by the child—but on the other hand, it was much safer, the Japanese had already decided, to put the land in the hands of the American child than to keep it in their own alien hands. What Yamamoto saw in Los Angeles was the rankest sort of American racism, and as it was with every Japanese, it could not help but hurt.

Then Yamamoto went up to San Francisco, where more Nagaokan people had settled, and he visited them.

Then it was back to Japan. After his return, he went down to Eta Jima to give a lecture. He talked about American manners and morals, not about military affairs. His audience was taken aback, although he was still well received. There was obviously method in Yamamoto's madness. He knew something most Japanese did not—that beneath the propaganda war and the racism that colored Japanese-American relationships and had since the early years of the twentieth century, there lay a need to understand the Americans, which the Japanese military was failing to do. Yamamoto tried to help remedy that situation. It was part of his sense of having a rising star, which had been the case, as one magazine pointed out, ever since this son of samurai had taken the celebrated name of Yamamoto.

SHIP CAPTAIN

In the biography of Admiral Yamamoto written by Eichi Sorimachi there is a photograph of Captain Yamamoto and the other senior officers of the First Air Battle Squadron of the Imperial Japanese Navy. That squadron was built around the new carrier *Akagi* late in the 1920s, and captain of the *Akagi* was to be Yamamoto's next assignment.

But first the naval general staff believed Yamamoto needed some refreshment at sea. After a brief tour with the naval general staff that summer of 1928, Captain Yamamoto was sent to command the light cruiser *Isuzu*, but it was understood from the beginning that this was only to be sure he was thoroughly refreshed in ship handling before he took on the pride of the Japanese carrier fleet.

For a few months, then, Captain Yamamoto was involved in training exercises in the Inland Sea and elsewhere with the *Isuzu*. He showed himself to be an adept ship handler, as well as a very efficient captain who had the respect of all his officers. More than that, unlike some ship captains, Yamamoto was very friendly with his officers. He used to step into the wardroom from time to time and watch them playing go or shoji or mah-jongg. He sometimes played shogi with them, and he tried to teach several of them to play bridge but ultimately gave up on them as too unimaginative to become good players.

Soon, on December 10, 1928, he was shipped up to the *Akagi*, and he reported for duty aboard the ship in January of 1929. It was a bad year for the carriers. Shortly after Captain Yamamoto joined the ship, they went out on maneuvers in the Sea of Japan, in an area bounded by Kyushu, Korea, and the China coast. The fleet was split into two units for the maneuvers, and the two units were to attack each other. It was a choppy day on the sea, with a good breeze blowing and rain, with some gusts and heavy squalls from time to time. After all, it was winter in the Sea of Japan. The squalls were heavy like those of the rainy season, and it was not good weather in any way for operations. But, of course, this did not make any difference. The order from the admiral was to operate, so they operated. The *Akagi* launched its planes in weather that was not too bad. But about an hour after launch, the front began to close in. Soon the sky was dark and the overcast heavy, and the ship was plunging through heavy seas.

They stood by for a while, more or less milling around in their assigned area and keeping a sharp eye out for the "enemy" planes, which never appeared.

Then from the *Akagi* strike force leader aloft came a radio message: "We are bombing the enemy's main force." And then, "We have bombed the enemy force and conducted a successful torpedo attack."

This was good news! It made Captain Yamamoto and the others on the bridge very happy.

But then someone looked at the clock and estimated the time out for the carrier planes. They were getting very short on time and should be coming in at any moment.

More time went by, however, and the planes could still not be heard overhead. They were definitely running out of time.

Captain Yamamoto and the others on the bridge strained their eyes, but still they could not see their aircraft. The weather had closed in, and they were surrounded by squalls. Then from the attack planes they heard the plaintive message over the air: "We cannot see the ship."

Very shortly thereafter, a plane came down to only thirty meters above the water, headed straight for the carrier, and then it zoomed up to avoid hitting the ship. It clipped the mast and zoomed off again. Once more nothing could be seen, and the pilot could not see the ship in the murk.

Then came another message from the pilot: "We only have gas left for twenty-five minutes flying time."

And the chronometer continued to click along: "Gas for twenty minutes. . . ." "Gas for ten minutes. . . ." "Gas for five minutes more. . . ." And finally there was silence.

All this while Captain Yamamoto stood on the bridge, his face a mask of gloom. The entire ship's crew was out on the flight deck, straining their eyes at the heavens, trying to see something. There was nothing to see but gray clouds, gray sea.

The carrier changed course, Captain Yamamoto trying to find a way out of the front. The clouds stayed with them. Time had run completely out. Every plane had to be out of gas.

That day the entire attack force landed in the sea after their gas ran out. Naturally, the exercises were suspended and the *Akagi* and the cruisers and destroyers of the squadron spent the next twenty-four hours searching the seas, in terrible weather that grew worse every hour it seemed, and they found nothing.

All during the search, Captain Yamamoto was on the bridge, and he did not eat or drink anything. At one point one of his officers looked at him and saw that his eyes were wet with tears. His behavior convinced everyone around him that this tragedy was a personal matter to him, and indeed it was, for he regarded his shipmates as his family.

No one knew how many square miles of sea they searched in those twenty-four hours, but it was useless. The weather was too bad to see very far, and of course in those days the planes did not carry any survival gear. So once the planes went into the water and broke up, the men had nothing to cling to in the freezing sea. It was doubtful if they could have survived an hour.

The men of the task force never found much. No trace of any of the men, and only a few bits of wood and fabric on the surface of the sea.

One would think that Yamamoto might have been broken by this tragedy or that he might have been terribly discouraged and dispirited after such an appalling accident, but the reverse was true. Instead of brooding about it, he determined that something must be done to get the pilots home to the ship in such weather as this, and he set about tackling the job. What the pilots needed was homing equipment and better navigation devices. Yamamoto was determined that they would have them, and he began a campaign.

* * *

A few weeks later, another tragedy struck the *Akagi* while she was operating off the Watashu Islands in the open sea.

Lieutenant Watanabe and Lieutenant Oshima died at their posts in a ship's accident, which was a lieutenant's fault. But Yamamoto refused to shift the responsibility. He was the captain of the ship. Anything that happened on the ship was his responsibility, and so he took the blame for an accident that was not his fault. Because of his character, however, and because of the esteem in which he was now held in all the navy, such incidents did not seem to hurt his career when they might have wrecked that of a lesser man.

By 1929 it was apparent that Captain Yamamoto would become an admiral. He was attentive to every detail about flying and carrier operations. He was constantly interested in improving the caliber of his aircraft and in training his airmen. The crew of the *Akagi* loved him even though he was a tough disciplinarian and was one of the first to begin the hard discipline program that was put into effect in the navy in 1928.

The proof that Yamamoto's superiors thought highly of him came at the end of 1929, when he was appointed to the Naval Affairs Bureau of the Navy Ministry. This bureau was one of the most important, in that it made navy policy concerning weapons and equipment. Yamamoto was in the right place to implement his ideas about air safety and navigation, and he did so. But he did not stay there very long, certainly not long enough to run out of ideas. He was well known in the navy as one of the most competent officers in the use of English, and so when the result of the Washington Naval Conference of 1920 began to become a bit frayed and plans were made for a new naval conference to be held in London in 1930, Captain Yamamoto was chosen to accompany the Japanese delegation as a special assistant. It was a major step in his career.

THE LONDON NAVAL CONFERENCE OF 1930

12

Biographer Eichi Sorimachi opened his discussion of the London Naval Conference of 1930 with the heading "the prospects seem increasingly tense and gloomy," and he was quite right. With the Washington treaties about to expire, Japan prepared to go to the conference table this time with a divided delegation.

One part of the Japanese group, representing the "fleet faction," insisted that Japan must have naval parity with the United States and Britain. If she did not get it, that faction was quite willing to throw the treaties to the winds and embark on a program of unrestricted naval building. In fact, the "fleet faction" wanted that more than a successful conference.

The "treaty faction," of which Captain Yamamoto was a junior member, was really quite content with the 5-5-3 ratio for naval forces. Although to preserve unity they agreed to go for more, they would have been eminently satisfied if all concerned had settled for a Japanese force seventy percent the size of the American and British forces. After all, as Yamamoto had often said, it was unthinkable that Japan could ever go to war with the United States, and anyone who appreciated the American production capacity and had seen the automobile factories of Detroit should have realized this. Yamamoto had been repeating this argument ever since he returned from the United States, but the arguments had fallen on ears that seemed to grow increasingly deaf after 1929.

The reason for the growing animosity of Japan toward the outer world was the depression that struck first in Japan in 1927. Since the end of World War I, the overblown Japanese economy had been propped up by a large military establishment. It cost money to keep troops stationed in Siberia, and the army insisted that this was necessary. At least part of this insistence was based on the reluctance of the military men to trim their new establishment down to a size the nation could afford. So it remained through the first half of the 1920s. But by 1925 Japan had been pushed to withdraw most of its forces from the Chinese province of Shandong, although the Kwantung Army in Manchuria was just waiting for an opportunity to move. The civilian elements within the government demanded that the army be cut, and it was. The result was a national recession. This was followed by the New York Stock Market crash of 1929, and that was followed by the collapse of financial markets in London and elsewhere in the world, including Japan.

How did it all happen so suddenly to Japan? The Japanese economy of the 1920s was apparently very prosperous, but extremely fragile, for the prosperity depended on Japan's ability to sell its manufactured goods—silks, cottons, ceramics, and the like—to other countries. The American market collapsed in the depression, and the enormous market in China also suffered. Silk was an extremely important product, because to the Japanese farm wife the silkworm provided the equivalent of the American farm wife's "egg money," that is, pocket money and, if necessary, a buffer against want. Suddenly there was no market for silk, and agricultural prices generally collapsed. Then began the dreadful period in which farm families were reduced to selling some of their children so the others might survive.

The new Japanese army and navy, built during the Meiji years, rested on a foundation of the peasantry. Most of the young officers came from farms or small towns, and when they went home, they found poverty and want. One answer, offered by senior officers and politicians, was expansion of Japanese markets to Manchuria and China. Such expansion, however, was now being resisted by Chiang Kai-shek and some of the warlords of the north. The army wanted to move into Manchuria.

It is ironic that as all this pressure was building, there had come to the throne of Japan a young man with high ideals and a sense of kinship with the British throne. As crown prince, Hirohito had visited England and had come away with a longing to be a constitutional monarch like his hero George V. The name chosen for his era, *Showa*, means peace and enlightenment, and in 1926, both aims seemed attainable in the world. Within a year, however, General Giichi Tanaka became Prime Minister of Japan, and he was avowedly bent on expansion and pursuit of empire. Tanaka and his government set out to take over Manchuria for a starter. In the spring of 1927, the Japanese army was mobilized, against the will of the navy. The Kwantung Army, a force of only about 12,000 men, was ready to move in Manchuria. But America issued a stern warning: Manchuria belonged to China, it said. The implication was clear that if the Japanese moved, so would the Americans—to stop them.

So the Japanese backed away from seizure of Manchuria in 1927, against the will of the activist faction of the army. The Kwantung Army did not stop its machinations, however. The army arranged the assassination that year, of Marshal Zhang Zoulin, the warlord of Manchuria, and this action threw the whole area into a crisis. In these muddy waters the Japanese would fish for the next four years. The "fleet faction" of the navy wanted to support this move, and this was the center of the difficulty for the Japanese navy.

Yamamoto's second daughter, Masako, was born in May of 1929, several months before the New York Stock Market crash. Five months later, when the Naval General Board moved to appoint the delegation to the London Naval Conference, the Japanese economy was tottering. The price of silk had fallen by half. Exports, on which Japan's economic life depended, were cut by a quarter, and by January of 1930, when Captain Yamamoto was selected to join the naval delegation, the depression was on.

This was how the schism between the advocates of peace and prosperity and those of aggressive nationalism became wider even as Yamamoto and the others headed for London. The extent of the schism was shown in the attitude of Admiral Kanji Kato, a leader of the navy's aggressive faction. He was asked to be a delegate to the London Naval Conference, and he refused rudely, saying that it was his job to fight wars, not to prevent them.

The chief naval officer of the Japanese delegation was Admiral Seizo Sakonji, but the head of the whole delegation was a politician named Reiijiro Wakatsuki.

* * *

The delegation set out in November. Yamamoto was promoted to Rear Admiral a few weeks later, which increased his stature for the meetings. In London, Yamamoto soon made a reputation for himself. His manners were excellent, and his behavior was impeccable. He never wasted time in recriminations or specious arguments. He listened well, and when he spoke, it was openly and only when he had something to say. For important matters, he spoke in Japanese, although there was no need. But it was his right, and he felt that by speaking his native language he could gain time and read the faces of his audience, which could be of inestimable advantage to him.

The problems of the meetings were serious. The Americans and the British wanted a moratorium on building battleships. The Japanese did not. The British wanted to outlaw the submarine. The Japanese and Americans did not. The Japanese wanted at least seventy percent of the naval power of Great Britain and the United States. The British and Americans insisted on the two-thirds figure. In addition, some members of the Japanese delegation wanted to fight for more concessions from the Americans and the British, but Yamamoto counseled patience.

As the conference continued, the British and Americans wondered aloud why the Japanese had professed to be satisfied with the Washington Treaty but now were talking about needing a larger force. Yamamoto undertook to answer them.

The world had shrunk, he said. The strides made in ship propulsion, in fueling at sea, in the building of aircraft carriers, and in aircraft design all had their impact. Now the strategic balances were all out of whack, not the result of any particular behavior, but because of technological advancement.

Of course, Yamamoto talked about parity in London, but he would have been satisfied with much less, as would the delegation. Instead, however, they came away with virtually no concessions, and this did not sit well at home. In fact, at the end of five weeks, the conference seemed doomed to failure, because the "fleet faction" was holding out for the seventy percent figure. Then Hirohito stepped in. It would be unthinkable, said the Emperor, for the conference to fail. It would bring ignominy upon Japan to have destroyed the alliances and would disgrace the Showa era by controverting the contention that it was dedicated to peace and good will. So the "fleet faction" was quelled, temporarily. The apparent concession of the British and Americans was to give Japan sixty-nine percent of their own strength, but it was illusory. Japan would actually have to reduce her number of submarines, and she could maintain only sixty percent of the cruiser force of the others. But Emperor Hirohito insisted on a treaty, and Chief Delegate Wakatsuki said that this was the best he could get.

Home was where the problem lay, of course. As the delegates talked, the economy of Japan grew worse. And as the economy worsened, the jingoists and the shouters were more often heard. In the army the "young Turks" were meeting in geisha houses and conspiring, talking loftily about the day when the army would take over the government of Japan and bring real unity to the country, throwing out all the politicians.

In London, the treaty delegation was wined and dined at various embassies, and there were many cocktail parties, at which Admiral Yamamoto held forth with aplomb and gusto. He was good at small talk in English, and he almost invariably made a good impression.

For his fellow delegates, Yamamoto had some sage advice. The important matter was a country's will to defend itself, not its military strength alone. The delegates of the "fleet faction," wanting to build their navy, ought to remember the tale of the Spanish Armada, and how the British, with help from the weather, defeated a numerically superior Spanish fleet. It was not so much different a tale than that of the Divine Wind (*Kamikaze*) that had struck the forces of Kublai Khan, an enormous array of 165,000 men, and destroyed almost all the invasion fleet.

Armed with his twin tales from history and modern technology about Britain and America, Admiral Yamamoto thus sought compromise at London. In the end, the Japanese got very little of what the "fleet faction" was seeking. The 5-5-3 ratio of naval forces remained, in essence. There was a change, but it was not a positive one. As the delegation headed home from London, a fire was being built within the naval establishment, seconded by the army, and even the public was growing restive. In fact, the London Treaty played right into the hands of the jingoists who were moving to take over the Japanese government.

POLITICS OR AERONAUTICS?

13

Admiral Yamamoto and the other members of the delegation arrived back in a Tokyo that was buzzing like a disturbed beehive, and the cause was the treaty they had just accepted in principle.

Of course, it was not their place to accept or reject the treaty as such. They said they had done their best to get more concessions but this was all they could secure, and they advocated acceptance of the treaty by the cabinet and the Diet.

Within the naval establishment, however, the breach between the "fleet" and "treaty" factions now became open warfare. Admiral Kanji Kato and Admiral Nobumasa Suetsugu discussed the treaty. Suetsugu leaked a draft copy of the treaty to the press, hoping to provoke a storm of public criticism. He did. A large segment of the public, already inflamed by the Kwantung Army propaganda about Manchuria and the growing interest of the Zaibatsu (the big business cartels) in expansion, now gave vent to its frustrations and antiforeign feelings in loud denunciation of the treaty.

As Yamamoto had said and would say again, what was the difference between sixty and seventy percent of the other fellow's strength? In neither case would Japan be able to win a war against the United States and Britain. But the "fleet faction" was not interested in argument. It was interested in expansion and power.

Five days after unleashing the press, Admiral Suetsugu prepared to hold a press conference. However, Prime Minister Osachi Hamaguchi told Naval Minister Takeishi Takarabe that this was a breach of the navy's role in life, and the minister called Admiral Suetsugu and told him to desist. Still, the admiral managed an "informal session" with the press in which he expressed the "fleet faction" view that the treaty should be rejected out of hand.

Admiral Kanji Kato and others of the "fleet faction" drew up their own proposals for naval construction and took them to Prime Minister Hamaguchi. The Prime Minister said that the Japanese economy was in such terrible shape that Japan could not afford any enlargement of her naval establishment at this point and that the cuts in tonnage and elimination of many submarines would help the economy.

The admirals could not argue openly against helping the economy, but they neither believed nor accepted the Prime Minister's argument.

Admiral Kanji Kato then sent a complaint directly to the Emperor. This he could do under the Japanese system of government, in which the Emperor held two roles, one as head of the government and the other as direct commander in chief of the armed forces. But the emperor was not sympathetic to the "fleet faction," and he ignored the petition.

The "fleet faction" then managed to arrange a meeting of the Supreme War Council of the army and navy leaders. There Admiral Kanji Kato quarreled with Navy Minister Takarabe, saying that the treaty would damage Japan's power to defend herself. This idea appealed to the *kodo ha*, or activist element in the army, which was seeking to end political rule of Japan altogether. And so the navy was fragmented over this issue. The admirals of the naval establishment, Makoto Saito, Keisuke Okada, and Mitsumasa Yonai, all favored the treaty. Among the younger leaders, so did Shigeyoshi Inouye, Yamamoto, and Takeichi Hori, his old friend, who now held the important post of director of the Naval Affairs Bureau. In other words, the leaders of the current naval establishment backed the treaty. But the "fleet faction" made up for its weakness in influence by its vociferation, as well as by its appeal to that radical young element of the navy that was the duplicate of the radical element of young officers who wanted to reshape the army and all Japan into a military mold.

So in the summer of 1930 the debate raged in Japan. The Emperor backed the treaty. Prime Minister Hamaguchi sent it to the Privy Council. The chairman of the Privy Council Treaty Examination Committee sympathized with the "fleet faction" of the navy and the *kodo ha* faction of the army. He loaded his committee with members who opposed the treaty. The committee suggested that since the military and naval establishments were split over the treaty, it ought to be rejected. The Prime Minister reminded them that this was a matter of diplomacy and foreign relations and that foreign relations was not the province of the military.

The Supreme War Council tried to intervene against the treaty. Prime Minister Hamaguchi warned them sternly that unless they minded their own business, he would ask Emperor Hirohito to make changes in the council.

The debate involved officials at every level. Prince Saionji, one of Hirohito's most valued advisors, backed the treaty. Chairman Ito was forced into a corner, and ultimately, the Privy Council approved the treaty. In the process, Admiral Kanji Kato resigned in protest. His resignation brought forth a storm of protest from younger officers, and the naval establishment became very tense. The matter was so serious, coinciding with the frustrations and unhappiness of the Japanese people over economic events, that it brought violence to Japan. On November 14, 1930, at Tokyo's main railroad station, Prime Minister Hamaguchi was the victim of an assassination attempt. A young man named Tomeo Sagoya, a member of the Love of Country Association, shot him.

The Love of Country Association was a small group of revolutionaries who wanted to bring military power to Japan. It was just one of dozens of supersecret associations that were springing up in 1930.

Prime Minister Hamaguchi did not die, but he had to retire from politics very shortly thereafter. A new era had come to Japan. The foreign correspondents had a name for it: The era of "Government by Assassination" they were to term this next decade of Japanese life.

It was in this atmosphere, as one of the announced members of the "treaty faction" of the navy, that Admiral Yamamoto had to pursue his career. Since Yamamoto had been a member of the treaty delegation, his views on the future of Japan's naval establishment were well known, but in this difficult period he was fortunate to be removed from the political scene by an appointment that took all of his energies: He was appointed director of the technical division of the navy's Aeronautics Department. In essence, this meant that Yamamoto was responsible for

the development of new naval air craft and air weapons. It was a new
appointment to a new job: Yamamoto's task was to build an air force
for the navy: not just a flying service, but a real air force.

Also, here was Yamamoto's opportunity to do something about that
memory that haunted his dreams—that day when the entire strike force
of the *Akagi* was lost in bad weather and ran out of fuel.

In those early days of carriers, the fleet depended largely on float
planes, which had about a 200-mile search radius. Yamamoto set out
to change all this.

What had to be developed were planes for search and planes for
scouting and planes for air strikes, both with bombs and torpedoes,
planes that could fly fast and deliver the maximum payload. The radius
should double the 1929 figure.

What Yamamoto began was a program under which the carrier force
supplanted the battleship force as the major striking unit of the navy.
This was done by Japan at a time when the British and American navies
continued to consider the battleship as the key weapon of the sea.
Yamamoto also was influential in the development of a long-range search
bomber for hunting submarines.

In his first twelve months in office, Yamamoto began to turn the air
force around. It was not long before people in the navy were talking
about the "air navy" instead of the "naval air unit." In 1930, Yamamoto formed fourteen new squadrons of wheeled aircraft. In 1931
came the Zero-type fighter plane, which was undoubtedly then the best
in the world, and the Nakajima-type attack plane, which also was very
efficient in delivering torpedoes.

Yamamoto was then also influential in straightening out the navy's
pilot training program, increasing its rigorousness. He was always a
great believer in training to the nth degree.

Although Yamamoto's job as head of the naval air technical division
was essentially a shore job, this did not mean that he spent a great deal
of time at home. The fact is that Yamamoto never did become domes-
ticated in the usual sense of the word. Since the year of his marriage,
he had spent too much time abroad to be a very good family man. And
even when he was ashore as he was now, he was more often to be found
in a club or a geisha house than at home, or in 1931 at the house of
Fleet Admiral Gentaro Yamashita, a family connection through Yamamoto's wife Reiko. He was a great admirer of the stiff-necked old
admiral, and he liked the admiral's wife, Tokuko. Sometimes when he

had nothing else important to do he would call on the family and "talk navy" with the admiral. In the winter of 1931, however, the old admiral began to fail and took to his bed. He was a demanding man, and he liked to have his wife by his side. So the loyal Tokuko sat for hours on end. If she tried to leave, the admiral would awaken and become fretful.

Thus Tokuko Yamashita was getting almost no sleep, and the regimen was wearing on her. During this period, Yamamoto was coming every day to visit his old friend. He saw what was happening, and he persuaded Tokuko to lend him a dark blue informal kimono that she often wore around the house. He went into the admiral's room and sat down in the chair Tokuko always occupied. The old admiral awakened, saw the familiar form in the blue kimono and went back to sleep. For several days Yamamoto made it possible for Tokuko to get some rest. Finally, on February 18, 1931, the old man died and the ordeal was over.

In 1933 Admiral Yamamoto's tenure as chief of the navy's air technology came to an end. He had added a great deal to the Imperial Navy's fighting capability, especially with the Zero fighter, and he had improved the facilities for air navigation and the techniques of operation from carriers. Now he was to put his theories into practice, because he was appointed to command the First Air Division of the navy.

THE COMPLEAT ADMIRAL

14

On October 3, 1933, Admiral Yamamoto was appointed to command the First Air Division of the Imperial Combined Fleet. He moved his flag to the carrier *Akagi*, where he had served earlier as ship's captain.

Almost immediately he had the division out to sea, carrying on his usual program of very hard training. Lt. Comdr. Yoshitake Miwa, who had been one of Yamamoto's assistants during the Washington naval attaché days, and was now air officer aboard the *Akagi*, had this tale to tell about that training cruise.

On board the carrier, command of the air unit was in the hands of the ship's captain and the flight control officers, but once the unit got into the air, command was in the hands of the attack leader, who was a pilot officer.

On this cruise, after one extremely difficult morning of trying to meet Admiral Yamamoto's very rigorous specifications for performance, the fliers stopped for the midday meal. As was the usual habit, they had some sake to drink. It had been a hard few days, perhaps too hard, for the attack leader and some of the pilots suddenly found that they were drunk. When the order came to man their planes and resume the afternoon exercises, they could not. The exercise had to be canceled that afternoon.

When Yamamoto heard of this matter, he was very seriously concerned. As a matter of discipline, the captain of the ship called the attack leader on the carpet and announced that the offenders would be punished as severely as their conduct warranted. Immediately they were sent letters of reprimand, which were attached to their performance records. As they all knew, this sort of document could wreck a man's career. Further, they were promised that the admiral would have other punishments in mind.

The attack leader was a stubborn and belligerent young man, and he began trying to raise a furor. All they had done, he said, was what hundreds of other pilots had done before. The other pilots and the air crews all came to their leader's side, and the *Akagi* became almost an armed camp, with airmen against the ship's officers and crew.

During the next few days, the atmosphere aboard the *Akagi* became so tense that Admiral Yamamoto knew he was going to have to intervene. The problem was how to intervene without destroying the morale of the First Carrier Division and creating problems that would require rebuilding of the whole organization.

Finally, Yamamoto called a general assembly of the ship's crew. A staff officer who sat down among the flight personnel reported that the attitude of the flying personnel was very resentful and ugly.

Admiral Yamamoto then made a speech to the assembled crew. He cited the incident in which the attack force from the carrier had failed to get off the ship and into action at the appointed hour. Drunk on duty was the charge. As everyone knew, no matter what the traditions of the Japanese flying corps were, it was punishable by court-martial.

He said people were wondering what would be appropriate punishment for this action. Well, what would be appropriate? The admiral pursued the subject. In his younger years, he said, he too had broken many naval regulations. So he understood their feelings. But did they understand what they had done?

The flight crews who had gotten themselves into a situation where they were unable to operate had endangered the entire fleet. Their job was to search for the enemy, and to search for and destroy submarines, and they had not gotten off the deck of the *Akagi* to do it. What if this were wartime? What would there have been to prevent the enemy from launching an attack, by submarine or by air on the Japanese fleet?

Admiral Yamamoto paused to let that information and that last question sink in. Then he went on. And so, he said, the war might well be lost in the bottom of a sake bottle. The attack commander and his friends had endangered the fleet, had endangered the navy, had endangered the nation, and had endangered the life and welfare of the Emperor. Now, he said, what was to be the punishment for the attack leader and the others involved?

Let them decide for themselves, he said. Let them decide. If they wished to place the nation in jeopardy, then they could bear the responsibility. It was all theirs.

The admiral stopped speaking. It had been a masterful address, pointing out quite truthfully the responsibility that every naval man had to the Emperor, a direct responsibility for his own conduct. He had not had to call directly to their attention Emperor Meiji's rescript to soldiers and sailors, setting forth their responsibilities. They all knew it by heart. The auditorium was silent for a moment, and then it erupted in a pandemonium of cheers. The airmen realized that they would not after all be punished individually. But the attack leader was now in a most embarrassing position. He had endangered the welfare of the nation. Now he seemed to realize it and he came to the admiral and made his deepest apologies. Soon the tensions of the past week were forgotten. Good will was established. And later that day others besides the attack leader came to Admiral Yamamoto; all of them apologized deeply and promised to do their utmost in the future to live up to the high standards that he was setting for them.

Admiral Yamamoto's fliers were brash young men, however, and they clashed often with the staff officers and, other officers of the carrier. One particular flight leader never would take any advice. Staff officers would tell him, "Your landings are too fast, you are too careless about takeoffs and landings, and one day your plane is going to catch fire."

He would listen, say "Okay," and then go right back to doing things his own way. He was a very headstrong young man. Then one day when he was preparing for takeoff, he revved the engine too fast when the handlers were still working with the plane, and it caught fire. Before they could get him out he was half dead, half alive, half alright, and half roasted. So he learned—the hard way.

Admiral Yamamoto tried to persuade his fliers to learn from other people's experience, so they would not have to undergo all the trials themselves. He was very patient with them, although the steel fist of discipline was never fully relaxed.

As with all his efforts, the months that Yamamoto spent as com-

mander of the First Air Division of the Combined Fleet were valuable
to him and to the Imperial Navy. He made a powerful fighting unit of
the First Air Division.

And once again, Admiral Yamamoto was at sea, completely divorced
from a political scene that was growing ever more tense.

In 1931, when Yamamoto was busy perfecting new aircraft for the
Imperial Navy, the *kodo ha* faction of the Imperial Army was planning
to take over the army and to move into Manchuria to guarantee expansion
of the army in the future. By August of 1931, a storm stirred by the
statements of military men and jingoists and fanned by an overeager
press created what foreigners called "Manchuria fever." It raged
throughout Japan, mass meetings were called, and threats were made
against anyone who opposed the move into Manchuria.

That month, Minister of War Jiro Minami called for the use of
military force to seize Manchuria and made insulting remarks about
civilian politicians. Prime Minister Wakatsuki—the man who had
headed the Japanese delegation to the 1930 London Disarmament
Conference—did not really have the power to call the war minister on
the carpet and get him fired. Under the system that existed, if he fired
this general, Minami would simply be replaced by another, because the
Japanese constitution demanded that the war minister be a general on
active service. The reason for this in the past—a technical one—had
long since vanished, and many in Japan thought it would be better to
have civilian control of the armed forces. But not the generals. They
knew where the roots of power lay, and they were beginning realize
that they controlled them.

So in 1931 the army maneuvered the seizure of Manchuria, against
the wishes of the Emperor and his council and the cabinet. In 1932 they
moved into North China in the guise of "expeditions" to chase
"bandits."

Late in 1931, a group of army officers plotted to seize power. Their
plot was uncovered and the event failed to happen, but so powerful was
this *kodo ha* clique in the army that the most serious sentence meted
out to these traitors was twenty days' confinement for one officer, which
he spent in the luxury of a geisha house.

So, in 1932, when Admiral Yamamoto was developing the Mitsubishi Zero fighter plane, the army was in control of Japan's government

for all intents and purposes. The next year at Shanghai, the navy also was brought into the scene of violence, with a carrier used to fight the Chinese in the Chapei District. For the first time since the end of World War I, navy planes were being used to kill people.

Admiral Yamamoto knew what was going on, but he was being most discreet in these dangerous days, not even making any public statements. None were required of him; his position as chief technologist just then protected him from political harm. In May of 1932, young navy officers shot Prime Minister Inukai in his official residence. This was a matter of great concern to Admiral Yamamoto, for it showed unmistakably that the "fleet faction" of the navy was preparing to assume control in alliance with the *kodo ha* faction of the army.

To an advocate of peace, which Yamamoto was, disaster followed disaster. Japan withdrew from the League of Nations. General Araki, the war minister, began talking about "the Imperial Way," which meant turning Japan into a police state run by the army and navy, in which every citizen would be expected to die "for the Emperor" on the command of army and navy officers. This was never envisioned by the mild-mannered Hirohito, who had longed to be a constitutional monarch. But now Emperor worship, in the guise of Shinto, became the new religion of Japan.

In 1933, as Yamamoto sailed the ocean training his fliers for a war that he now saw coming, the Japanese occupied more of North China.

And then came 1934 and a new attempt by the moderates in Japan to check the power of the military. One of their principal instruments in this attempt was to be Admiral Yamamoto.

LONDON FAILURE

15

In the spring of 1934, while Admiral Yamamoto was at sea with the fleet, the "fleet faction" of the Imperial Japanese Navy had been busy taking control of naval affairs. Huge new naval guns had been designed, built, and tested. These guns were 18.1 inches in bore, more than two inches larger than the most powerful naval guns in the Western world. Plans were laid for the construction of four new battleships of 72,000 tons, which would make them by far the largest in the world and proper platforms for the 18.1-inch guns. The "fleet faction" leaders were planning many new cruisers and destroyers too. All of this, of course, was in violation of the spirit if not the letter of the London Treaty of 1930, which would expire in 1935.

The masters of the "fleet faction" had done everything but actually begin construction, and they were restrained from this only by the watchfulness of the "treaty faction." For the fact was that after the invasion of Manchuria the naval "fleet faction" and the army *kodo ha* faction became intertwined, both bent on expansion and conquest.

The figures for the year's government budget were announced, and it was revealed that military and naval expenditures were going to take forty-three percent of the national budget. Civilians in the Diet complained and went to Finance Minister Takahashi for answers. Takahashi went to War Minister Araki. The figures were not disclosable, said the general—military secret—and that was that.

The enormous expenditures were partly for planning naval expansion and partly for actual expansion of the army's operations in China. The Japanese moved into Inner Mongolia and even penetrated Hubei Province, where the old capital city of Beijing was located. All this military activity was supported by most of the public, which had been convinced by the depression's effects and by army propaganda that expansion into China was absolutely essential to the "survival" of Japan. The myth of "overpopulation" (fewer than 100 million people, as opposed to 120 million in 1980) had been established by the expansionists.

In the past year, the "fleet faction" had been conducting open warfare against the "treaty faction." In January of 1933, when Admiral Yamamoto had taken over the First Air Division of the Combined Fleet, Admiral Mineo Osumi had become minister of the navy. He was not a notable member of the "fleet faction," but he was a will-o'-the-wisp who blew with the wind. With the reemergence of Admiral Kanji Kato (who had become a member of the Supreme Military Council) and Admiral Nobumasa Suetsugu into positions of influence, supported by their army friends, Minister Osumi became their creature.

Admiral Kanji Kato met with the minister and with others of the "fleet faction," and soon they demanded that the minister clear out the enemies of the "treaty faction" from positions of influence in the navy. Admiral Seizo Sakonji had been forced to retire, as had Admiral Takeshi Terashima and Admiral Naomi Tanaguchi. These were all friends of Yamamoto's and people who believed, as he did, that Japan would be stupid to undertake a war against the great powers of England and the United States. Just now the followers of Admiral Kato were after the scalp of Admiral Takeichi Hori, Yamamoto's best friend.

This campaign was in full swing on September 7, 1934, when Admiral Yamamoto was suddenly appointed chief delegate for the navy to represent Japan at preliminary talks in London aimed at revising the London Disarmament Treaty of 1930 and extending it past 1935.

Yamamoto was a logical choice. He had been moved out of the First Air Division command in the spring of 1934 to become a member of a special Committee for the Study of Disarmament Measures, a group sacrosanct from the attacks by the "fleet faction" because it had Emperor Hirohito's wholehearted approval. The navy, now controlled by the "fleet faction" through Minister Osumi, told Yamamoto that it demanded full parity with the Americans and the British. Emperor Hirohito said that he wanted an extension of the treaty and work toward general disarmament. So Yamamoto was to go to London with lesser lights and with Ambassador Matsudaira, an old friend, to negotiate as best he could.

On September 25, Yamamoto and his staff met at Tokyo station. They were surrounded by people, not all of them well-wishers. From some came angry demands that Admiral Yamamoto stand up to the vicious Westerners and demand full parity. He was harangued by unofficial and unwanted advisors at the station, on the quai at Yokohama, and even in his cabin on the *Hie Maru*, where he was lying on the berth when a man burst in and began reading him a lecture from a long scroll. Yamamoto did not say anything, but he was not happy, and later he wrote to his friend Hori denouncing these "patriots."

The *Hie Maru* took the party to Seattle, where they boarded the Great Northern Railway. They rode east to Chicago, stopping off there for three days (Yamamoto went to Evanston to see a football game between Northwestern University and Iowa State), and then took the New York Central Railroad to New York. There they stayed at the Astor Hotel for a few more days, sailing on the *Berengaria* for England on October 10.

The ship landed at Southampton, and they took the boat train to Waterloo station. Then they went to Grosvenor House on Park Lane, where they would lodge in luxury.

On October 17, Admiral Yamamoto called on Ambassador Matsudaira, and they conferred about their plans for the meetings. Then they paid courtesy calls at the British Foreign Office, and the admiral called on the British Admiralty. Next day he called on the chief of staff of the Royal Navy, and then he had four days off to go sightseeing and amuse himself. On October 23, the meetings began at No. 10 Downing Street, the Prime Minister's residence. There the Japanese conferred with the British. Next day they went to Claridge's Hotel, where they conferred with the Americans. So it was not really a general conference at all, but a series of bilateral meetings that really could not have been expected to produce anything but confusion.

The problem was, or one problem was, that the Americans and the British could not agree among themselves as to what they really wanted. They sensed the growing irritation of Japan with the naval status quo, but they were very much worried about the Japanese army's encroachments in China. They also recognized that the navy had been employed in the "Shanghai incident" and had fired on the Chinese, while Japanese carrier planes had attacked Shanghai. Japan was therefore suspect, and it was difficult for the Western allies to come to grips with the Japanese demands for parity in naval terms.

The London meetings were seen as a last opportunity to save both the Washington and London Treaties of the past. The Washington Treaty would expire in 1936 and the London Treaty in 1935. Some elements in all three powers wanted to preserve at least some sort of treaty, but other elements, particularly in Japan, wanted to dump any restrictions on naval building whatsoever. This was the problem Yamamoto faced at home, as he knew very well.

The meetings proceeded through November, Ambassador Matsudaira and Admiral Yamamoto representing Japan, Prime Minister MacDonald, Foreign Secretary Simon and several British admirals representing the host country, and Ambassador Norman Davis and Admiral Standley representing the United States.

On November 15, Admiral Yamamoto was promoted again, this time to vice admiral. He was negotiating from strength this time, and he knew that his opponents were very much worried about Japan's emerging power. In a letter to his young protégé Lieutenant Commander Miwa, he showed that he was not immune to hopes for national aggrandizement himself:

> . . . I feel keenly that the time has come for this mighty empire rising in the east to devote itself, with all due circumspection, to advancing its own fortunes.
>
> The example afforded before the World War by Germany—which if it had only exercised forbearance for another five or ten years would by now be unrivaled in Europe—indicates that the task facing us is to build up our strength quietly and with circumspection. Even though the present conference may not be successful, I sense that the day may not be so distant when we shall have Britain and the United States kowtowing to us. . . .

And he also told Miwa that their shared field, naval aviation, was the wave of the future for Japan's navy.

* * *

Admiral Yamamoto was now moving in the highest circles, quite a feat for a poor boy from Nagaoka. He was entertained, along with Ambassador Matsudaira, by Prime Minister MacDonald at the official country estate, Chequers. They visited former Prime Minister Lloyd George. Yamamoto played bridge with various British admirals and usually won their money. In the evenings, Yamamoto and his aides played poker or bridge for a time, and then Yamamoto would write letters. He received hundreds of letters, from school children, well-wishers, and critics, and he tried to answer them all personally. He did not sleep a great deal, perhaps five or six hours a night, and the fact that he did not drink gave him increased stamina for the jobs to which he set himself.

While Yamamoto was in London, he received the bad news that the "fleet faction" had finally "gotten" his friend Admiral Takeichi Hori. He had been pushed out of his job by the naval minister and put on the reserve list—which meant an end to his naval career. The charges were a trumped up accusation of "cowardice" during the "Shanghai incident," when Hori had been commander of a squadron that was supposed to start firing on the Chinese and had delayed because there were civilians in the area.

It did not matter; the "fleet faction" would have found some way to get at Hori anyhow. He was even stronger in his denunciation of the "fleet faction's" warlike aims than Yamamoto had been in the past. In fact, Yamamoto just now was in the equivocal position of having to seek a parity with Britain and the United States that he did not really think was meaningful. However, he continued to try.

Meanwhile, he had discouraging reports about affairs at home. Not only was Admiral Hori disgraced, but so too were several other admirals, including Rear Admiral Tsuneyoshi Banno. Banno had been entrapped by a self-seeking journalist into making an unwise remark about factions within the Japanese navy and then found that the journalist had expanded and perverted his views. The resulting article gave Minister Osumi the opportunity he was looking for—to knock over another member of the "treaty faction" of the navy—and he did so immediately. Thus Yamamoto learned from afar that the situation in the navy was deteriorating very rapidly.

By late November, the situation in London was approaching stalemate. The big powers were not willing to grant Japan the naval parity that Admiral Yamamoto had been instructed to seek. He had cabled once or twice to the Navy Ministry for instructions, hoping to achieve some compromise, but the Navy Ministry was unyielding, spurred by the "fleet faction." No one could find a formula—largely because Japan wanted no compromises this time, only the right to build a big fleet. The British tried to approach the problem in another way, limiting the size and gunnery of individual types of ships, but no one was able to agree on that. So as December came, Admiral Yamamoto sensed that the conference would end in failure. Five days before Christmas, the Americans left suddenly for home, and that was the end of it.

By this time, the "young Turks" were in control of the naval affairs office in Tokyo, and they were saying privately that Yamamoto could not be trusted, that he would give everything away to the Americans and the British.

So, with nothing more to be done, on January 28, Admiral Yamamoto and Ambassador Matsudaira headed east, toward Moscow and the Trans-Siberian Railroad that would take them homeward.

They stopped off in Berlin, where the Germans had been taking a big interest in the naval talks and hoped to work out an alliance with the Japanese against the British and Americans. But Yamamoto, although he met German Foreign Minister von Ribbentrop, had no taste for Germans, particularly Adolf Hitler. It was indicated that he could be invited to meet Hitler, but he declined and got out of Berlin, heading for the East.

Yamamoto gambled his way across Siberia with those captive partners of his staff and arrived at Tokyo station on February 12, 1935. He was greeted by a large crowd of officials and well-wishers. While responding to them, a bit of the imp in him came out. A group of geisha from the Akasaka area of Tokyo were there, and someone said he stuck his tongue out at them as he passed.

After the platform reception, Yamamoto boarded his limousine and went to the Imperial Palace to sign the visitors book and thus announce to the Emperor that he had returned. After that he was free, and he went home to his family for the first time in five months.

Two days later he appeared at the Navy Ministry to report on the failure of the talks. The Navy Ministry was delighted, but not really caring. All the decisions had already been made, and the preparations by the "fleet faction" to begin the furious naval building program that had already been planned for two years were complete.

Yamamoto was now assigned to the Naval Affairs Bureau in Tokyo, but there he was given a room and nothing to do. He had come home famous, but he was ignored by the Navy Minister and the "fleet faction." The authorities seemed to want him to get so disgusted with inaction that he would resign. They very nearly succeeded; he considered this course seriously, but friends counseled against it.

But, he would argue, just now he would rather go back to Monaco and become a professional gambler. He could support himself without trouble.

In the end he did not resign, but rather consoled himself by making a number of trips to his home town of Nagaoka. He also consoled himself more personally by spending many hours at the geisha houses of Rappongi, where he was known fondly by the geisha as "eighty sen Yamamoto" because of the two missing fingers on his left hand; the geisha charged one yen for a manicure, but they said laughingly that they could not charge "old eighty sen" that much because he didn't have all his fingers. He had long-standing personal relationships with several geisha. Now, in the loneliness of rank without power, he had time to pursue them.

The isolation of Yamamoto continued for some time. The "fleet faction" wanted to see him destroyed, but he had too great a reputation, and now that he was back in Japan, he kept quiet about his views. There was no point in enunciating them any more because the treaties were dead and Japan was already embarked on its massive naval building program that was supposed to put it ahead of the United States within five years. Finally, friends in high places overruled the "fleet faction" and got Yamamoto an appointment through which he could once again be very valuable to Japan. He was made head of the aeronautics department of the navy, which meant all the naval air program, carriers, sea planes, and land-based airplanes.

YAMAMOTO AND THE AIR FORCE

16

Later, when the dust of World War II had settled, the Japanese naval historians would recall Admiral Isoroku Yamamoto not only as the "Nelson of Japan," but also as one of the learned pioneers of naval aviation. At first almost alone among the senior Japanese naval officers he saw the value of naval aviation. As a captain, and then as a rear admiral, he had the clout in the Imperial Navy to do something about it.

Yamamoto was a captain when he learned to fly and became an expert in flight operations. From afar, in America, he saw how naval aviation might be used, and he decided that Japan must become the pioneer. Then he set out to convince his peers. The Japanese navy, like those of the United States and Great Britain, was still heavily committed to the battleship. In the 1930s, Yamamoto set out to change this, but he had certainly not done so by 1935 when he came to the air force again.

In the early 1930s, as head of the technical division of the naval air force, Admiral Yamamoto had undertaken developmental work on a number of naval aircraft, including the Zero fighter, the Type 97 single-engined attack plane, and the twin-engined Type 96 attack plane and general-purpose aircraft, which in its most common manifestation came to be known to the Allied airmen as the "Betty." In 1935, when

Yamamoto was taken from the oblivion of the Naval Affairs Bureau back room and put in charge of the naval air forces, he once more encountered these aircraft, which at the time were just coming into operational use.

To Yamamoto, the job as head of the air department was the most desirable one in the navy. The appointment was traditionally for one year only, but Yamamoto would have liked to keep it forever. It gave him a chance to do for naval aviation all those things he wanted to do.

One of his first priorities was to improve the quality of naval combat flying to the point where the number of operational accidents was cut way down. Until Yamamoto's day, when a pilot had perfected his landing techniques and was stationed aboard a carrier, he thought his training was pretty well over. Yamamoto was of a different view: He wanted constant training. He wanted fliers who could fly rings around the pilots of other countries, and the only way to get them was to keep them in the air until they made virtually no more mistakes. So Yamamoto training came back to the naval air force.

He then began to devise tactics for the employment of aircraft. He foresaw the day when the navy would have large sea areas to protect, when naval aircraft could not be confined to float planes for battleships and cruisers and wheeled planes for carriers. They would need all sorts of aircraft for all sorts of purposes. The Japanese then developed the giant four-engined Kawanishi flying boat, which was the most effective long-range search plane in the Pacific during the Great War. Yamamoto also foresaw the day when long-range bombers (the Bettys) operating from land bases could bomb targets a thousand miles away or attack an enemy fleet.

In 1930, as chief of the technical division, Admiral Yamamoto had persuaded the giants of industry at Osaka to back the concept of a large carrier force. In 1935 he went to work on the giants of aircraft production—Mitsubishi, Aichi, and Nakajima—and persuaded them to back the concepts he wanted for naval aircraft production. And Yamamoto knew what he wanted, because, unlike almost any other air admiral in the world at this point in history, he flew in the airplanes himself and knew what was needed.

This year, 1935, was probably Yamamoto's happiest in the navy. He was building the air organization he wanted, he was slowly convincing a number of his peers that the aviation arm was vital to the fleet, and he was beginning to get the sort of aircraft that would catapult

Japan's air fleet into world leadership. Also, he was out of the political scene altogether, which delighted him.

In fact, 1935 was a watershed year in Japanese politics. Since 1931, the *kodo ha* element of the army had been in control of military policy, and the expansion had gone apace. The navy counterparts had also begun to have more influence than in the past, although they were more restrained than the army.

The fact was, however, that at the beginning of 1936 the political atmosphere in Japan had become very dangerous. In the summer of 1934, a young officer named Aizawa became furious with General Tetsuzan Nagara of the Military Affairs Bureau for guiding the army in the wrong way, he said, and he shot the general dead. The reform faction within the army insisted that the young lieutenant colonel be disciplined, and he was ordered to stand trial by court-martial. This action brought the condemnation of hundreds of young officers who backed the *kodo ha* and its new manifestation, the Imperial Way movement.

As the year dragged on, it became apparent that the *kodo ha* faction of the army was losing political ground in Japan. The Seiyukai party of Japan, which backed the *kodo ha* faction, lost many seats in an election called that fall. The Minseito party, which was moderate, was brought to power, showing that, underneath, the Japanese people really favored moderation.

The army men realized this and saw that if they were going to have power, they were going to have to seize it by violent action. Thus were laid the seeds of open rebellion in the army right wing.

A plot was hatched and triggered through a newspaper announcement. Early on the morning of February 26, 1936, four regiments of the army, including one of the special Imperial Guards, set about a campaign of assassination. Generals, admirals, and political leaders fell. The young officers seized the War Office and occupied the Diet building, but they did not manage to seize the Navy Ministry and other key offices. They very nearly killed Prime Minister Okada; he was saved only because the young officers charged with the job did not know Okada, and they killed his brother-in-law by mistake.

On this black morning of treason, Admiral Yamamoto was staying at the Navy Ministry as duty officer. When the word came to him that dreadful things were happening in the other government offices of Tokyo, he did what he could to help.

Many of the navy's senior officers had been waiting for some sort of move from the army activists. For months the younger officers of the navy staff had been bombarded with propaganda calling for action. Some of them, of course, followed the *kodo ha* faction, but some did not, and from those who did not, the senior officers of the "treaty faction" learned what was happening.

One of them, Admiral Mitsumasa Yonai, was commander of the Yokosuka Naval Station, and Admiral Shigeyoshi Inouye was his chief of staff. They were prepared. In fact, Inouye had already managed to have a navy tank stationed in front of the Navy Ministry, just in case. Its reported purpose was "to familiarize the Japanese people with weapons." Now they also prepared the First and Second Fleets for action. If the army seized the Diet and other buildings, the navy was prepared to fight it out and pulverize the buildings. It would take about three salvos from the guns of the ships in the harbor to do the job, the admiral in command suggested. They also had trained special troops to be used in such a fracas.

As it turned out, however, the army's coup was anything but complete. After it had begun, Admiral Yamamoto learned the facts. He had no authority, as air officer, to call out ships or troops, but he could send an ambulance to the residence of Admiral Kantaro Suzuki, the grand chamberlain to the Emperor, who had been wounded in the assassination attempts.

Suzuki had four bullet wounds, but he survived; the attempt to assassinate him was an indication of the bungling of the day. The rebellion really lasted four days; army officers occupied several government buildings and would not leave, but they did not have enough strength to carry off the revolution. Before many hours passed, the Emperor declared martial law in Tokyo. When his military aide (who was an old army man) objected, Hirohito turned on the aide and told him that if nothing was done, he would personally lead the Imperial guards to put down the rebels. When that word got out, the rebels suddenly collapsed. Ultimately, thirteen officers were convicted of treason and executed.

In the next few months, the *kodo ha* faction of the army was quieter, and so was the "fleet faction" of the navy. In this period, a number of generals retired. Moreover, during this period, the "treaty faction" of the navy gained power under the government formed by Koki Hirota, a moderate. Admiral Mineo Osumi, who did the bidding of the "fleet faction" of the navy, was relieved as Navy Minister, and Admiral Osami Nagano was selected. At the end of 1936, Nagano lost his vice minister of the navy, Admiral Kiyoshi Hasegawa, who went back to sea, as was mandatory for an admiral seeking success in the chain of command. Minister Nagano wanted Admiral Yamamoto to be his new vice minister. The reasons were simple enough: Yamamoto spoke English very well and understood the British and the Americans, which few Japanese naval persons did. Also, he had shown himself in London to be a skilled diplomat, and in this touchy period—with Japan out of the League of Nations, the army mistreating visitors, and the situation in China worsening almost weekly—diplomacy was certainly valuable. And finally, Yamamoto's moderate views toward Great Britain and the United States coincided with those of Prime Minister Hirota and the navy minister.

The trouble was that Yamamoto did not want the job. He hated politics, and he loved what he was doing, creating a powerful air force. At first he refused the post, but the navy minister came back to him again. When it was put to him on patriotic terms, he had no choice but to accept.

At the end of 1936, therefore, Admiral Isoroku Yamamoto for the first time took on a job that was more political and diplomatic than military. He did it to help those who shared his views, and to try to keep the naval "fleet faction" from taking over. He was entering the most dangerous period of his life. He had scarcely been in office more than a few days when it was rumored that one of the superpatriotic societies had declared him a primary target for assassination.

TARGET OF THE RIGHT

17

The announcement of appointment of Vice Admiral Isoroku Yamamoto to the post of vice minister of the navy brought groans and complaints from the members of the "fleet faction." Yamamoto's views about the various naval treaties were very well known in Japan, as was his belief that Japan would be committing suicide to go to war with the United States.

By 1936, the "fleet faction" had managed to put out of its collective mind any consideration of the nation's natural resources. A cool head would have told them the following:

Copper	75,000 tons yearly (less than half of military requirement)
Iron ore	12 percent of national requirement
Coking coal	None
Petroleum	10 percent of need
Rubber	None

Japan's industrial capacity, too, was extremely limited. In 1936, three million people were employed in factories with five or more workers, but an equal number of persons were employed in "cottage industries," which meant fewer than five persons per working unit.

The "fleet faction" dismissed these statistics as misleading, however. Manchuria had plenty of iron and coking coal. Copper could be obtained from the Philippines and other Southeast Asian countries. Petroleum was available in the Dutch East Indies. Rubber was plentiful in Malaya.

How would Japan get these resources? She would take them, after her fleet had dealt with the Americans, the British, and the Dutch and Japan had assumed her rightful place as leader of the Asian bloc of nations.

How would Japan convert to a wartime industrial footing? She would pass new laws putting the people at the service of the new government. By 1936, the activists had blinded themselves to the statistical needs of Japan, and they completely disregarded a factor that Yamamoto placed even ahead of natural resources: the resilience of the United States and its amazing ability to produce manufactured goods in quantity.

Soon Admiral Yamamoto's views on another subject quieted his enemies for a time, however: "As for myself," he said, "I would much rather be chief of the air department of the navy than involved in the government role. This is what I have wanted to do all my life long."

Certainly no naval faction could complain about those views, since it was also known that Admiral Yamamoto's management of the air arm was the most aggressive possible and that he was a strong believer in a powerful attack force. Still, he accepted the post of vice minister with very little enthusiasm. He was not very pleased with his minister in the first place. Yamamoto had shown how he felt about Nazi Germany when he left the London talks in December of 1934 by showing no interest at all in German Foreign Minister von Ribbentrop's attempts to take him into camp in Berlin. He had not even wanted to meet Hitler. And now he was to work for a man who had already announced his support of a treaty of alliance with Hitler and Italy's Benito Mussolini. To be sure, the navy had a clear-cut tradition of apolitical service. The Navy minister was a political appointee and as a member of the cabinet had to engage in politics. But no one else in the navy, including the vice minister, had ever engaged in politics. The vice minister's job was administrative and supportive. He was to support the minister's policies, no matter how he felt about them personally. This was the way it had always been.

Therefore, when the congratulations began to come in, such as those from Yamamoto's friend (and later biographer) Eiichi Sorimachi, the admiral said brusquely: "There's no cause for rejoicing."

Yamamoto stuck out what must have been a rather unpleasant assignment, working for a man he did not really respect, but bound by Imperial Navy protocol to accept an appointment from a superior, until the fall of the Hirota cabinet. It was a dreadful period in Yamamoto's life, for he was like a circus acrobat walking a tightrope.

The *tosei ha* (control) faction of the army had gained control after the unwise attempt of the *kodo ha* to create the revolution of February 2, 1936. The "control faction" generals were going to make certain that no such uprising was tried again, so they ruthlessly rooted out the malcontents and replaced them with their own men. One control officer was General Hideki Tojo, promoted to become the chief of the Kempeitai of the Kwantung Army in Manchuria. This was the "control faction's" way of controlling the Kwantung Army, which had been so difficult for so long.

As the "control faction" secured power, however, its aims and those of the old *kodo ha* faction seemed almost to coincide. The Hirota government, dedicated to peace and civilian government control, was losing power steadily and swiftly. Japanese incursions in North China grew ever more obvious, until, in December of 1936, the month that Yamamoto was appointed to the navy vice ministry, two desperate generals in North China abducted General Chiang Kai-shek at Xian in northwest China and forced him to agree to stop his anticommunist campaign in China and turn a united front against the Japanese.

Early in 1937, the Hirota government fell in a dispute with the army. The army had a simple mechanism of control at this point, brought in as the army's latchkey to power. No cabinet could function unless it had a war minister. The army got the supreme council to pass a constitutional requirement that the war minister must be an army officer on active service. Thus, if a war minister began to side with the civilians, the army could retire him, and a new man would have to be appointed. No one could be appointed who did not have the approval of the "control faction." If the "control faction" generals did not like the actions of the cabinet, they could force its fall by telling the war minister to resign.

And this is what happened with Hirota. The war minister resigned, and no one else from the army would serve. Hirota could not form a new cabinet. He resigned.

The next cabinet was formed by General Senjuro Hayashi, a moderate. At first he had the support of the "control faction." He appointed a new navy minister, Admiral Mitsumasa Yonai. The admiral, of course, had the privilege of choosing his own vice minister, but Yamamato and Yonai were suited to work with each other like a pair of draft horses. They were old friends, having become acquainted shortly after the Russo-Japanese War, when Ensign Yamamoto had been sent to gunnery school. Lieutenant Yonai and Ensign Yamamoto had shared quarters and had soon found that they had much in common. They agreed on most naval matters, and they worked together so well that biographer Sorimachi termed their relationship a "famous combination." It would persist until virtually the end of constitutional government in Japan, and one of Yonai's last acts as a political figure would be to save Yamamoto's life by "putting him on ice."

Yonai arrived in the cabinet in the same month that a book about him—*The Life of a Navy Man*—was published. Theoretically, it was an excellent bit of timing for such a book. Yonai had recently been appointed commander of the Combined Fleet, which in those years was the apex of a distinguished naval career. He could be expected to serve two or three years and then to step down and retire at the top of his form. As it turned out, however, this was not entirely a salutary moment, in terms of political life, because it brought Yonai to the attention and scrutiny of the army authorities, who were looking over their shoulders with enormous suspicion. Preparing to seize absolute power, they were worried lest they be frustrated. And indeed, a very intelligent combination of men—Admiral Yonai, Admiral Yamamoto, and Admiral Inouye (who had been Yonai's deputy during the Yokosuka Naval Station days and the abortive February 26, 1936 putsch)—was going to do their best to throw obstacles in the face of the military takeover.

Although Prime Minister Hayashi was a general, he could not control the army, and his government lasted only until May of 1937. It collapsed over what by now had become the usual issue: a quarrel between the civilian and military factions of the government. The Emperor and his council were then faced with a knotty problem. If they took on a new general as Prime Minister, they were putting the empire into the hands of the army. There was no doubt about that. The army candidate was General Sugiyama, one of the leaders of the "control faction." But who else could there be? The army had already declared its unremitting opposition to "politicians."

There was one figure, Prince Fumimaro Konoye. The prince was bred to royal privilege and luxury, and yet he had a sort of magic common touch as well, although it was not matched by the inner strength of character that marks a statesman. Still, he was considered by the Emperor to be the best bet in the hard game of trying to stop the army from running roughshod over civil government. And so the prince acceded to the Prime Ministry, and the army adopted a wait and see policy about him. Prince Konoye was advised to keep Admirals Yonai and Yamamoto in office as counterbalances to the army, and he did so. But Konoye also appointed General Araki to be minister of education, a disastrous move that threw the whole Japanese educational system into the hands of the army. Immediately the army took advantage of the offer; Bushido became the new philosophy of education. Everything for the Emperor. *Tenno heika Banzai!* No one living in Japan in the summer of 1937 could miss the implications of what was going on.

And, of course, the political pot boiled over all too soon.

In June, from Mukden, General Tojo sent down a politicomilitary report that warned that the Chinese were growing stronger all the time and that they had just signed a pact of mutual defense with Outer Mongolia that threatened Japanese intentions toward Inner Mongolia. General Tojo advocated a preemptive strike before Chiang Kai-shek could get his house in order. The army high command agreed. And so in June the cards were stacked.

On June 25, Yamamoto's elder brother Kihachi died up in Nagaoka. Although the admiral had long been living under the name Yamamoto, he was still a Takano at heart, and he loved his family. From time to time he had visited Nagaoka, spending as much time as possible there, in fact. Now he attended the funeral but stayed only hours, returning to the capital by the night train of June 27.

So Yamamoto was back in Tokyo when the pot boiled over in North China on July 7. The Japanese garrison forces around Beijing had gotten

General Tojo's message, and they created an incident at the Marco Polo Bridge outside the city. A column of Chinese troops, who had every right to be in the area, was passing on the Marco Polo Bridge going one way and a column of Japanese troops, who said they had every right to be there, was passing in the other direction. Shots were fired, men were killed, and the two columns dropped off the bridge and assumed defensive positions facing one another.

The troops remained facing one another, while the politicians took up the matter.

Prime Minister Konoye had constituted the five key members of the cabinet—war, navy, home, finance, and himself—as a sort of super-cabinet to make quick decisions. He called this cabinet committee into session and asked for advice. The army wanted to go all out to conquer China. Admiral Yonai, the navy minister, wanted quite the opposite. He and Yamamoto wanted to keep the poison from spreading. When the army insisted on sending troops, Yonai and Yamamoto objected, but the army said that it must save the 5000-man Tianjin garrison. This would solve everything, said the war minister—they would see that as soon as the announcement came, the Chinese would give in and become reasonable.

Admiral Yonai did not believe it, and he was right. The staff of the army wanted a war, and they were determined to have it. Every time General Sugiyama, the war minister, made an agreement with the other four ministers, the army high command vetoed it. If anybody objected, they threatened to withdraw General Sugiyama from the cabinet, thus forcing the fall of the government. And so the "China incident" at Marco Polo Bridge made a full-scale war out of what had been a smouldering fire.

It took a while, largly because of the determined opposition of Admirals Yonai and Yamamoto to every hostile act of the army. But they were beaten down on issue after issue and came to be known in army circles as principal obfuscators. Yamamoto was so frustrated that he gave up smoking, one of his few habits. In London he had bought a large supply of expensive cigars, which he had been smoking and giving out to visitors. Now he suddenly gave them all away. Friends tried to give him cigars. No, he said, he would not take them. Not until "this mess" was over would he smoke again. Friends thought he meant the "China incident," but that was not precisely what he said. All the signs in 1937, to a man of Yamamoto's intelligence, knowledge, and prescience, pointed to a collision course between Japan and the Western powers.

Japan's naval rebuilding program was the talk of the Western world. Sometimes the Westerners threw jibes at Japan, as with the contention that the Japanese were good at copying but could not produce original designs. One common story was "The Tale of the Purloined Destroyer Plans."

Japanese spies had stolen the American plans for a new destroyer, so the story went, and they used them to build a new destroyer in their own program. The destroyer was launched and went down the ways, flags flying and bands playing, and went down, down, down, straight down to the bottom of the sea, because the Americans had made some slight alterations in the plans they had "carelessly" laid out for the Japanese to steal.

The story made the rounds of American cocktail parties and brought great laughter. The Japanese were noted for copying. Why, had they not even named a town "USA" so they could stamp on their cheap copies of good old American goods "Made in USA"? Who could take seriously any nation who did things like that?

The fact was, of course, as the students of naval affairs in the West knew, that the Japanese were building a great fleet, the most powerful in the Pacific by far, and, courtesy of the indefatigable lobbying of Admiral Yamamoto, the most powerful carrier force in the world. The new super battleships *Yamato* and *Musashi* were coming along on schedule, and others were planned. Cruisers and destroyers were coming off the ways. The Japanese naval torpedo was at least two generations ahead of the best American torpedo. Japanese naval gunnery was better than either American or British gunnery. Japanese aircraft, far from being copies of British, American, and German designs, as they once had been, were now original, and mostly far ahead of the West.

Yamamoto knew this, and so did the hawks, Admiral Kanji Kato, Admiral Nobumasa Suetsugu, and Admiral Chuichi Nagumo. And these days, the hawks were beginning to speak out, loudly and clearly.

One day Admiral Nagumo saw Admiral Inouye at a party at Prince Fushimi's house and, as usual, led an argument for the "fleet faction" against the "treaty faction" that Inouye was known to represent. In the end Nagumo became angry and threatened Inouye: "You're a fool," he said. "One thrust with a dagger up under the ribs and that would be it. . . ."

Among all the treaty advocates, Admiral Inouye was perhaps the most outspoken. Certainly he was much more outspoken than Yamamoto. But Inouye was no fool. In 1937 he wrote his will, and after that he spoke out quite freely, with no apparent concern for what might happen to him.

On September 20, 1937, Admirals Yonai and Yamamoto got a new ally. Admiral Shigeyoshi Inouye became head of the Naval Affairs Bureau. Since he was of like mind with Yonai and Yamamoto, there seemed to be some hope of limiting the navy's role in the "China incident."

By that time, everyone in Japan knew that the "China incident" had become something very serious indeed. Three divisions of troops had been sent to Tianjin. The Japanese army air force was bombing North China, the Japanese captured Tianjin, and then Beijing, but the Chinese retreated and fought on.

From Yamamoto's point of view, the most serious aspect of the affairs of that late summer was the spread of the war to Shanghai and the employment of naval forces. The cruiser *Idzumo*, lying in the Whangpoo, was bombed by Chinese planes, and this brought the call to bring naval forces into Shanghai. The cabinet authorized (over Admiral Yonai's disapproval) two more divisions of troops for China. General Sugiyama personally told the Emperor not to worry, he would end the "China incident" within thirty days.

Japanese carriers, cruisers, battleships, and destroyers were now all employed: blockading the China coast, lying in the Whangpoo, and supporting Japanese troops with gunfire and bombing raids.

In September, the army rammed through the Diet a two-billion-yen supplementary military budget, all brought about by the "China incident." Prime Minister Konoye opened a drive for "national unity" at Hibiya Park in Tokyo and made a rousing speech.

In the West, the Americans suspended shipments of scrap iron to Japan. President Franklin D. Roosevelt came out and said it: "Japan is an aggressor nation!"

Admiral Yamamoto could see the clouds darkening. His reaction was to do nothing at all, that is, to work hard during the day and then at about five o'clock in the evening to disappear from the office without telling anyone where he was to be found. Usually he was in the geisha quarter visiting one of several geisha with whom he had long relationships. If anyone spoke to him about this, he indicated that what he did on his own time was nobody's business but his own. The young militants of the navy grew bolder. One day a delegation of ardent young officers stormed into the Navy Ministry and demanded to see Vice Minister Yamamoto. Another might have turned them away. He did not. They came in carrying petitions and with stern looks on their young faces.

It was most unseemly, they said, for a man in the position of the admiral to be seen so often in the geisha quarter of Tokyo.

The admiral looked them up and down. "Any of you that doesn't fart or shit and has never screwed a woman speak up. I'm willing to listen." And then he sent them on their way without another word.

The Japanese army captured Shanghai and then began to march on Nanjing. By December 11, they were fighting in Nanjing's suburbs.

And on that day a squadron of Admiral Yamamoto's men carried out an act that to him would have been unthinkable. They were supposedly attacking the Chinese upriver from Nanjing. But they bombed and sank three steamers of the Standard Oil Company and the American gunboat USS *Panay*. At about the same time, a Japanese artillery commander on the shore attacked the British gunboats *Ladybird*, *Bee*, *Cricket*, and *Scarab*.

However, the sinking of the American gunboat was the serious matter. As Admiral Yamamoto expected, it brought a storm of fury from the United States. In Tokyo, Ambassador Grew began packing, half sure that the United States would break diplomatic relations. Admiral Yamamoto rushed to the American Embassy to put the best possible face on the terrible affair, to apologize profusely, to offer indemnity, and to do all that a man of good will could do.

One basic problem, however, was that Yamamoto's sincere protestations were not echoed in the navy itself. The young officers were jubilant at what they had done, and many of their superiors agreed.

Yamamoto and Minister Yonai sent their own agents to China to try to avoid any further incidents. But with the set of mind of the naval forces in the field, this was almost impossible. When Admiral Mitsunami, the man in charge of the task force that had sunk the *Panay*, came back to Tokyo, Minister Yonai fired him immediately and publicly. It was a precedent and a warning to the ''fleet faction.'' All these efforts, cemented by Foreign Minister Koki Hirota (the former Prime Minister) with his own heartfelt expressions of goodwill, convinced the Americans that it might really have been a mistake, which Yamamoto knew it was not, although he detested the men who had carried it out.

So finally, largely through Yamamoto's offices, the *Panay* incident came to an end without blowing up into war. Vice Minister Yamamoto issued a public statement:

> The imperial Navy, which bore responsibility for this incident, takes this opportunity to express its gratification at the fairness and perspicacity shown, despite a barrage of misunderstanding and propaganda, by the American public in appreciating the true facts of the incident and Japan's good faith in dealing with it. It also expresses the deep gratitude for the dispassionate and understanding attitude adopted by the Japanese public since the occurrence of the incident.
>
> The navy will, of course, take redoubled precaution henceforth to ensure the eradication of incidents of this type, but at the same time it earnestly hopes that the entire nation will help turn misfortune to good advantage by cooperating in the furthering of international understanding and friendship via the removal of misapprehension and suspicions that come between Japan and other nations concerned in the ''China incident.''

After the *Panay* incident, the hawks within the navy were temporarily cowed. The triumvirate at the Navy Ministry let it be known that the fools had brought Japan very near to war with the United States, at a time when Japan was certainly not ready. Thus the triumvirate gained a few steps on the hawks of the right. In the navy they managed to secure the appointment of Admiral Suetsugu, one of the principal leaders of the ''fleet faction,'' as a cabinet councillor. This put him on the naval reserve list and took him out of the picture.

So 1937 came to an end. The following year brought new troubles. The worst of them was the Tripartite Pact—the Rome-Berlin-Tokyo alliance sought by Hitler and Mussolini and endorsed enthusiastically by the army and the ''fleet faction'' of the navy.

This move was heartily detested by the Navy Ministry triumvirate.

As Yamamoto put it, to form an alliance with the worst enemies of the United States and Great Britain was to court war. "The way things are going," he would say gloomily, "we shall have war with the United States."

It was 1938 when the young naval and army officers began to speak openly against Admirals Yonai, Yamamoto, and Inouye, to complain about their attitudes toward the Tripartite Pact and toward "Japan's national interests." Admiral Yamamoto began to receive a steady stream of hate mail. At first Yamamoto was upset by these letters, and he spent many hours reading them and checking on the bonafides of the senders. Then he came to the conclusion that this was part of an organized fright campaign and that the senders were all members of the right wing. After this he was inclined to pay very little attention to the complaints. But soon the complaints became threats, as the young officers grew ever more hysterical under the pressure of the "China incident," which just would not go away, but spread and spread and spread.

So the complainants began to parrot Admiral Nagumo's words— how easy it would be to stick a knife under the ribs of the three of them. And the wish was father to the thought, for in 1938, Admirals Yamamoto, Yonai, and Inouye all began receiving death threats. Some of them promised to come the next day and kill Yamamoto. The threats did not change Admiral Yamamoto's way of life a bit. He often went to the British Embassy to dinner or to see a film. He continued to go, although sometimes he had to push his way through angry demonstrators crowding the front of the Embassy. One tale of threats and action was told by Shigeharu Enemoto, a friend of Yamamoto's who was secretary of the Navy Ministry Secretariat:

One day in June 1939, Vice Minister Yamamoto invited me to dinner, to which I consented readily.

Before going to dinner, Admiral Yamamoto wanted to visit his niece who was sick in the hospital. We walked right by the British Embassy. At that time outside the British Embassy a huge crowd was gathered for a demonstration, and they were shouting slogans and cursing Admiral Yamamoto. He did not pay the slightest bit of attention, except to laugh. I was struck dumb by this show of courage.

At that time his opposition to the Japan-Germany-Italy Tripartite Pact was well known and aroused hundreds of complaints. He was prepared to die.

Yamamoto wrote:

To die for Emperor and Nation is the highest hope of a military man.
After a brave hard fight the blossoms are scattered on the fighting field.
But if some person wants to take a life instead, still the fighting man
will go to eternity for Emperor and country. One man's life or death
is a matter of no importance. All that matters is the Empire. As Con-
fucius said, "They may crush cinnabar, yet they do not take away its
color; one may burn a fragrant herb, yet it will not destroy the scent."
They may destroy my body, yet they will not take away my will.

Usually Yamamoto was not so solemn about the prospects. Yamamoto's friend Sorimachi visited him one day at the Ministry and they
went out for a meal. On their way back to Sorimachi's hotel, they
stopped at a shop in the Kanda, the literary section of Tokyo, to look
at something. The something turned out to be a piece of Admiral Yamamoto's calligraphy in a nice, neat frame.

It was, of course, the mark of prominence that someone would want
to collect Yamamoto's calligraphy, quite common practice in China and
Japan. Some generals, admirals, and statesmen were really very skillful
at this fine art. Yamamoto was not one of the best, just as he was not
much of a poet, although he wrote a lot of poetry.

Admiral Yamamoto told his friend a story about this piece of calligraphy. It seems that their mutual friend, Admiral Shiozawa, had come
to the shop a few days earlier on some other errand and had noticed the
calligraphy.

"How much?" he had asked the shopowner.

"Eighty yen, sir," said the shopkeeper.

"Oh, that's far too much," said the admiral. "Why, Yamamoto's
calligraphy is not worth buying. It's no good at all."

"That's right, sir," said the shopkeeper. "I'm afraid the calligraphy
is no good, but the frame alone cost me ninety yen. I think eighty yen
is a reasonable price—it's still ten yen less than the cost of the frame.
This is a big bargain!"

And Admiral Yamamoto had laughed aloud as he told the story on
himself.

As the political situation developed, however, the prospect ceased
to be humorous. The army, annoyed by Yamamoto's unflinching opposition to the Rome-Berlin-Tokyo treaty, sent military police to

"guard" Yamamoto. He was quite certain that at some point they would make an attempt on his life, so he avoided them as much as possible and made sure that he always had a couple of sailors around when the military police were near. The trouble was the navy did not have a shore police system to match the Kempeitai. It was another coup for the army. In the guise of "protecting" all the national leaders, the army kept a watchful eye on them.

Early in January of 1939, the Konoye cabinet fell, over the issue of the Rome-Berlin-Tokyo treaty. A new cabinet was formed by Kiichiro Hiranuma. Navy Minister Yonai retained his post, as did Yamamoto. By this time it was apparent that the Rome-Berlin-Tokyo axis was going to be forced on Japan by the army. Yonai and Yamamoto struggled to turn it into a sort of anti-Comintern pact, which would not be operable if, for example, Hitler went to war with Great Britain. Japan would not have to follow. This matter dominated that cabinet all its life, and seventy-five meetings were held on the subject of the treaty.

That summer of 1939 the threats against Yamamoto became more numerous. Against his wishes, the "fleet faction" had extended its doctrine, and now the United States was openly considered to be the prime enemy. Yamamoto lamented this state of affairs, but there was nothing he could do about it.

The Hiranuma government collapsed in August of 1939 when suddenly the Germans announced the signing of a nonaggression pact with the Soviet Union. The announcement threw the army and all the supporters of the Rome-Berlin-Tokyo alliance into confusion.

A few days later the European war began when the Germans marched into Poland. General Abe was chosen to lead the new Japanese government, and he wanted a less militant navy minister who would not balk the army so often. So Admiral Yonai was out, and so was Admiral Yamamoto. One of Yonai's last acts as minister was to secure the appointment of Admiral Yamamoto as Commander in Chief of the Combined Fleet. He did it because he was quite certain that if Yamamoto stayed ashore, he would be assassinated before the year was out.

And so Vice Admiral Yamamoto cleared out his desk at the Navy Ministry. It had almost been cleared anyhow, for since the threats of assassination had begun, he had started carrying away all his personal possessions. Now he finished the job. On August 30, 1939, Yamamoto went to the Imperial Palace for investiture as Commander in Chief of the Combined Fleet. His wife was off in Karuizawa visiting. The next day, wearing his splendid white uniform with all the gold braid and the Order of the Sacred Treasure, First Class, he boarded a train at Tokyo station and traveled to Osaka. Offshore, the great Combined Fleet rode at anchor, some seventy ships, the third most powerful fleet in all the world. Here would be Admiral Yamamoto's new home, and his last one.

PLANNING FOR PEARL HARBOR

18

What is remarkable about the coming of Admiral Yamamoto to the Combined Fleet (as described in Chapter 1) is how Admiral Yamamoto the political creature, who had served in four cabinets as vice minister of the navy, could become Admiral Yamamoto the military creature, whose only interest from the day he hoisted his flag above the *Nagato* was the perfection of the fleet as a fighting machine and a plan of attack designed to win the war he knew was coming within a few months. It indicates a rare sort of detachment for a fighting man.

On the surface in 1939, even after the war in Europe began, the prospects for Japan seemed bright. Prime Minister Abe claimed that Japan would not become involved in the European conflict. But that thought passed quickly, and so did the Abe government, which lasted only four months.

Then someone in the Imperial entourage had one last card to play against army control. Admiral Yonai was appointed to form a government and did. The reason was Emperor Hirohito's hope that he could avoid the signing of the pact with Berlin and Rome.

Admiral Yamamoto had no confidence in the whole idea. Too much was happening that indicated Japan was going the other way. The press was running heavily jingoist. Former Prime Minister Konoye was talking about the need to disband all political parties and turn to "national movements" instead in the search for Japanese unity of purpose.

Yonai could not achieve that. His cabinet, even with the imperial blessing, staggered along and finally collapsed in July of 1940. By this time, Admiral Yamamoto seemed oblivious to the politics that had earlier intrigued him. Therefore, when a friend wrote him asking what he would think about going into politics himself, he said flatly that the idea was most unappealing and that for him the best place to be was at sea.

And from the standpoint of the Imperial Japanese Navy, Yamamoto was certainly proving that contention.

The first year of Admiral Yamamoto's tenure as Commander in Chief of the Combined Fleet was devoted to creating a powerful fighting machine. How powerful was shown in the completion of the mighty *Yamato* and *Musashi*, 76,000-ton battleships, about ready in 1940, as compared to the five 35,000-ton battleships added to the British navy, as announced by Prime Minister Churchill that year. Three more such giant battleships were planned by the Japanese.

The fact was, however, that Admiral Yamamoto was not thinking in terms of battleships, particularly after November 13, 1940. This was the day that British carrier planes found the Italian Fleet at anchor in the inner harbor at the Italian naval base at Taranto and knocked out half the fleet in one afternoon.

Here was proof of the contention Admiral Yamamoto had shared with American General Billy Mitchell for years, that naval aircraft were superior to battleships and that the ships of the future were the carriers. Now, in the fall of 1940, Admiral Yamamoto began thinking about the best way he could use his naval forces to strike a fierce blow at the Americans when the war came.

By the fall of 1940, Yamamoto was certain that the war was not far away. He and Admiral Yonai had failed to stop the drive for the Rome-Berlin-Tokyo pact, and it was signed that fall, putting Japan in league with Great Britain's enemy Germany.

With the signing of the pact, Yamamoto made his famous statement to Prime Minister Konoye that he could run wild across the Pacific for six months or a year, but after that the American productive capacity would begin to show and Japan would most certainly lose a war against America.

Of course, the army pushed Japan steadily forward on the China front, and the drift toward war continued. By December of 1940, Admiral Yamamoto was writing to Admiral Shigetaro Shimada, the commander of the China Fleet, that he had no confidence in Prince Konoye and Foreign Minister Yosuke Matsuoka. The former was vacillating, and the latter was an Americanophobe.

So, if there was going to be a war, as a loyal Japanese naval officer, Admiral Yamamoto had to do his best to plan for winning. As he trained his officers and men, he considered the problems of war against the United States. Just as the U.S. Navy had its Plan Orange, which envisioned a war against Japan, so the Japanese had their Kantai Kessen Plan, or decisive battle plan. They expected the U.S. Pacific Fleet to steam out from San Diego, heading west, preparing to attack Japan in Asian waters. First of all, Japanese submarines would find and harry the American fleet, destroying as many capital ships as possible. Then someplace favorable to Japan, where the navy could employ its major fleet elements, the sea battle would be joined, the Americans would be defeated, and Japan would control the Asian seas.

But as 1940 came to an end, it became obvious that the problem was not so simple. Without fuel resources, Japan had to drive to the south; the only ones available to her were those in the Dutch East Indies. So the drive must be to Borneo and Malaya, to secure the natural resources, and then to resume the battle to conquer China.

Yamamoto recognized this, but he also recognized another problem that seemed to have eluded almost all his colleagues. From time to time he warned associates that unless the American fleet was knocked out very early in the war they would begin bombing Japan and burning Tokyo. If this happened, he said, the Japanese people might lose heart and give up the whole war very quickly.

Yamamoto was then evolving his own war plan, which he based on the practicalities as he knew them. He told the Imperial Palace that the size of the Combined Fleet ought to be doubled, the number of carriers increased, and the number of planes more than doubled.

When the United States split its fleet in 1940 and created the Pacific Fleet at the forward base of Pearl Harbor, Admiral Yamamoto saw both danger and opportunity. The new base gave the Americans a major advantage, but it also concentrated the American Pacific Fleet in one small basin, where under certain conditions it would be very vulnerable. The lesson of Taranto came back to Yamamoto that fall. He began talking to Rear Admiral Shigeru Fukudome, then his chief of staff, and more and more often he mentioned Pearl Harbor. By the end of the year, an idea had gotten into his head.

For a number of years Japanese naval strategists had talked about a possible attack on Pearl Harbor, but until it became the permanent fleet base, there was not much to the talk. Besides, as everyone knew, Pearl Harbor was an extremely well protected port, and very difficult to get into. The best chance had always been believed to be to put submarines around the Hawaiian Islands and let them attack the fleet as it came out of Pearl Harbor.

But in 1939 and 1940, Admiral Yamamoto's dreams about practical naval aircraft had begun to come true. A squadron of "Betty" bombers had flown across the China Sea from Formosa to attack in China and then had flown back—an unprecedented feat. The fast torpedo bombers of the carriers had proved themselves with the fleet, and so had the dive bombers. The naval torpedo called "the long lance" was a very effective weapon. Yamamoto was convinced that aerially delivered torpedoes would play a big part in any new war. This was all new doctrine, and in retrospect it seems almost incredible that Admiral Yamamoto could have persuaded his naval peers, most of them battleship men by training, to accept all these innovations in so short a time as the fall of 1939 until the winter of 1941.

By the end of 1940, Yamamoto had turned over consideration of a plan to attack Pearl Harbor and the U.S. Pacific Fleet to Rear Admiral Takejiro Ohnishi, one of his most trusted officers. First of all, he had to convince Admiral Ohnishi that this was possible, because Ohnishi did not believe. Ohnishi said that they were liable to lose five or six warships in this fight, and they could ill afford it. The potential sacrifice was too great.

To this Yamamoto replied that if they did not make a preemptive strike, they would be on an equal footing with the U.S. forces and that America's productive capacity would soon overwhelm them. He made a powerful case; Ohnishi knew as well as he did the story of Admiral Togo's swift strike at Port Arthur and how it had caught the Russians off guard and caused enough destruction to keep them off balance for all the war. It was true that several ships might be lost, but this was to be expected of battle; the test was whether or not the losses were justified by the aim. If the carriers were lost, but they knocked out the American Pacific Fleet, they would have done their job, and Japan would have the time to turn around and rebuild its fleet while the enemy was at a disadvantage.

So, once Admiral Ohnishi was convinced that the preemptive strike was necessary, Ohnishi came up with a report that the idea was possible and desirable, and this, by the end of 1940, became the new Japanese fleet doctrine.

By January of 1941, the plan was established in Yamamoto's mind and he was in the process of convincing Admiral Kashiro Oikawa, the Navy Minister, of its validity. The navy had to be changed so that its major striking force was not the battle fleet but the carrier fleet.

What was happening that year was something swift in the processes of naval evolution. Not only was the Pearl Harbor attack plan under consideration in the naval heirarchy, pushed by Admiral Yamamoto, but plans were afoot for an entire reorganization of the navy around a carrier-based force. No other nation was even thinking in these terms.

Yamamoto was a leader, of course, but many of the younger officers were of the same mind. To understand why this was important, one must realize that in the Japanese naval system, staff officers—bright young "brains" as they were called by the commanders—were given an enormous amount of authority. The commander always had the responsibility, but his willingness to delegate authority to his staff was quite unlike anything of the sort in any other navy. Thus you had commanders and lieutenant commanders of the navy exerting major policy influence at the fleet level. One such commander was Minoru Genda, who did much of the detailed planning work for the attack on Pearl Harbor. He also was the architect of a plan to reorganize the navy so that the carrier attack force became all powerful. The doctrine here was to mass the carriers and mass the attack. It would work very well at Pearl Harbor and at Trincomalee, as well as down in the South Pacific in the early days of the war, but it would fail at Midway and cost the Japanese very dearly. This was not because the danger was forgotten at the Combined Fleet level—at Midway the striking force would be warned to spread out—but the striking force would not listen to orders. Once again, this independence was characteristic of the Japanese navy, an indication, perhaps, of a reason that doctrinal changes did not seem so difficult as with other navies.

While all this was occurring, so were the discussions about the Tokyo-Berlin-Rome axis. Once that hated treaty had been made a part of Japanese political life, Yamamoto felt an ever greater need to prepare for the coming war against the United States.

And he also wanted to take as active a part in the coming war as he could. A friend from Nagaoka came down to visit Yamamoto aboard the flagship and asked his views. What Yamamoto wanted, he said, was to get Yonai to take command of the Combined Fleet, so that Yamamoto could take the striking force into action against the enemy.

But that is one wish he was never to have satisfied. The naval high command did not want to make a change. Having gone along with Yamamoto's revision of basic naval theory, it had been decided that Yamamoto was the man to carry it out, and that had to be done at the level of command of the Combined Fleet. So Yamamoto was destined not to have the fighting command that he dearly wanted or the chance to supervise the effective operations of his beloved carriers. Until the end he was to hold the lonely job at the top.

YEAR OF DECISION

19

1941. Barring a miracle, Admiral Yamamoto now knew that war with the United States and Great Britain was inevitable. The seal was put on the cap in the spring, when it became apparent that the policy of the United States was not all bluster and blow, as Japanese Foreign Minister Yosuke Matsuoka had claimed, but had turned very firm indeed.

For years the navy men—who generally opposed war with the West for very good reasons—had been accused of "crying wolf" when they spoke of the strength of America. But in the spring of 1941, when the movement of the Japanese army into French Indochina was greeted by an American cutoff of steel and oil exports to Japan, the Konoye cabinet was completely shocked. The politicians had told themselves that America was a paper tiger for so long that they really believed it.

Prime Minister Konoye, who had vacillated for years on this subject, made a desperate stab to repair a desperate situation. He sent a message to President Franklin Roosevelt asking for a Pacific Conference to resolve the problems between the two countries. But it was already too late for such "ordinary" special diplomacy. The Americans replied coolly and not until fifty days had passed that such a conference was possible only if the Japanese moved out of Indochina and China.

The navy men still wanted to negotiate, even on such hard conditions.

And so did Prince Konoye and the civilian elements in the government.
But the army, which had gained almost total power over the government
by 1941, refused to consider such a course. And so, as Admiral Yamamoto prepared to make a speech of instruction to the officers of the
fleet, new words and new ideas crept in. The talk was now openly of
war for the first time outside the supersecret sessions of cabinet and the
navy high command:

> Once the cabinet decision is made, our Combined Fleet will proceed
> to its post with the mission of placing the empire in a position of perfect
> security, breaking down our powerful enemy through the utmost efforts
> of officers and men. This is an unusual mission. Though the way to
> victory will not be easy, yet there is nothing we cannot do if we are
> prepared, and we will work out a far-sighted plan. Officers and men
> will, of course, remain faithful to the Emperor and carry out all orders
> with dauntless resolution. (Ugaki diary)

And so, by the beginning of October 1941, all the plans were made,
all the major decisions had been made, and all the options had been
considered. Now the Combined Fleet was playing out the moves on the
naval chessboard, with Admiral Yamamoto putting out of his mind as
much as possible his continued opposition to the coming war and his
belief that it would mean disaster for Japan.

On October 16, the fleet was conducting maneuvers off Murozu-
mioki, a secluded little spot in the inland waters of Japan. The mighty
flagship *Nagato* was the guinea pig, and she was being attacked at
anchor by planes and submarines of the fleet.

Admiral Yamamoto was observing with some approval the activities
of his fleet after all these months of fierce training, when at 6:30 that
evening came word that the cabinet of Prince Konoye had resigned.
Yamamoto knew precisely what this meant: The last hope of averting
the war had now been lost. In this third Konoye cabinet, the navy had
had a strong part. Admiral Soemu Toyoda had succeeded the warlike
Yosuke Matsuoka as foreign minister. Admiral Oikawa had become
navy minister. Both had counseled Prince Konoye that he must be
prepared to make concessions to the United States relative to China in
order to avert war. Konoye was known as "a lord who wears long
sleeves at court"—an easygoing fellow who liked to propitiate everyone. But at this point there was no propitiating the army as far as China

was concerned. The army had millions of men in China and an enormous stake in the China war as the instrument of its own survival. Every general officer could remember the barren years when there was no money and no room for expansion. And so the army remained rocklike, and on this rock the Konoye cabinet foundered, as Admiral Yamamoto had known it would.

The resignation of this third Konoye cabinet meant that there was no alternative but to put an army man into power, and that meant war without doubt.

The exercises continued, but so upset was the staff of the Combined Fleet about the turn of events that although October 17 was the day of the Harvest Thanksgiving Festival, Yamamoto forgot it and so did all his staff officers save Admiral Ugaki, the chief of staff. Next morning a signal was flashed, and the men of the fleet faced the eastern sky at 8 A.M. and bowed reverently, but they did not change out of battle dress and they did not move from their battle stations. The ways of peace were already being left behind.

October 17 was a day of excitement at sea as it was a day of decision in Tokyo. Yamamoto's Combined Fleet continued the exercises, and that day's run called for gunnery practice against Koiwai Island. The exercise was most satisfactory to the admiral from a military point of view. But he was also poring over bulletins extracted from Radio Tokyo by the staff, and the news was disquieting. That morning in Tokyo the Council of Elders met at the Imperial Palace, and out of this meeting came what Yamamoto had feared most: Lieutenant General Hideki Tojo, his old opponent of the days when he had been deputy navy minister, had now been instructed to form a cabinet. The army was in the saddle. Tojo, a prime mover in the Manchurian takeover, was now the most important man (the Emperor was a god) in Japan.

Events moved rapidly that day: Tojo's official residence as war minister was already the headquarters of the new cabinet that had not been appointed! Visitors were coming to see the new "Prime Minister," although he was not yet that. The pressure was unremitting. And throughout the fleet went the question: What will happen to Yamamoto now? Many, including his own staff, believed that his days were numbered. They knew of his opposition to war and his basic quarrel with General Tojo. It seemed impossible that he could remain as commander of the Combined Fleet given his known views about war with the United States. Admiral Ugaki suggested that he might become commander of

Yokosuka Naval Base, a nice, safe demotion with a big house and no power at all. Yamamoto, of course, was half bent on retirement anyhow; he had been serving the navy for forty years. The news kept coming in. Who would the new navy minister be? There were rumors that it would be either Admiral Shigetaro Shimada, a balding, prune-faced man with a tiny mustache, lately chief of naval affairs in China, or Admiral Soemu Toyoda. Shimada had been rumored to be the next commander of the Combined Fleet but was now appointed navy minister instead. What did this mean?

On October 18, the tempo of events in Tokyo was made more frantic by a grand festival held at the Yasukuni Shrine, a temple for the heroes who had fallen in the wars of Japan. In recent years, since the beginning of the "China incident" in 1937, the importance of the Yasukuni Shrine had steadily increased, as the army wedded together love of country, Emperor worship, and the Shinto religion to create a mystic amalgam of patriotic fervor. This day fifteen thousand "spirits of heroes" were enshrined, and the Emperor came to pay his own respects, which gave the occasion great importance. Aboard the fleet the news brought a surge of piety and decisions to give gladly every life for the preservation of Emperor and Yamato, the spirit of Japan.

That day Admiral Yamamoto read the dispatches again. Shimada would indeed be the new navy minister, which meant that General Tojo had a toady in place. Not that Shimada had all the wrong ideas. Not at all. He was not a member of the "fleet faction" of the navy, but neither was he a member of the "peace faction." He would go along; he would do what Tojo ordered. He might first make a stab at stating a different point of view, but he did not have the character to press his claims. So the way of the navy was set: It would follow the army into this war to come.

The tension in the fleet was very great. To break it, Admiral Yamamoto declared a holiday and took the staff ashore at Murozumi. They went to a tourist hotel and took rooms. They overlooked the harbor where Shinsaku Takasugi, one of the great generals of the Meiji period, had trained his troops. They had an excellent lunch at a long table, with fresh fish and vegetables, and then the staff members scattered to follow their own pursuits. The admiral went fishing for sea bream, his favorite fish. Some of the staff officers began drinking, and they drank until three o'clock the next morning. Admiral Yamamoto looked on this with a benign eye, although he did not drink himself and had not since that day as an ensign at Eta Jima when he had gotten so drunk.

That day and the next the officers of the fleet forgot about events in Tokyo and amused themselves in the Hikari area. But then in the afternoon came the call back to duty, and they took their boats from the pier at the Hikari Naval Arsenal and went back to the big ships. There the radio reports had piled up: The cabinet had been confirmed, General Tojo was leading the country, and Admiral Shimada was the navy minister. The only even remotely bright light was the fact that Shigenori Togo, a known moderate, was the new foreign minister. How much that meant, Admiral Yamamoto did not know, but he did not think any moderate could do much in the present political climate.

On October 19 the cabinet organized, and Yamamoto and his staff watched a little nervously to see what would happen to the active fleet. That day it was announced that Vice Admiral Hirata had been appointed to command the Yokosuka Naval Base, which meant that the crisis was over as far as Yamamoto was concerned. Why, he never knew, but in spite of his attitude toward war with the United States and his old conflicts with General Tojo and the other leaders of the army oligarchy, Yamamoto was left strictly alone in this hour of crisis. One reason was undoubtedly his popularity within the fleet: Never had an admiral commanded the respect of the men and younger officers to a greater degree. His training program, so much tougher than anything that had gone before, had made them all realize that they could rise above themselves, even the ship captains who were forced to navigate in close waters and thus run the constant danger of collision of their ships. Another reason was Yamamoto's undeniable popularity with the royal family and the Emperor himself, who shared Yamamoto's respect for the West, although he now found himself a captive within the new system of Emperor worship invented by the army to stabilize its own position. And still a third reason was probably the understanding within the naval establishment that there was no officer more competent to lead the Combined Fleet to victory than Admiral Yamamoto. His daring plan for the Pearl Harbor attack had passed through the crucible of the Japanese naval establishment, and after many expressed misgivings, his fellow admirals had realized that Yamamoto spoke no more than the truth when he said that Japan's hope for victory in this war to come was limited by time and oil. Every sensible officer of the navy was well aware of the perennial oil problems, and those who made any sort of study at all also recognized the difficulties of using Borneo oil, which was full of sulfur that corroded the boiler mechanisms of their ships. Also, it had to be recognized that if the enemy could seriously disturb Japanese merchant shipping, then the fleet would be endangered even more.

The same day that the appointment to Yokosuka was announced, it was also announced that Vice Admiral Jisaburo Ozawa had been promoted to become commander of the Second Fleet. Here was another of the younger admirals who was coming up. Yamamoto had much regard for Ozawa and would have liked to have him closer to his own establishment, but a major problem within the Japanese navy was the tight control exercised by the Naval Personnel Bureau in Tokyo. Unlike the American navy, for example, where Admiral Husband E. Kimmel, commander of the American Pacific Fleet, had control over the selection of his own staff, Admiral Yamamoto never did. Even his chief of staff was chosen for him, and the best he could do was to pull whatever strings he could grasp and hope for the best. Nor was he consulted in the changes of commanders at the secondary level.

In fact, he was not particularly pleased with his chief of staff, Vice Admiral Matome Ugaki, who was another of the hard-drinking set of naval officers. The night before the fleet sailed on new maneuvers, many of the officers stayed up late drinking, among them Admiral Ugaki, and next morning Yamamoto bantered with him: "You got up this morning just after you had gone to bed, eh?"

That remark was not made totally in fun, because Yamamoto disapproved most heartily of any social activity that would lead a man even to appear to neglect his duty. The admiral's own proclivities were well known within the fleet: He loved women, and he loved gambling. The shoji board and the go board were never absent from his cabin. But when he was at sea and involved in the matters of the fleet, nothing came between Yamamoto and his duty, and this is how he wanted it to be with all the men who served under him.

That day, October 20, the mighty battleship *Yamato* joined with the fleet for the first time since it had been commissioned. Captain Murozato came to the flagship to pay his respects. Soon this new behemoth would become the admiral's flagship. She was enormous!—863 feet long on deck with her six 18.1-inch guns, 71,000 tons, the largest ship in the world. The Imperial Navy had planned to build five such ships, but by 1941 only two of them had been completed, the *Yamato* and her sister ship the *Musashi*.

On October 21, the fleet moved again—more training exercises, bedeviled by a collision between the modern submarine *I-66* and the older *I-7*, sinking the *I-66* and doing serious damage to the *I-7*. This was a deplorable situation in view of the seriousness of the international situation and what was now the almost certain probability of war with the United States.

What was on Admiral Yamamoto's mind just now was more than the appointment of the new cabinet with its warlike tendencies. If there was to be war, Yamamoto had held steadily, then he must be allowed to make his preemptive strike, which was now called the A Mo Operation. He had already told Admiral Ugaki that he intended to stand or fall on the attack on the American fleet at Pearl Harbor. There was still a good deal of opposition within the fleet, and most of it came from the flagship of Admiral Nagumo, the officer who had been entrusted with the command of the carrier strike force and who would actually carry out Admiral Yamamoto's orders. Nagumo complained constantly; Yamamoto had no faith in him at all, and he told his staff as much.

"That man Nagumo not only has words with others but is given to bluffing when drunk, and he is not prepared even yet" was the verdict of Admiral Ugaki. Admiral Yamamoto felt even more strongly. He said that if Nagumo could not stop his carping, and his chief of staff continued to agree with him, then both of them should resign and let others take over the task. Yamamoto's choice would have been Admiral Ozawa, but he had been sent off to command the Southern Fleet.

On October 23, Admiral Yamamoto was particularly incensed with Admiral Nagumo because the latter more or less poo-pooed the seriousness of a collision between the two submarines attached to his strike force. He said he intended to give a full report to the commission that would investigate the incident, and he indicated that, in his belief, Admiral Nagumo was failing to do his job. Staff officers tried to persuade Yamamoto to soften his position, but he was stern. Weakness was not to be tolerated, particularly when they were facing war.

On October 24, the flagship put in at the Sasebo Naval Base. Admiral Yamamoto had some inquiries to make about the submarine accident, and anyhow, it was time for a rest again after so much hard training, he said. So he let the staff go off to the resort town of Beppu while he took care of his duty. So the staff went on to Beppu, and Yamamoto indicated that he would come along later. There was a big party at the Tsutaya Restaurant that night, but the fact was that Yamamoto had no intention of joining it. He headed straight for the tea house called Togo,

located on the steep side of one of Sasebo's hills. The house was operated
by the geisha Masako Tsurushima, who had been Yamamoto's lover
since the days when he was a lieutenant.

On the next day, Yamamoto had talked about going out in Beppu
harbor to shoot ducks, but he never appeared at Beppu, leaving behind
Admiral Ugaki, who had wanted to go along. Yamamoto was feeling
the need for a little solitude, and that particular geisha house was operated by his favorite geisha. Admiral Ugaki lazed around Beppu, had
breakfast at 11 A.M., and went over to the Nakayama Hotel to see
Admiral Takasu, commander of the First Fleet. When he met the admiral, he had a geisha on each arm. That night the party became very
animated, and everybody, including the chief of staff, was very late in
getting to bed. Admiral Ugaki, in fact, had a nice long shampoo before
he retired in the wee hours of the morning.

Admiral Yamamoto never did appear at Beppu on this trip. The staff
assembled and went back to their ships in midafternoon. Then, at about
five o'clock, Yamamoto came up by flying boat and boarded the flagship.
Ugaki noted with some relief that much of the tension the admiral seemed
to have shown in recent days had disappeared. Nothing at all was said
about where the admiral had spent his evenings.

Everyone on Yamamoto's staff was awaiting the outcome of the negotiations between the Japanese delegation that had gone to Washington
and the American government, knowing that this was the last possible
chance to avoid the war. The wheels that would grind out the Pearl
Harbor attack were already turning furiously. On October 28, Admiral
Yamamoto learned from Tokyo that Admiral Harold R. Stark, chief of
U.S. Naval operations, had sent a record sixteen top secret telegrams
to his fleet, most of them to Pearl Harbor. He also learned that day that
the Emperor had told Prime Minister Tojo to make a complete resurvey
of the Pacific situation before proceeding in any direction. But the
planning continued. On October 29, a delegation came down from navy
headquarters in Tokyo bringing a draft directive for operations, and this
occupied Yamamoto most of the day. Yamamoto again stated his feelings: They were moving inevitably toward the war the navy did not
want and the war he did not think Japan could win.

Was there a chance of drawing back? Not now. "Procrastination
means to fall into the enemy's hands." At this point the enemy had to

The house in Nagaoka City where Isoroku Takano was born.

His father, Sadayoshi Takano.

His mother, Mineko.

Isoroku as a high school
boy.

As a cadet at Eta Jima Naval
Academy.

Ensign Yamamoto at the time of the
Russo-Japanese War.

Admiral Heihachiro Togo, the hero of the Russo-Japanese War.

The Navy Staff College Class of 1915. Lieutenant Commander Yamamoto is in the front row, far left.

Yamamoto and his bride Reiko at the time of their marriage in 1918.

Captain Yamamoto as naval attaché in his Washington office in 1927.

Captain Yamamoto, commander of the carrier *Akagi*, in 1928.

Officers and passengers of the *Seiberia Maru* (Siberia) en route to America in 1930. Yamamoto is in the third row, immediately in front of the woman in furs.

Yamamoto (*right*) at Tokyo station, on his way to the London Disarmament Conference of 1930.

The Japanese delegation to the London Disarmament Conference of 1930. Yamamoto is on the left.

Admiral Yamamoto (*right*) with Admiral Yonai, the navy minister, in 1934.

Admiral Yamamoto as
Commander in Chief of
the Combined Fleet.

The battleship *Nagato*, the fleet flagship until 1941.

An artist's conception of the Pearl Harbor raid of December 7, 1941.

Admiral Yamamoto in the operations room of the flagship *Yamato*.

Rear Admiral Gunichi Mikawa.

Rear Admiral Raizo Tanaka.

Vice Admiral Nobutake Kondo.

General Imamura, the
Rabaul army commander.

Vice Admiral Chuichi Nagumo,
Admiral Yamamoto's bête noir.

Vice Admiral Matome Ugaki,
Admiral Yamamoto's last
chief of staff.

Rear Admiral Daniel J. Callaghan.

Rear Admiral Norman Scott.

Admiral Yamamoto addressing the fliers of the Eleventh Air Fleet at Rabaul before takeoff on one of the I Go missions, spring 1943.

Admiral Yamamoto in Rabaul with Admiral Kusaka (*second from left*) and other officers of the Southeast Area Fleet just before Yamamoto's fatal flight to Ballele.

Remains of the bomber in which Admiral Yamamoto was riding when attacked by American P-38 fighters.

Yamamoto's state funeral in Tokyo, June 1943.

Yamamoto's tomb in Tokyo. Inset shows monument in Nagaoka City.

Yamamoto Memorial Park in Nagaoka City.

make concessions, or Japan had to use military power, even though it was painfully apparent that she did not have the material resources to wage a long war. "It is a long way that has no turning."

On October 30, a typhoon came heading west and the fleet stood uneasily at anchor off Tosa. Waiting, waiting, waiting. Admiral Nagumo visited the flagship, and once again, Admiral Yamamoto was displeased. Nagumo was visibly shaken by the importance of his mission to attack Pearl Harbor, and his attitude continued to be querulous and negative.

On October 31, Admiral Yamamoto ordered more exercises, involving the entire Combined Fleet: from morning until noon, from noon until dusk, and then a night battle simulation. He could not control Nagumo's talk, but he could force Nagumo into that last inch of preparation. Another "day battle" and another "night battle" were staged on November 1.

Late that afternoon, Admiral Yamamoto received a secret message from Navy Minister Shimada summoning him to Tokyo without calling attention to the fact. What did that mean, Admiral Ugaki asked his commander in chief.

"I can't say," was all that Yamamoto could reply. For indeed, he sensed that on the eve of the great and terrible adventure, there were still enough doubts left in Tokyo to leave the barest of chances for peace—but not really. As Yamamoto had told Ugaki, with the benefit of his considerable experience with Americans, if there was to be peace, the Japanese would have to make concessions about China, and Tojo was adamant against such concessions.

Still, they were calling him back to Tokyo for consultation about something. "How long can the navy stand the suspense of these negotiations?" he asked Ugaki, for that was probably the first question Admiral Shimada would ask the commander in chief when he came up to Tokyo.

If it had to come, Ugaki said, then December 8, the planned day (December 7 in Hawaii) was the best. If negotiations should string on, say until summer, the fleet would be worn to a frazzle.

Why did the commander in chief think he was being summoned to Tokyo, asked Chief of Staff Ugaki. Was it perhaps that they would make him Prime Minister because of his known views?

This was complete nonsense, said Yamamoto. Wishful thinking.

The course was set, and all that was happening now was vacillation against the horror of it.

Against this backdrop the accelerated training continued, day and night. On the morning of November 2, a fine sunny autumn day, the fleet anchored off Tosa Bay and Admiral Yamamoto got into a seaplane and flew to Kure. From there he took the express train to Tokyo.

Immediately on arrival at Tokyo station, in his civilian clothes, he took a taxi to the house of Minister Shimada and went into conference. He also met with Prime Minister Tojo. The reason for the many meetings, Yamamoto learned, was the contention of Foreign Minister Togo that something might be gained by agreeing to move the troops out of Indochina, thus restoring the situation to what it was before the Americans cut off the oil and steel. But the army was totally opposed to any such concession.

There were a dozen meetings, and on November 4 they all boiled down to the decisions, as Yamamoto had known they would. The war preparations would continue unabated, but so would the negotiations, in the hopes that the Americans would make concessions in their demand that the Japanese evacuate China and Indochina. The final decision to launch the attacks against Pearl Harbor, Malaya, the Philippines, and the Dutch East Indies would be made on December 1. The agreement of the roles of army and navy in these operations had already been drawn.

After that last meeting, Admiral Yamamoto got back on the train and hurried back to his flagship.

The admiral and his staff went up to Tokyo again on November 6, this time to prepare the operational order to the Combined Fleet that would unleash the Pearl Harbor attack.

Imperial Japanese Naval Order Number One:

1. The Commander in Chief of the Combined Fleet will make necessary forces advance to the starting points of the coming operation, expecting the breakout of war against the United States, England, and Holland sometime around the beginning of December.

2. The Commander in Chief of the Combined Fleet will keep strict watch for any unexpected attack by the United States, England, and Holland.

3. The Commander in Chief of the Combined Fleet will not be allowed to carry out any reconnaissance except one very secret one.

4. The Commander in Chief of the Combined Fleet will make the Fourth Fleet begin to lay mines around the southern islands as part of the defense program.

5. The plan for army-navy operations will be controlled by the Army-Navy Central Agreement.

6. The Commander in Chief of the Combined Fleet will consult with the commanding general of the army about army-navy cooperation. Y Day, the day of supposed outbreak of hostilities, will be 8 December.

There, it was done. All the talk, all the planning, was now committed to paper and would have a life of its own.

On Saturday, November 8, Admiral Yamamoto and Admiral Ugaki attended a day-long series of meetings with army officials at the Military Staff College. The dispositions of enemy fleets and troops were laid out by the intelligence people, and strategies were discussed. But there was no more agreement between army and navy than was usual. The army would be responsible for battles on land, the navy for battles on the sea. The one difficult point, air operations, was most unsatisfactorily resolved. The army, in effect, took no responsibility for defending any coastlines or coastal areas, but continued to eat up its half share of aircraft for use to support purely army operations.

That night, Yamamoto and Ugaki dined with Navy Minister Shimada. They ate elegantly and drank champagne.

Sunday was a day of rest, but on Monday, Admiral Yamamoto and his staff went back to a Military Staff College conference room. They sat at one side of a long table, and General Terauchi, commander in chief of the army and his staff, sat on the other side. Solemnly they all signed the joint army-navy agreement and then held a formal luncheon.

The afternoon was spent tidying up affairs at the Navy Ministry. The next day they took the train to Yokosuka and then went by air back to the *Nagato*, passing over an assemblage of a hundred transport ships off Okayama. Indeed, the whole nation seemed to be moving toward war.

On November 13, Admiral Yamamoto went ashore to the Iwakuni Naval Air Station to meet with the senior officers of the Combined Fleet. He made an inspirational address calling all of them to do their best for Emperor and country.

"His address was extremely wonderful, as it should be as the supreme commander at the start of a grand expedition," wrote Admiral Ugaki in his diary.

After the address, the staff had their pictures taken, sitting in the rain in the open outside the base club. Then they went to a party and drank ceremonial sake and ate dried chestnuts and slices of dried shellfish and seaweed, whose Japanese names symbolized fight, win, and be happy. The festivities lasted until 6 P.M., and then the staff went to the Fukagawa Restaurant for a dinner party with fifteen geisha. The admiral was not much impressed by the geisha, who were not very stimulating. "The countryside is still the countryside," said Admiral Ugaki. At 9 P.M. the party broke up and the admiral went back to the flagship.

On November 14, Yamamoto was ashore again, meeting with the generals who had come down for the ceremonial affair, which lasted until after lunch. Back to the ship, more detail, and it all seemed to be just marking time. Waiting. Waiting.

On November 15, the Emperor opened an extraordinary session of the Diet to appropriate four billion yen for special war purposes. Already the "China incident" and what came after had cost the Japanese government about a hundred billion yen, and there seemed to be no end to it. Yamamoto was depressed, but buoyed a little that day with the news of the graduation of cadets from the naval academy at Eta Jima. It took him back to his own days nearly forty years before, and now these new ensigns would be joining the fleet within days.

On Sunday, November 16, Admiral Yamamoto had his last meeting with General Terauchi, and all declared themselves satisfied that cooperation between army and navy would be extensive. (It never was.) The soldiers went away, and the admiral could now devote his entire attention to the last problems of readying the fleet for action.

From the radio came the news that Ambassador Kurusu had just arrived in Washington to join Admiral Nomura in talks with the Americans, having received new instructions in Tokyo. The discussions with the Americans, everybody knew, were entering the final phases, and Admiral Yamamoto now had no hope at all.

On Monday, November 17, the flagship sailed to Saeki, and Admiral Yamamoto went aboard the *Akagi*, supercarrier and flagship of Admiral Nagumo's First Striking Force. The admiral was going to wish godspeed to the aircrews who would carry out the Pearl Harbor attack. They assembled on the flight deck and the admiral made a stirring speech. The young men pledged themselves to die for the Emperor and their country.

That midnight, the *Akagi* sailed for the assembly point in the Kuril Islands where the striking force would jump off for the Eastern Pacific. Now all signs were pointing toward the war that would begin within three weeks.

WAVES OF WAR

We have fourteen days left. They seem so long.
—Admiral Ugaki in his diary, November 17, 1941

20

November 18 dawned fine but soon clouded up. No matter, the training went on. The *Nagato* left port at 7:45 A.M. for the first exercise, every man to his action station. Then anti-aircraft firing, and then shooting the big guns. The fog came in and hung over the ship, but the shooting went on as scheduled, at 30,000 yards. The smell of cordite and sweat hung over the ship, and the men were exhausted when the ship returned to port at 9 P.M.

On November 19, there was training again. The officers on the bridge spotted a strange-looking craft heading south. Finally, Admiral Yamamoto figured it out: It was a submarine of the I class, but it was carrying a midget submarine on deck. She was headed for Pearl Harbor—the first warship to be actually on her way. Five I-boats were moving out, with a distance of ten miles separating one from the next.

"The surprise attack on X Day will be an entirely unexpected storm," said Admiral Ugaki.

He and Yamamoto saw young lieutenants smiling at them from the submarines, and they knew these men expected never to return alive to Japan. "*Kesshitai no seishin*"—the decision to seek death.

On the afternoon of November 20, Rear Admiral Yasutomi, the commander of the Fourth Submarine Squadron, came to the flagship to say farewell to Admiral Yamamoto. Yasutomi did not expect to survive the attack either. And also up came Rear Admiral Kurita, commander of the Seventh Squadron and one of Yamamoto's admirers. He was a man that Yamamoto trusted.

Several admirals came down from Tokyo to confer with Yamamoto on the eve of battle. The admiral invited them all to dinner at the Iwakuni Air Base. He fed them sukiyaki, because one of them had noted that in Tokyo these days there was not much beef, and then the admiral sent them home with five pounds of precious beef as well.

On November 22, Admiral Hashimura, who would command the Fourth Destroyer Squadron, came up to say goodbye. He was another friend of Yamamoto, and he was going off to support the landing in the Philippines.

November 23 was a cold, rainy day, and Yamamoto thought of the officers and men of the First Striking Force, on their way to the Kuriles jumpoff point. How cold it must be for them up there in the north!

Aboard the flagship the atmosphere was solemn and highly charged with emotion; there was no forgetting of the Harvest Festival this day, and at 9:15 A.M. all the officers and men faced to the east and worshipped. Thought of the harvest brought thought of the rice crop (which was down slightly from 1940), and that brought thoughts of discussions with visitors from Tokyo about the shortages of some foods these days. Thoughts of food shortages brought thoughts about the length and seriousness of the China war, which had already cost Japan enormously, and for what? But the army would not be propitiated with anything less than total victory in China, and that was the rub.

The radio that day spoke of the negotiations in Washington. No change. Admiral Yamamoto had a feeling of time closing in on him. The deadline—at which the order to move must be made irrevocably —was only seven days away. Yamamoto had to thrust all thoughts of propitiation from his mind; Tojo had now told the world that Japan's freedom to act in China was unimpingeable, and that was the crux of the matter. As Yamamoto knew better than anyone else, the might of the Western world would be arrayed against Japan, and there was no better time to strike than right now.

On Monday, November 24, Yamamoto and his chief of staff went to the operations room for a briefing about enemy forces and were struck by the amount of red (representing the enemy) penciled around the Pacific. They spoke now of "the coming war," and Admiral Ugaki indicated that he was coming around to the view long held by his commander in chief that only audacity would serve Japan.

On November 25 the fleet pulled out of Hashirajima and headed for

Kure. There Yamamoto and his chief of staff boarded the *Yamato*, which was soon to become the flagship of the fleet. Yamamoto was not very pleased with the prospect. The *Nagato* was a very comfortable ship, while the bright, shining *Yamato* was a huge, modern fighting machine, too efficient looking to be comfortable.

For two days the admiral carried out ceremonial duties at Kure, receiving delegations, speeding parting fleet units northward on their way. On November 27 he had a secret message from naval headquarters in Tokyo: The American meetings were deadlocked. The prediction was for failure. Ambassador Kurusu had put it openly to Secretary of State Hull. The Americans wanted Japan to evacuate Indochina and all China and to withdraw from the Rome-Berlin-Tokyo alliance, but the Americans would not agree to stop helping Chiang Kai-shek. What more was there to talk about?

The tension grew, and thus so did the forced gaiety ashore at Kure. The staff gave a party at the Kazan Restaurant, and Yamamoto agreed to appear, although he would not get involved in their drinking bout. By the time he got there, most of the officers were in their cups. Admiral Ugaki joined with a will. Yamamoto had a glass or two and then turned over his sake cup and involved himself in conversation with several of the geisha. Shortly, he broke away, but Ugaki stayed and went on to the next party, given that evening by Admiral Toyoda.

On Saturday, November 29, the last portion of the First Striking Force sailed for the east. They would supply Admiral Nagumo's fighting ships at sea, given any sort of good weather. Tokyo reported that the Americans in Washington had presented a new declaration of policy and course of steps to be taken by Japan that gave no concession to Japan's occupation of Indochina and eastern China. There was no hope.

"Is there any room for our study of the above and its reconsideration now that things have come to this?" wrote Admiral Ugaki in his diary. "The only way for us is to make short work of the U.S."

Sunday, November 30, was a fine wintry day. The fleet left Hashirajima before dawn and moved into Bungo Channel, where the day's exercises began. The concentration was on fleet firing and antisubmarine defense, and the admiral was upset because the antisubmarine defense was not well coordinated. Yamamoto was firm: The training would be repeated that night until they got it right. Chief of Staff Ugaki spent the night on the bridge, supervising.

Midnight came, and Admiral Yamamoto, too, was up. The day of decision had arrived. Yamamoto prepared to go up to Tokyo to hear personally the Imperial Rescript calling for war and to respond. Chief of Staff Ugaki sat down to write up some notes for the speech Yamamoto would give in reply.

Late in the afternoon the admiral left the ship and took the train from Iwakuni to Tokyo. Yamamoto stopped off at Umenoshima, at the geisha house where Chiyoko Kawai held forth. But she had gone to attend a party with the Marquis Kido, several other important figures, and Yamamoto's old friend Takeichi Hori. Having been forced to retire from the navy by the "fleet faction," Hori had now gained an appointment as president of a big shipyard, and this party was to celebrate his new job.

The admiral wanted to see the geisha, but more he wanted to see his friend Hori for what spiritual help that would give him, for he was very depressed with the feeling that war was now inevitable. He telephoned the house where the party was in progress and told the geisha to get Hori, which she did. After a while Hori left the party quietly and came to the geisha house, where he found Yamamoto lying on the tatami of his room looking unhappy. The two old friends had a long talk that night. Yamamoto told about the meetings with the army and how General Terauchi had been immutable on the subject of the negotiations with the United States and that the decision had been forced: The war was going to happen at any moment.

For a few seconds Yamamoto considered the last slender chance. "The arrangements have been made to recall the force if anything should come of the negotiations, but. . ."

As Yamamoto knew very well, the stiffening attitude of the Americans in recent weeks had made it almost impossible to believe anything would happen to change the situation. He told Hori how he had laid the groundwork with the strike force before they left and how he had told Admiral Nagumo that he had to be ready to "switch off"—to recall the planes even as they were in the air. This announcement had brought groans and cries that it would be impossible, a response that had in turn irritated Yamamoto. The admiral had informed all concerned that if they could not obey orders, no matter when they were received, then those concerned should resign from the service then and there. This strong talk had quelled the rebels, but in his heart Yamamoto had known that his was so much empty talk. There would be no recall. There would be no turning back. There would be war. And this night he poured out his feelings to his friend Hori, for the last time.

He was seeing the Emperor the next day, he said, to receive the Imperial Rescript, and that was just about the last step.

Meanwhile, back with the Combined Fleet, Admiral Ugaki had opened the sealed order that had been delivered several days earlier. The order announced that Japan had decided to begin war against the United States, England, and Holland during the first ten days of December. So as Admiral Yamamoto was preparing to receive the Imperial Rescript, the messages were already going out to the commanders of the various units of the fleet warning them of war and announcing that the exact times and places would be given to them in a matter of hours.

On December 2 the Japanese strike force crossed the international dateline. Admiral Yamamoto and Admiral Ugaki drafted the message Yamamoto would send to the fleet in a few hours:

> THE FATE OF THE EMPIRE DEPENDS UPON THIS
> WAR. DO YOUR DUTY.

At five o'clock that afternoon Yamamoto said it was time, and the chief of staff sent a message to the first striking force:

> CLIMB MOUNT NIITAKA.

This was the signal for which Admiral Nagumo had been waiting, the news that the conferences had indeed failed and that he was to move as rapidly as possible to the attack on Pearl Harbor.

And as all this occurred, Ambassadors Nomura and Kurusu were still talking in Washington. They spent an hour that day with Undersecretary of State Sumner Welles, while President Roosevelt, who had returned to Washington from his winter retreat in Warm Springs, Georgia, conferred with Secretary of State Hull and Admiral Stark. The Japanese were aware that the situation was indeed grave, but they were unaware that the attack on Pearl Harbor had already been launched.

On December 3 at 10:45 A.M., Admiral Yamamoto presented himself at the Imperial Palace and crossed the moat. He was dressed now in his full uniform with medals, and he was ushered into the Imperial presence. There the Emperor read to him the Imperial Rescript announcing war.

> In issuing the order, we trust you with the duty of commanding the Combined Fleets. On considering the responsibility of the Combined Fleets, remember that the prosperity of our Empire depends on them. Since you have trustworthy experience in many years' training of the fleets, we expect you will satisfy our desires by displaying our authority and force through victory over the enemy.

"Your humble subject is filled with trepidation and inspiration," Yamamoto replied, "to have received your Gracious Precept prior to the opening of war. The officers and men of the Combined Fleet will swear to do their duty. With confidence we face operations."

Afterwards the admiral went to interviews with Prince Fushimi and Prince Takamatsu, old friends who wanted to talk about the coming war. Back on the flagship, Chief of Staff Ugaki noted that President Roosevelt met that day with his secretaries of war and navy and the chiefs of operations of the army and the navy.

When Admiral Ugaki read that news in the radio bulletins, he permitted himself a little gloating. "Don't you know a big dagger is thrusting into your throat in four days?" Admiral Ugaki said. But, as if troubled by conscience, he confided in his diary: "It is not unfair to assault one who is sleeping. This means a victory over a most careless enemy."

Ugaki knew, however, as Yamamoto had so often said, that the preemptive strike was Japan's only chance to win the war on the old Samurai principle of "win first and fight later."

Pearl Harbor was not the only matter on the minds of Yamamoto and his staff, however. Forces were moving from Taiwan to make the attack on Malaya.

Even if by some miracle the talks in Washington were to succeed, it would have been almost impossible to stop the other military groups that were already heading out to attack Malaya, occupy southern Thailand, attack the Philippines, and attack the Dutch East Indies. For on December 3 the army's wheels also were in motion, and the army had no hesitation whatsoever about what was going to happen. Tojo had opted for war, General Terauchi had already headed south to Indochina to be close in order to supervise southern operations, and as far as the army was concerned, there was never any possibility of turning back. Yamamoto knew all this, and he was very depressed that afternoon.

On the evening of December 3, Admiral Yamamoto showed up without notice at his own house in Tokyo—much to the surprise of his wife and four children, who hadn't the slightest idea that he was away from the fleet. That night he ate with the family—a most unusual occurrence—but he was preoccupied. Since he was often preoccupied on those infrequent occasions when he was at home, no one was terribly surprised.

The evening passed amicably, Yamamoto stayed in the house for the night, and the next morning he went off to Navy Minister Shimada's residence for an official party that celebrated the Imperial Rescript and what was about to happen to the world. Those at the party included Yamamoto's friend Prince Takamatsu, the Emperor's naval aide, Vice Admiral Tomoshige Samejima, and Prince Fushimi's aide. Takeichi Hori was there—by special invitation from Yamamoto, because he was still looked upon askance by much of the naval community for his extreme liberal views toward foreigners. Some other friends of Yamamoto's were there, and all the brass hats from the Navy Ministry and Naval Headquarters. The Emperor had sent over a number of bottles of ceremonial sake from his own supply, which was of course an extreme honor, and the officers opened it with reverence. They drank to the success of Yamamoto's mission. The party ended around lunch time. Yamamoto set off for a flower shop, where he bought a dozen red roses, and then for the geisha house at Umenoshima, where he met Chiyoko Kawai for a late lunch.

After lunch, Yamamoto and Chiyoko left the geisha house and took a taxi down to the Ginza. They parted company there, and Yamamoto hailed a passing taxi and went to Tokyo station. There he found Takeichi Hori, who had come along earlier to buy his ticket for him, and they had time for a few words before Yamamoto's train was ready to leave the station.

"Look after yourself," said Hori to the admiral.

"Thanks," said Yamamoto laconically. "I don't imagine I'll be back."

And the admiral got on his train, which pulled out a few seconds later. As both men suspected, it was the last meeting the two friends from boyhood would ever have.

* * *

On December 4, the tranquility of the flagship *Nagato* in the fleet anchorage was disturbed by an urgent message from Tokyo indicating unusual activity off the shore of Hawaii. Had the attacking force been discovered? No, the activity suddenly ceased, and all was again serene on the flagship.

But not for long. A few hours later came another disturbing message: A plane carrying the army's operational orders was reported missing while on its way to Canton. Tokyo feared that the crew had been captured by the Chinese.

So the tension continued. Admiral Ugaki was so tense that he clipped bits of his fingernails and a lock of hair to send home; he was overwhelmed with a sense of fateful undertaking. And as for Yamamoto, he had sensed long ago that he would not survive this war. He fully expected to go down with his flagship somewhere in the eastern or southern seas. He had already entrusted the welfare of his wife and four children to his old friend Takeichi Hori. He had said his last farewell to the geisha Masako Tsurushima, the great love of his life and most frequent companion of the last fifteen years, and to Chiyoko Kawai. He had no such painful parting with his wife and children, but he had told Hori all.

As Admiral Yamamoto returned to the flagship, the fate of Hawaii (like a rat in a trap, Ugaki declared) renewed in these two men their sense of mortality and frailty. The stirrings became more frequent. That day a report arrived from Tokyo of a large British plane shadowing the force at sea that was heading to occupy southern Thailand.

December 7, Tokyo time, dawned bright and sunny. Admiral Yamamoto sent his war message out to the fleet, and it was read to the men of every ship at sea, including the intrepid fliers and sailors of the Nagumo Pearl Harbor attack force.

And then, that night, a message arrived on the flagship from Tokyo, informing Admiral Yamamoto that a Japanese army plane had shot down a British seaplane just off the coast of Thailand. The seaplane had been snooping around the Japanese invasion fleet. The message referred to "an enemy plane." That had to be the first shot of the Pacific War!

There were no other messages as darkness closed down over southern Japan. Now Admiral Yamamoto waited for morning to come to Hawaii.

WAR ON THREE FRONTS

21

In those last few hours before the dawn of December 7, 1941, over Pearl Harbor, the tension aboard Admiral Yamamoto's flagship was almost visible. Chief of Staff Ugaki wrapped himself in a mantle of self-justification for the sneak attack that the Japanese forces were about to carry out before war was declared, even before the talks between the Americans and the Japanese envoys were broken off.

Not so Yamamoto. He harked back to the precepts of his namesake Tsunetomo Yamamoto, seventeenth-century author of the book of *Hagakure*, the bible of the samurai, for his own justification: What he had done was done to serve his Emperor and to save Japan.

This did not mean, however, that Yamamoto was untroubled by the turn of events. Indeed, as one of the earliest and most vociferous opponents of war against the United States and Great Britain, he was troubled all the way. He had never believed that such a war was in the best interests of Japan or that, ultimately, Japan would win it. The best he had ever hoped for was a quick false victory that would give the Japanese a chance to make some concession, get the Americans to the conference table, and continue their China adventure. By the late autumn of 1941 he was not even sure that this was possible.

The first news of the war did not come from Pearl Harbor, but from the south, where Japanese convoys were heading toward Thailand and Malaya. On the night of December 7 (Tokyo time), Admiral Yamamoto retired with the information that the convoys to the south were steaming along as planned, without incident.

At 3 A.M. on December 8, Admiral Yamamoto had the word from the wireless room that the order *Totsugeki* (Charge!) was being sent repeatedly on the wireless from the *Akagi* off in the Western Hemisphere. So he knew that the two hundred aircraft of the attacking force were getting into the air to attack Pearl Harbor.

And then the messages from the attack fleet began coming in on the flagship:

> I HIT AN ENEMY BATTLESHIP. . . .
> I BOMBED HICKAM FIELD. . . .

Then intercepts from the American message centers began to arrive:

> ALL SHIPS IN PEARL HARBOR GET UNDER
> WAY. . . .
> SWEEP MINES SOUTH OF FORD ISLAND. . . .
> THE COMMANDER OF THE ASIATIC FLEET WILL
> OPERATE ACCORDING TO PLAN. . . .
> SOS . . . ATTACKED BY JAP BOMBERS HERE. . . .
> PEARL HARBOR PRIORITY . . . SHIPS NATIONALITY
> UNKNOWN TEN MILES OFF POINT. . . .
> JAPS . . . THIS IS THE REAL THING. . . .

From these fragments, a picture began to emerge, a picture of a successful attack. The admiral realized that the order to sweep mines must have been caused by someone seeing something inside the harbor, and that meant the midget submarines had gotten in. The rest would have to wait a while, because the flagship was now deluged with messages.

The Eleventh Air Fleet was preparing to attack Malayan targets but was delayed by fog on Formosa. The amphibious landings on the Malayan coast began.

From Tokyo came word of much activity. That morning the privy council had held a meeting and the Emperor issued his formal declaration of war against the United States and Great Britain. Then the Emperor called in the ministers of army and navy and gave them messages for the troops and sailors.

The Thai government succumbed to force majeure and agreed to let the Japanese troops, who had already landed, occupy the south, but Japanese troops entering Bangkok met armed resistance.

From Hong Kong came word that the attack had begun; from Shanghai they heard that an American gunboat had been captured and a British gunboat sunk.

From Admiral Nagumo's strike force came preliminary claims that two battleships had been sunk at Pearl Harbor and four damaged, while four cruisers were damaged, about 300 American planes were destroyed, and "a carrier was probably sunk" by a Japanese submarine. Thirty Japanese planes were lost, said the message.

From Wake Island came report of the attack on that American base, but no final results.

From the Philippines came reports of the Japanese landings near Manila and the bombing of Clark Field. From Singapore came reports of air raids on the airfields around the city.

Later reports told of landings at four spots on the Malay Peninsula and hard fighting. And from the submarine command came the news that the *I-22* had gone missing off Singapore and that the *I-23* was heading home to Japan, having suffered serious damage in a fight with antisubmarine forces.

And then came an Imperial Rescript:

> Since the "China incident" our army and navy valiantly have fought and done their best for the past four and a half years. When we consider the cause of the difficulty, we cannot but conclude that the sources of difficulty are the United States and England. Although we tried to resolve the differences in peace, they did not show any sincerity for settlement but made economic and military threats against us. At this juncture we decided to declare war against the United States and England to guarantee Japanese self-existence and self-defense and the eternal peace of the Far East. We rely on the fidelity and valor of the army and the navy to complete their task of establishing the safety of the empire.

December 9, 1941, Tokyo time. Aboard the flagship, they called it X + 1 Day. On this day Admiral Yamamoto had congratulations on his glorious victory at Pearl Harbor: from the chief of the naval general staff, from Navy Minister Shimada, and from the army minister and General Terauchi. He was not much impressed; he continued to believe the attack had been a serious error.

Not much was yet known about what had happened at Pearl Harbor, although the frantic nature of a message sent by U.S. Navy Secretary Frank Knox indicated to Yamamoto that the shock had been very great. Knox spoke of just that, "tremendous shock," and said that no time was to be lost in getting more ships, more planes, and more personnel out to fight.

In midafternoon on December 9, the submarine *I-65*, which was operating off the Malay Peninsula, reported that two major capital ships were in sight, and the operations room of the flagship suddenly grew hushed. These could be only two ships: the ships the British sent to reinforce their Asian strength. They were in fact the great new British battleship *Prince of Wales* and her consort, the battlecruiser *Repulse*, which, although of World War I vintage, was still a pride of the British Fleet. These two vessels had been sent down to Singapore a few weeks earlier to show the flag and indicate to the Japanese the British determination to defend this area.

The submarine was ordered to keep in contact with the ships, and search planes were sent out. But the British ships were still too far off the Indochina shore for land-based naval aircraft to attack them. Everything would have to wait until tomorrow, but meanwhile all the ships in the area were alerted to watch for the enemy.

Admiral Yamamoto wanted a battle if possible. The Seventh Destroyer Squadron was ordered to search for the enemy, and search planes were ordered around at different angles. But the British force changed course, and the ships were lost to view as night fell.

What Yamamoto did not know, and what worried him, was Admiral Tom Phillips's purpose in being out in these waters just then. Was he coming to intercept the Japanese landing fleet off Kotabar? Yamamoto did not know, but he had to have respect for his enemy. Still, the British ships were only two, no matter how powerful, and they had no air cover. The Japanese had many battleships, many destroyers, many submarines, and many planes in this area.

That day Admiral Yamamoto also received some news from the First Striking Force that made him extremely angry. Admiral Nagumo had turned away from Pearl Harbor without finishing the job. In the first two waves of attack, the Japanese had lost no more than thirty planes and a handful of miniature submarines. The striking force had expected—at least Yamamoto had told them to be ready to accept— losses of up to fifty percent, and there had been virtually no losses. Still, Admiral Nagumo had moved away from the scene. As Ya- mamoto said, it was a prime example of sneakiness and second-class thinking.

Admiral Ugaki and the staff of the Combined Fleet proposed that Admiral Nagumo be ordered to turn around and return to Hawaii to finish the job begun. But Admiral Yamamoto refused to order Nagumo back. There was always the chance, he said, that Nagumo had a really good reason for retiring, although personally he did not believe it. Since Nagumo had not wanted to finish the job properly, there was no way to force him to do so. So Yamamoto contented himself with ordering Admiral Nagumo to make an attack on Midway on the way back to Japan, to knock out the facilities there so it could not be used as a submarine base.

December 10. X + 2 Day on the Japanese war calendar. The Combined Fleet headquarters contingent was at sea, sailing between Hahajima and Iwojima. Landings continued in the Philippines, against considerable resistance, and on Guam, where there was virtually no resistance.

The matter that occupied Admiral Yamamoto's attention this day was the whereabouts of Admiral Tom Phillips and the British Force Z, the two battleships and their attendant destroyers. They had disappeared. One submarine had found them the night before and fired torpedoes, but all torpedoes missed and the ships disappeared in the night.

Still, Yamamoto knew the general area where they must be, so he ordered an attack, and that morning the planes took off from Indochina bases to find the ships. Soon the enemy was sighted and attacked by a formation of fifty-one torpedo bombers. Of course, the British ships had no air cover, and the end result was to prove once and for all the contention of American General Billy Mitchell back in the 1920s that airplanes, unassisted, could certainly sink heavily armored battleships. The *Repulse* went down shortly after 2 P.M., and the *Prince of Wales* (which the Japanese believed to be the *King George V*) sank a few minutes later. Three Japanese planes were lost and a few damaged.

That day Admiral Yamamoto received another Imperial Rescript:

The Combined Fleets, just at the outset of war, have gained great merit by destroying the enemy fleet and air strength at Hawaii. We highly approve of this and hope our subjects will strive for future victory.

And that day, from the air waves, they learned that the Americans had blamed Admiral Kimmel, commander in chief of the U.S. Pacific Fleet, and General Short, commander of the American army forces in Hawaii, for the defeat. Admiral Ugaki summed up Yamamoto's feelings in his diary.

This tells us much about the shock they received. But it is a gross error for the authorities to want to punish their subordinates when some misfortune occurs. When a government wants to exert its national will, it must be prepared for war, and if it is not fully prepared, then it must be ready for defeat. The responsibility always rests on the chief officer.

From Wake Island came a shock to the Japanese, however. The occupation force was repulsed by the American defenders. Something went wrong, the Japanese task force commander sailed away for reinforcements, and the situation was confused. Yamamoto was not happy.

Nor was he happy with the army's claim now that their planes had done all the damage to the Philippines and to other areas. The fact was, said the staff, that the army had done virtually nothing, but was making great claims for successes that were actually navy successes. "A trivial cheat," said Chief of Staff Ugaki.

This day, Yamamoto knew that the war to come was going to be long and difficult, and his heart sank, because this was just the sort of war that Japan could not withstand. Nagumo's failure to knock out the American aircraft carriers and to destroy the submarine and other facilities at Pearl Harbor rankled very badly. It was the difference between success and failure, really, because the only success that would have served Japan would have been total success, which had been within Nagumo's grasp. He had lost only thirty planes in the initial Pearl Harbor attacks, scarcely more than would be lost in a training exercise, and yet he had turned around with the job half finished. This was almost as bad as not having attacked. No matter the Imperial Rescript, no matter the paeans of praise over Radio Tokyo, Yamamoto was depressed by a sense that he had lost his gambit because of the timidity of a subordinate.

Now, it was realized aboard the flagship, the world was really plunged into a world war. The declaration of war by Germany against America and by America against Germany and Italy as well as Japan underlined this newest development.

December 12. X + 4 Day. The landings in the Philippines were going very well, the admiral observed with some satisfaction. But down at Wake Island, things were going very badly indeed. Admiral Kajioka, the commander of the invasion force, had suffered serious damage to several ships, and now he demanded the use of an aircraft carrier. Admiral Ugaki, who got the message, put it aside. He did not want to disturb Yamamoto.

If Yamamoto had wished, he could have basked again this day in the glory reflected by another Imperial Rescript:

> The air forces of the Combined Fleet have displayed their brilliant merits by destroying the fleet of the British navy in the South China Sea. We highly appreciate the achievement.

December 13. X + 5 Day. The Combined Fleet, still at sea, passed through the Hayasui Channel and came to anchor at Hashirajima, the fleet anchorage. There the admiral got bad news: Two destroyers had been sunk at Wake Island, and the invasion had turned into a fiasco. The whole force withdrew. And then there was no report of the air raid on Midway ordered earlier; what could Nagumo be doing now? Certainly he was not following his orders.

The fleet was sorely troubled at this period by a whole group of submarine sighting reports, which occasioned many alarms and excursions by patrol boats, destroyers, and aircraft. No submarines were sunk.

December 15. X + 7 Day. The disappointing word came from Admiral Nagumo that he had given up the attack against Midway because of bad weather and was hurrying home, much to the disgust of Admiral Yamamoto. Yamamoto wanted the force to make a strike at Wake Island, but Nagumo stalled. It was a difficult situation. On December 17 the official results of the Pearl Harbor attack were announced, and Japan erupted in glee because four battleships were reported sunk, four more damaged, and many other ships hit. Given this praise, how could Nagumo be told that he had failed?

That day aboard the flagship, the irony was noted: Japan had fought since 1920 at the adverse ratio of naval forces demanded by America and Britain 5-5-3. Now, in a few days, the ratio had been reversed by the sinkings at Pearl Harbor and off Malaya and the joining of the great *Yamato* to the Combined Fleet that week.

On Saturday, December 20, the navy minister came down to the anchorage for a celebration and to distribute some medals. The two of them talked for a long time about the war, and the minister said the government was very pleased. Yamamoto said very little.

The occupation of Wake Island was finally finished, to everyone's vast relief, on December 22. It had been a complete foulup, and the responsibility was laid at the door of the commander of the Fourth Fleet. Admiral Yamamoto removed him from command that day.

December 24. X + 16 Day. The Nagumo task force returned to Hashirajima, and Nagumo and the staff came to the flagship. Admiral Nagano, chief of the naval general staff, came down again from Tokyo and met with Yamamoto, Nagumo, and the others. The story of the Hawaii raid was told in detail, and Admiral Yamamoto said very little about his views. After that the staffs held a long drinking party and some of the real views were exchanged.

That afternoon, Admiral Ugaki came down with a severe toothache. Admiral Yamamoto had pains elsewhere. And that day was the last of the celebrations. On December 25, the fleet war book stopped taking account of the number of days that the war had progressed. As everyone could tell, even though the successes were overwhelming, and the army in particular was buoyed to the point of self-satisfaction, it was going to be a long, long war.

SUCCESS UPON SUCCESS

22

Hong Kong fell on December 26.

The navy was occupied with expansion into the atolls of the South Pacific just now, an expansion that was more expensive than had been expected. Several destroyers and minesweepers were lost to submarine torpedoes and mines.

January 1 brought thoughts about the past—it was six years since the "China incident" had turned Japan upside down. Now the Great East Asia War—as it had been titled in Tokyo—was twenty-five days old, and the forces of Imperial Japan were moving very rapidly.

The navy now predicted for Admiral Yamamoto that the first stage of the war would be completed by March. This meant that Japan would have overrun that entire South Pacific area that was its target and would be ready to think about moving elsewhere—into Australia, Hawaii, and maybe even Alaska, with its all-important fishing grounds.

The big worry of the navy at this point was lest the unstable elements of the army (and Tojo was certainly the leader of this faction) foment a war with the Soviet Union as well. They had very nearly done this in the "Homonhon incident," in which the Japanese army had been roundly defeated.

As part of the usual ceremony for New Year's Day, Admiral Yamamoto had his picture taken with the staff. They assembled to salute the Emperor's portrait, pledge their honor, and drink sake in celebration. The war was going splendidly, and virtually no one but Yamamoto considered that day when industrial America would recover her strength and begin to fight back with enormous power.

"We will surely win," said Admiral Ugaki, with the confidence born of success.

That afternoon, the flagship was roused to action by a report of an enemy carrier with two cruisers moving out from Oahu Island. Was this going to be a raid? Admiral Yamamoto laid plans to ambush the carrier with a submarine flotilla that was preparing for sea at Kwajalein, in the new Marshalls Islands base. Meanwhile, the submarine flotilla that had been involved in the Pearl Harbor attack and was now off the western American coast would come back and attack from the rear. But the submarines did not find the American carrier, and in a day or two the excitement died down aboard the flagship.

Admiral Yamamoto was a very efficient fleet commander in terms of his attention to detail. He insisted on knowing everything that was going on in his Combined Fleet. For example, just after the new year, he led his staff on an expedition to see the lookout post established on Ohmishima and a naval shore battery on Nasake Jima. At one o'clock in the afternoon, they left the flagship in small boats and landed at Wasa. Then they started to climb up the steep mountain, the admiral leading. They climbed for an hour on a steep and rocky path, until, panting and perspiring, they reached the lookout post. The view below encompassed the two channels, Moroshina and Kodako, that led to the anchorage. Matsuyama castle stood in the background against the blue sea. Then they tumbled down the mountain again, and at four o'clock they were ready for the second part of the expedition. They went by the antisubmarine net and to Nasake Jima, where the admiral inspected the battery of four shore guns. Then they went back to the ship, arriving at 6 P.M.

Such attention to detail was a mark of the admiral. He had sanctioned the use of the new midget submarines in the attack on Pearl Harbor, and now he wanted to know what had happened. One of the boats was the *I-16*, and it was ordered to Hashirajima so that its captain could report to the admiral personally about the mission. The captain reported on the difficulties of carrying a midget submarine on the deck, launching it, and then trying to recover it. In fact, all the midget submarines that were used at Pearl Harbor were lost, and the admiral told his staff that there was still a lot to be learned before the next operation in which midget submarines seemed indicated.

Yamamoto was not very sanguine about the submarine and never had been. At the London naval conference he had joined the faction rejecting the British contention that the submarine should be abandoned altogether as a purely offensive weapon: In the naval conference Japan opposed the abolishment of the submarine on the ground that it was a defensive weapon, not an offensive one. Now that seemed to have become true; they were really defensive. At least that was the Japanese view.

And here Yamamoto showed a major weakness as a fleet commander: He did not understand the primary use of the submarine. Consequently, the Japanese fleet never made adequate use of its submarine fleet, although the I-boats were extremely efficient weapons, with longer range and better torpedoes than the American boats of that period. For one who had shown so much appreciation of air power in the war in Europe, Admiral Yamamoto showed no appreciation at all of the effectiveness of the German U-boat in the war against Britain. The concept of commerce destruction as a major factor in the war did not seem to interest Yamamoto.

Before the outbreak of war in 1939, Captain Karl Doenitz, chief of the German submarine service, had written the high command that if they gave him 300 U-boats he could bring England to her knees in less than a year. Fortunately for Britain, Hitler did not pay attention. The man who did pay attention to the concept was Winston Churchill, who shared with Doenitz a perfect understanding of the importance of commerce destruction. But not Yamamoto. He was constantly telling the Sixth Fleet, his submarine force, to concentrate on the sinking of warships. They did so, and they would sink a number, but within a matter of months the Americans were producing warships so rapidly that the sinkings were not a major factor in the war. Admiral Yamamoto's error here was major, and it had an enormous effect on the outcome of the Pacific war. As Admiral Nimitz said, shortly after his arrival at Pearl Harbor, with their I-boat force, the Japanese could have cut off Hawaii from the mainland, and thus crippled the American Pacific war effort, for many, many months. Yet Yamamoto, who had shown enormous prescience in leading Japan to preeminence as the first major carrier power, was not alone by far in his misapplication of the submarine warfare principle.

On January 2, 1942, Admiral Ugaki noted in his diary: "It is regrettable for the officers and men of the submarine service that they have not yet sunk any important men of war except merchantmen." So the myopia in the fleet was general, and it was shared in Tokyo. While Admiral Nimitz was pulling out all the stops to bring submarine forces into play against Japan, the Japanese I-boats were looking for American carriers and battleships, and this attitude would not change. A few days later, the Fourth Submarine Division reported the sinking of the carrier *Langley*, the only carrier in the U.S. Asiatic Fleet, and that whetted the submarine force's appetite for war ships. When another I-boat torpedoed the carrier *Lexington* a few days after that, the seal was put on the Japanese naval attitude.*

Admiral Yamamoto had promised five dozen bottles of beer to the first torpedo officer of a submarine to sink a fleet-class carrier, and he paid off to the torpedo officer of the *I-6*, the submarine that torpedoed the *Lexington*. She was actually not sunk, but the Japanese did not learn that until several months later when she appeared in the Coral Sea. So Radio Tokyo triumphantly announced her sinking and elaborated on the story for several days. And the commander in chief's approval of the search for capital warships diverted the whole submarine force. No one was talking about commerce raiding after that.

Japanese troops occupied Manila on January 2 and 3. The Americans and the Philippine Constabulary had fled, mostly to the Bataan Peninsula. The invasion was way ahead of schedule, as it was everywhere else. So Yamamoto reorganized the fleet. The Southern Expeditionary Fleet was renamed the First Southern Expeditionary Fleet, and it prepared for invasion of Rabaul because the other moves had been so successful. A new Third Southern Expeditionary Fleet was given charge of the Philippines operations, which now consisted of mopping up and the reduction of the Corregidor fortress with its big guns that controlled Manila harbor.

Along with the expeditionary fleet, Admiral Yamamoto prepared to send the carrier task force down south to make way for the Rabaul invasion by softening up the Australian defenses. Yamamoto now expected that the Rabaul phase would be complete by mid-March, and then some more plans would have to be made. In the back of his mind was a plan for the capture of Midway Island, which bothered him because

---

*The reports were in error. Both carriers were sunk in the Pacific, but not just then. The *Saratoga* was the ship torpedoed, but she was repaired.

of its usefulness as an American submarine and air base, and a simultaneous move against the Aleutian Islands, which would give the Japanese a foothold on the North American perimeter. The staff was talking about invading Hawaii, and in Tokyo plans even to the point of invasion currency were being drawn. Yamamoto's staff officers began studying alternative plans for future operations. Whatever the plans, they must be kept strictly within the overall aim of the war: the attainment of self-sufficiency for Japan, so that she could continue her major effort, which was to swallow China. Admiral Ugaki wanted to send submarines far afield, to the Indian Ocean and to the Panama Canal, but he was restrained by Yamamoto. Even the invasion of Hawaii, for which the staff officers were clamoring, would have to wait until that decisive fleet action, missed by Admiral Nagumo at Pearl Harbor, had been brought to successful completion.

The war was going splendidly, too splendidly for Admiral Yamamoto. The army announced that it was ready now to stage the invasion of Java, weeks ahead of schedule. But the problem with all this success was that no one in Tokyo was able to bring it into perspective. Yamamoto knew that the Americans would soon recover from the Pearl Harbor destruction. He had not achieved his decisive action, and it haunted him. Navy and army had more than carried out the tasks assigned to them so far. What was needed now was statesmanship in Tokyo to consolidate the victories without waste and strengthen the empire. Looking around him, Admiral Yamamoto saw no such statesman, no one of the caliber of Britain's Winston Churchill or America's Franklin D. Roosevelt. And he confided his fears to Admiral Ugaki, who capsulized them in his diary:

> However invincible the Imperial armed forces are, and however great their exploits may be, the great achievement done at the sacrifice of our lives will be only in vain, unless statesmen have a great policy for the country.

On January 8, Admiral Nagumo sailed for the south, and the next day Japanese troops moved into Tarakan and the Celebes Islands. Yes, the war was going splendidly.

On January 14, after four days of hard work, Admiral Ugaki completed the proposal directed by Admiral Yamamoto for the Midway operation, to be followed by the invasion of Hawaii. The justification was the need to destroy the American fleet and bring the war to a quick conclusion. This directive was turned over to the fleet staff officers for detailed study and recommendations. This, as we have seen, was the Japanese system, in which young staff officers were given enormous responsibility and latitude. In fact, they had almost full sway up to the time of final decision. Even Admiral Ugaki, the chief of staff, was not permitted in the junior officers' councils, lest his presence inhibit their free discussion of ideas.

The next day the Admiral and the staff of the Combined Fleet left the *Nagato* to take up operations aboard the new fleet flagship *Yamato*. The following few days were spent in furious training exercises as the commander of the flagship began to understand what Admiral Yamamoto required of him. The crew very nearly wrecked the new flagship one day, in Kudako strait, when the flagship ran afoul of a sailing ship in midchannel with a strong adverse tide running. The sailboat captain panicked and stopped dead, the battleship barely missed her stern by putting the helm hard to starboard, and the inertia of the huge vessel then carried her toward the shore of Nuwajima. It was only by stopping the starboard engine, casting both anchors, and starting both engines full speed astern that the ship came to rest, only 750 yards from the southeastern tip of Nuwa Jima.

That night the admiral moved the flag back to the *Nagato*, where it would remain until the captain of the *Yamato* learned a bit more about the capabilities and problems of his ship.

On January 20, Admiral Yamamoto directed the *Nagato* to Kure. He and the men of the flagship had been two months steadily at sea, and the crew needed a rest. The admiral went ashore that day, visited the naval hospital, and paid tribute to the navy's dead at a local shrine. That night the staff held a party at a local restaurant and stayed in a hotel. The party was a grand success because the operations in the south were again going splendidly.

Next day came favorable reports from Rabaul and Balikpapan: The Japanese were marching on Rangoon, Thailand had declared war on the British, and the advance in Malaya had nearly reached Singapore. The future of the Japanese empire had never seemed brighter.

On January 27, Yamamoto's young staff officers came up with their plan. They had considered an immediate attack on Hawaii but had not been able to figure out how to destroy the land-based air force brought into the islands in the past few weeks. So they had opted for Midway, where that problem did not really exist. The plan was taken to Admiral Yamamoto, and he began to study it. At the same time, Commander Yamamoto (no relation) of the naval general staff appeared aboard the flagship on other business, and Admiral Ugaki gave him a copy of the proposal to take back to Tokyo.

For some time Admiral Yamamoto had been concerned about the whereabouts and activities of America's aircraft carriers. On February 1 he had some unwelcome news. An American carrier force had moved to the Marshalls for a raid, with cruisers and several destroyers. They hit Wotje, Eniwetok, Kwajalein, and Jaluit. They destroyed a number of planes and several ships, and they killed Rear Admiral Yasuhiro Yukichi, the commander of the naval base. He was the first admiral killed in the war.

Yamamoto was very upset, because the Japanese had been caught just as much unaware here as the Americans had at Pearl Harbor, and there was really no excuse for it because everyone knew now that there was a war on. The attack had been successful, said the admiral, because the men of the fleet had grown cocksure after their many easy victories. Everyone felt the admiral's displeasure that day, including Admiral Ugaki, who indulged himself in a long session of self-recrimination.

From the outset of the war, Admiral Yamamoto had been concerned about the day when American naval air power would make it possible for planes to raid Tokyo. He read the press, and he knew that the Americans had diverted ten cruiser hulls to become carriers, so it would not be long before the danger became very real. At this time Tojo and the army were boasting that the Americans would never touch Tokyo, but Yamamoto knew these were empty promises. This was one of the major reasons he so urgently sought the decisive battle and looked with such favor on the Midway plan.

On Saturday, February 7, came the welcome reports of the Japanese success at the battle of the Java Sea, which destroyed most of the remnants of the U.S. Asiatic Fleet and British and Dutch sea power in the area.

On February 12, the admiral's flag was again shifted to the *Yamato*, and the admiral and staff celebrated a housewarming with chicken sukiyaki and sake. That night they celebrated again, because they learned of the fall of Singapore. This was considered in Tokyo as the supreme victory of the war. The Japanese government changed the name to Shonanto, and along came another rescript lauding Yamamoto and the navy, plus a hand-embroidered banner showing an airplane against the rising sun, done by no less a personage than the Empress herself. It was delivered by the Emperor's naval aide.

Once again, the next day, the whole staff had a picture taken on the foredeck. General Tojo made an important speech about the Greater East Asia Coprosperity sphere, calling on the Australians and New Zealanders to break their alliance with the Western powers and join up. The call was ignored in Canberra. Then, as if on signal, on February 19, Admiral Nagumo's task force attacked Darwin, sinking three destroyers, a subchaser, and eight merchant ships. The harbor was wrecked, and about thirty Allied planes were destroyed. Afterwards Admiral Nagumo sailed on to Truk to await further orders.

On March 1, 1942, Rear Admiral Takejiro Ohnishi came to the flagship for a courtesy call. He had been ordered to Tokyo to take up duties as chief of the general affairs bureau of the navy aeronautical department. Yamamoto was interested to see that Ohnishi, who had at first opposed the Pearl Harbor operation as foolhardy, had now come completely around in his view and believed that carriers were the center of power. This was a belief that Yamamoto himself had long held, but Ohnishi went further than Yamamoto, who had a fine respect for land-based air forces as well. All this came out while the two admirals played shogi half the night. Score: Yamamoto four wins, Ohnishi three wins.

Early in March, Admiral Halsey's task force raided Marcus Island, and although the damage was slight, it made Yamamoto think again about the possibility of American air raids on Tokyo.

The war surged on. In early April, Admiral Nagumo's carrier force hit Ceylon, damaging the harbor and sinking some ships at Colombo, and then it engaged elements of the British fleet off Trincomalee, sinking the carrier *Hermes*. Once again, Admiral Nagumo did not wait around long enough to complete the job: Two other British carriers got away. Admiral Yamamoto happened to be in Tokyo at that point, at the Navy club, where he encountered Prince Fushimi. The prince was all congratulations and smiles about the great job being done by the navy, so Yamamoto could not air his own negative views. Everything seemed to be going better than anyone had dared hope. Nagumo sank two cruisers as well.

The plans had been made, and the navy and army now agreed to begin the second stage of war operations, which involved the attack on Australia and Midway. On April 17, Admiral Yamamoto delivered his message to the fleet, and the task forces set out to make landings in the Solomon Islands and at Port Moresby on New Guinea.

"With this spirit," wrote Admiral Ugaki triumphantly, "the foundation of the empire can be said to be safe."

But the fact was that even as the admiral so wrote, forces were in motion to give the Japanese a great shock, and to bear out Admiral Yamamoto's most startling fears.

EARLY WARNING

23

Admiral Yamamoto had never expected that the Japanese surge across the Pacific would go unchallenged for long. This is why he was pressing for a naval operation that would bring forth the American fleet and make possible the decisive battle he sought while Japan still had the edge in strength of aircraft carriers and capital ships. The sinking and disabling of most of the battleship fleet at Pearl Harbor had created a feeling of victory in Japan, but the continued operations of the American carriers worried Yamamoto. Already the American carriers had made two strikes: one on the Marshall Islands and a less successful one on Marcus.

The real problem for Admiral Yamamoto was a failure in intelligence. He really did not know where the American carriers were or what strategy they might be following. A succession of sighting reports, usually from long-range aircraft, proved unsuccessful because the observers could not get a pattern and could not keep track of the American carriers.

Just now, in the spring of 1942, Admiral Yamamoto did not expect much trouble, except from the occasional raid. This is why, on Saturday, April 18, Tokyo time, a carrier raid on Tokyo and other parts of Japan proved to be a complete surprise and a matter of great chagrin to Yamamoto and the Combined Fleet.

The excitement began on the flagship at 7:30 A.M. Saturday. The admiral had just finished breakfast when a telephone message came from the chief of the naval general staff in Tokyo. Patrol Boat No. 23 of the patrol line that encircled the Japanese islands reported sighting three enemy carriers at a point 700 miles east of Tokyo. The report was made at 6:30 A.M., and the patrol boat had not been heard from since.

The fleet staff rushed into action. Most of the Japanese fleet carriers were at sea, on their way home from the raid on Trincomalee and just now west of Taiwan. Admiral Nagumo was ordered to hurry eastward to the east side of Japan. Meanwhile, the cruiser *Atago*, flagship of the Japanese Second Fleet, was lying in Yokosuka, and the commander of the fleet and his senior staff officers were at the offices of the naval general staff. They were given charge of a search and destroy operation, but it was badly hampered by the lack of carriers.

At naval headquarters the radio staff tried to make contact with Patrol Boat No. 23, the *Nitto Maru*, but she did not answer. Two auxiliary cruisers, the *Awata Maru* and the *Akagi Maru*, were sent to the scene, but they found no trace of the other craft. She had, of course, been sighted by Admiral William F. Halsey's task force and destroyed, but not before she had issued her warning message.

The American force was the celebrated "Shangri La" force entrusted by Admiral Ernest J. King, the American naval chief of staff, with the task of bombing Japan. The whole idea was a morale builder for the American people, who needed a lift very badly in that spring of 1942, with the war going so negatively everywhere: the forces on Bataan about to flee to Corregidor for a last stand, the east coast of the American mainland under siege by Admiral Doenitz's U-boats, to say nothing of the fall of Hong Kong, and Singapore, and the collapse of Dutch power in the Dutch East Indies. All this had suggested the need for some spectacular move, and in the person of a feisty little Army Air Corps lieutenant colonel named James Doolittle, the American high command found the answer: a bombing raid on Japan.

The American problem was that the navy did not have a carrier-based aircraft capable of the sort of flight that would be necessary to bomb Japan and then make an escape to China, which was the only nonsuicidal approach possible. Carriers in 1942 dared not approach the Japanese homeland close enough to operate in their usual fashion with their short-range fighters and bombers. But Doolittle had the answer in the B-25 Mitchell medium bomber, which did have the range to take off from about 700 miles out, bomb, and then make the China coast. A deckload of B-25 bombers was put aboard the carrier *Hornet*, and in company with the *Enterprise*, the Halsey force set out for Japan. What the men of Patrol Boat No. 23 saw on that Saturday morning was the approaching force of carriers and cruisers, ''spooked'' before they could reach the 600 mile point, which Halsey had hoped to do.

The Japanese search ships and search planes did not find the American carrier force that day, luckily for Halsey, and Admiral Nagumo's carrier strike force was too far away to become involved.

At 1 P.M., the flagship had the news of an enemy air raid on Tokyo, but no details. Then came many rumors and false reports. At sunset (about 5 P.M.), Admiral Yamamoto ordered a new search from the Japanese home islands, and about fifty planes went out 700 miles to the area where the carriers had been reported that morning.

That night the flagship had new reports from Tokyo. The planes had bombed nine places in Tokyo with incendiary and explosive bombs, twelve people had been killed and a hundred wounded, and fifty houses had burned down and fifty more were damaged. Other bombers had hit Yokohama and Yokosuka, damaging one warship, the *Taigei*, and others struck Nagoya, Wakayama, and Kobe. Yet the enemy force could not be found. Admiral Yamamoto correctly presumed that the Americans had withdrawn rapidly eastward immediately after launching the planes.

The damage obviously was not great, but the shock value was enormous. General Tojo was very much embarrassed, having promised the Japanese people that Japan would never be bombed. Immediately Yamamoto told Admiral Ugaki that the staff would have to begin considering new problems and new defenses against this sort of air attack. Since the Americans had done it once, it had to be assumed that they would do it again soon. In fact, some members of the staff suggested that the Americans might be moving north toward Hokkaido just now, and air searches were started in that area.

On Monday new reports began to come in that clarified the story. One of the American planes had crash landed near Nanchang, China, and its five-member crew was captured by Japanese troops. At first the American air crew refused to give any information, and then some members began to tell the Japanese cock and bull stories. These were believed in part at first, but then were discovered to be false. Finally, under torture and threat, the Americans began to tell the true story, that these were B-25 bombers, that they had taken off from Admiral Halsey's carrier, and that they had been instructed to land at Hangchow, if possible. In fact, none of the planes landed safely.

The Doolittle raid troubled Admiral Yamamoto for days, not because of the damage done, which was infinitesimal, but because of the possible implications. Chief of Staff Ugaki stated the admiral's views to the staff:

> In view of the recent success, the enemy will undoubtedly repeat this kind of operation, while attempting raids from China. Therefore, we must make an effort to find the enemy in the east and at the same time watch for a threat from the west.

The search planes worked diligently for three days but found nothing, and on Monday the operation was finally called off. Once the true story of the raid was told, Admiral Yamamoto's fears subsided, for it became apparent that the Doolittle raid was a "stunt" and not the beginning of a plan.

The admiral could now turn his attention to less pressing but more important matters. The Pearl Harbor raid and the success of the strike force in raiding Australia and Ceylon had shown Yamamoto and the others of the Imperial Navy that the day of the battleship had ended and the day of the aircraft carrier had arrived. On April 23, officers from the naval general staff came to Hashirajima to discuss the naval construction program. In 1940 the Japanese had planned to build five battleships of the size of the *Yamato*, but only the *Musashi* was nearly completed. Now Yamamoto advised against proceeding with more battleships. Instead, he suggested, they should convert the hulls to make aircraft carriers. The same was true with heavy cruisers. More destroyers were needed, and many more submarines.

But the most serious logistical problem of the navy was in the matter of airplanes. From the beginning of military aviation in Japan, the allocation of aircraft had been split down the middle, half for the army and half for the navy. Now that division seemed most unfair to Yamamoto. He was given the responsibility for air protection of all Japan's new empire, all those farflung islands in the South and Central Pacific. The army's responsibility was really for the land masses, and that meant the Japanese holdings on the continent of Asia, as well as Java, Sumatra, and the Philippines. Army planes supported army operations and did nothing else. Therefore, Yamamoto reasoned, the navy should get a bigger share of the aircraft production. But of course the army men in

Tokyo denied this and put every obstacle in the way of the navy. Since the Prime Minister was a general, and since the cabinet was loaded with army men, Yamamoto's was a forlorn hope.

Meanwhile, in the fleet, preparations for the Midway attack continued, with meetings and training exercises every day. The plan for invasion of Hawaii was brought out, and a "tabletop" exercise was held aboard the flagship. It lasted four days and was still in progress on Monday, May 4, when the Americans launched their first real counteroffensive of the war.

As part of the "second stage" of operations, Imperial General Headquarters had ordered the occupation of the island of Tulagi in the southern Solomons, the building of an air base on Guadalcanal Island, and the occupation of Port Moresby in Australian-held New Guinea. The occupations were slated for the first few days of May.

On May 3, a Japanese convoy made a successful landing at Tulagi and put off the seaplanes, which were moored in the natural harbor there. Supplies were taken ashore, the former Australian government administrative offices were occupied, and the Japanese began work on their new seaplane base.

But on May 4, American planes attacked the Tulagi base, sank all the planes afloat, and bombed and strafed the ships in the harbor and the installations ashore. These were planes from the American carrier *Yorktown*, the center of Vice Admiral Frank Jack Fletcher's task force, which had been sent to the South Pacific along with Rear Admiral Aubrey W. Fitch's *Lexington* task force.

Two days later the Americans set out to attack the Port Moresby invasion convoy and found the light carrier *Shoho*. They sank her in twenty minutes. Aboard the *Yamato*, the shock was enormous. Until this point the Japanese navy had been in complete command of its seas. But now the war had been brought to the navy.

Aboard the flagship, Admiral Yamamoto received a very rosy and very inaccurate report of the events of the next few hours. One of the major problems of the Japanese navy was a tendency to lionization at the expense of accuracy. Victory had come so easily in those early days that the naval general staff in Tokyo had become boastful. On May 7, eager pilots reported that they had found several American and Australian warships off DeBoine Island, which was correct, that they had found two carriers, apparently operating independently, which was correct, and that most of the bombers of the land-based Twenty-Fifth Air

Flotilla had attacked these ships and sunk a battleship and damaged another battleship, which was false. They had sunk a destroyer and seriously damaged the oiler *Neosho*.

On May 8 the air battle of the Coral Sea was joined, the first major carrier confrontation of the Pacific War. The Japanese sank the carrier *Lexington* and damaged the *Yorktown*, while in addition to the *Shoho* the Americans damaged the carrier *Shokaku* so badly that she had to go into drydock.

But once again, the question of reporting on the results of a battle created problems. Offhandedly, Vice Admiral Shigeyoshi Inouye, the Commander in Chief of the Fourth Japanese Fleet, said that his planes had hit two carriers, "which undoubtedly sank." This did not satisfy Yamamoto, and when the commander of the Fourth Fleet then broke off the action, although the *Zuikaku* had plenty of planes and there was strong land-based air support, Yamamoto and his staff were furious, and demanded an explanation. They did not get one. The staff wanted the head of the commander of the Fourth Fleet, but Admiral Yamamoto was more cautious. The Port Moresby invasion was called off. Japan had suffered her first strategic defeat of the war.

This fact was concealed in the reports from naval headquarters in Tokyo, which made much of the sinking of the *Lexington*, pointed out that the *Shoho* was only a converted transport, and claimed a major naval victory. But Admiral Yamamoto knew that all the torpedo bombers of the *Shoho* had been lost, as well as many planes of the *Zuikaku*, that he would not have the *Shokaku* and the *Zuikaku* with him in the coming battle of Midway, and that the Port Moresby invasion was a failure. In a letter to Admirals Inouye and Takagi, the commander of the carrier force, Yamamoto pointed out some of the errors that had led to failure. In Japanese fashion this had to be done very carefully, lest the officers involved feel disgraced. The result was not very salutory, because Tokyo was trumpeting the news of the "great victory." Yamamoto was extremely disgusted, but what was to be done? Japan was riding a wave of euphoria. Corregidor had surrendered that week, and Japanese forces were rapidly overrunning northern Burma. They crossed over into China's Yunnan Province, thus sealing off the Burma Road, the Chinese Nationalist Government's single link to the outside world.

On May 9, Admiral Yamamoto's importunations to Admirals Inouye and Takagi seemed to have some results. The two of them announced that they were going to resume the battle with the Americans, which they had broken off the day before. But it was too late. They had lost the American task force, which was now preparing to return to Pearl Harbor, and they never found it again. To Admiral Yamamoto this was just another missed opportunity.

For the next few days, while completing the plans for the Midway invasion, Admiral Yamamoto considered the problem of the Port Moresby invasion, now delayed. The army wanted to get on with it, but Chief of Staff Ugaki did not. The trouble was that there were now no carriers in the South Pacific to support the operation, since the *Shokaku* and *Zuikaku* were heading for Truk. Only the carrier *Kaga* could possibly be spared, in view of the coming Midway operation. After two days of discussion, Yamamoto agreed to delay the Port Moresby operation until July. The army, which wanted to speed up its operations, decided to try an overland attack, and brought the Seventeenth Army, which had been in the Dutch East Indies, down to the South Pacific.

The change in the war was now most apparent aboard the flagship. Japan had begun losing ships at a significant rate. The 4400-ton minelayer *Okinoshima*, the flagship of the Nineteenth Division, was torpedoed by an American submarine east of Rabaul. The repair ship *Shoei Maru* also was sunk off Cape St. George. And on May 17, the *Shokaku* appeared at Hashirajima and anchored. She could not be moored because of the damage caused by three American bombs.

Admiral Yamamoto was now eager to move toward Midway, to stage his great battle and stop the erosion of his naval forces. Aboard the flagship the preparations were hurried. Officers went ashore to deposit their precious possessions. Yamamoto left his medals and extra uniforms, and on May 19 the *Yamato* sailed for maneuvers and training. It would not be long before it headed out to the rendezvous point where the fleet would assemble to begin the voyage across the Pacific. The training continued. No detail was too small to escape the admiral's notice. As the *Yamato* sailed out of Hashirajima, and had just reached the narrowest section of Nasami Channel, the light carrier *Junyo* came steaming up at high speed, and the flagship just barely got by without damage. On the admiral's bridge there was muttering about "cowboys" and captains who treated 10,000-ton carriers like motorboats. Admiral Yamamoto did not like "cowboys," and the name of the captain of the *Junyo* was put down by Admiral Ugaki. It would be a long time before that captain made the admirals list.

As if to emphasize Admiral Yamamoto's sense of urgency on the eve of the Battle of Midway, the repair ship *Asahi*, steaming up toward Camranh Bay on her way home from Singapore, was attacked and sunk on the night of May 25 by a submarine.

That day the admiral held another "tabletop battle" depicting the coming Midway and Aleutian Islands operations. The Emperor had sent along some presents, including a case of sake, so that night Yamamoto and his senior staff gathered on the upper deck of the flagship and had a picnic.

As was customary, the admiral wrote a final letter home asking the members of his family to support the Great East Asia War fully, to do their duty cheerfully, and to keep the household honorable while he was away. It was not a farewell letter, just sort of an insurance letter, leaving behind his legacy, just in case.

MIDWAY

**2
4** Admiral Yamamoto was as nervous as the most callow young seaman as the Combined Fleet set sail for Midway and the Aleutians on the great adventure that he hoped would bring a victorious end to the Pacific war. Admiral Ugaki believed that the Combined Fleet was blessed by God, but Yamamoto was not so sure. He was a gambler, and now he was taking the greatest gamble of his life.

Others in the fleet were even more worried. One of these was Vice Admiral Nobutake Kondo, commander of the Second Fleet, which had been designated to make the Aleutians attack. When the Combined Fleet staff plans for Midway and the Aleutians had been circulated among the senior officers, Admiral Kondo had made his objections to Admiral Ugaki. But since the detail of the plan was Ugaki's, the complaint fell on deaf ears. Then Admiral Kondo asked how the Japanese would supply Midway once they had taken it; the atoll stands lonely sentinel in the middle of the Pacific 1100 miles from Hawaii. American submarines would be around that spot like sharks at a feeding ground. That complaint too fell on deaf ears, and so did all others. The objections from Naval Headquarters, which were many, were suppressed, and largely for the wrong reason. Admiral Yamamoto's Hawaii attack plan had been opposed by many in the beginning, and then it had been a success. Imperial

General Headquarters had even blown its success out of all proportion, as Admiral Yamamoto knew. So now Tokyo had let Admiral Yamamoto have his way, although there were still mutterings in the halls of the naval ministry. The opposition had been cowed, bulldozed, and manipulated. Even Yamamoto did not know the extent to which the matter had been manipulated, because the dirty work had been done by Chief of Staff Ugaki.

The Japanese naval system, as previously noted, endowed staff officers with an enormous amount of influence, if not real power. As a child of the system, Admiral Yamamoto accepted this situation and left details to the staff. He did not know that in the war games he had ordered to test the viability of his plan, Ugaki had doctored the results by overruling the judges on several vital decisions.

Admiral Nagumo had complained that the radio facilities of his flagship, the *Akagi*, were not adequate to manage the Midway attack as planned. If Admiral Yamamoto was coming along on the *Yamato*, which had excellent communications equipment, then let Yamamoto take personal command of the operation. This suggestion did not even get to Yamamoto, who might have liked it just as much as Admiral Halsey would have. When Halsey was riding with the fleet, he was in command and no one else. But Yamamoto did not get a chance to make such a decision. The whole matter was dismissed offhand by the fleet staff.

And so the whole fleet was out, with Admiral Kondo heading toward the Aleutians in the van and Admiral Nagumo heading toward Midway. Admiral Yamamoto and the battleships and cruisers came along in case of a fleet engagement at sea, one of the old-style surface engagements.

There were two reasons for this decision. First, because it was a dual operation, someone had to be responsible for both. But this could have been managed by delegating authority—to Admiral Nagumo for the Midway invasion and to someone like Admiral Ozawa, whom Yamamoto trusted, for the Aleutians attack. The problem was, and this was the second reason, that Yamamoto did not trust Nagumo, who had failed him twice already, at Pearl Harbor and at Trincomalee.

So, at 6 A.M. on May 29, the fleet left the Hashirajima anchorage, passed through the Bungo Strait and the Inland Sea, and headed south at sixteen knots. Intelligence indicated that no fewer than thirteen enemy submarines were operating off the Japanese coast. The danger point for the invasion fleet was the outer end of the Bungo Channel, and a destroyer squadron had been sent to that area the day before to work it over and keep enemy submarines away. Two submarines had been detected and attacked, with the primary purpose of driving them out of the area. By the time the main elements of the fleet arrived, the area was clear, paravanes were lifted, and the fleet increased its speed to eighteen knots. The major fleet elements had been equipped with radar now, including the old battleship *Hyuga*, which had recently suffered a major explosion in one of its turrets and had been modernized while undergoing repairs. So it was with comparative confidence that the admiral set out to cross the Pacific, radar antennas twirling in the moonlight.

The fleet maintained complete radio silence, and everything was going very smoothly. Admiral Ugaki observed that the difficult maneuver of changing over to night fleet disposition was "like taking kids to their beds." Well-disciplined kids, he meant, for the results of Admiral Yamamoto's constant training program were now showing. A few weeks earlier the senior officers of the carrier strike force had asked Yamamoto to permit long leaves—two weeks or more—so that officers and men could go home and visit their families. But Yamamoto had refused. As long as the war remained in a critical situation, the entire fleet must be ready for action at short notice. Naval headquarters might be supremely confident and the information section might continue to spout its cacaphony of victory cries, but Yamamoto saw a grim future unless the fleet could destroy American naval power in a hurry.

Not long before, Yamamoto had written to his friend Admiral Mineichi Koga, who was in command of the naval forces at Shanghai, complaining about what was going on in Tokyo: "The mindless rejoicing at home is really deplorable," he said. "We are far from being able to relax at this stage. I only wish that they had had, say, three carriers at Hawaii as well."

Almost since the day of the Pearl Harbor attack, naval headquarters had adopted a publicity policy of trumpet blowing, which Yamamoto decried. The Imperial General Headquarters announcements over the radio were accompanied by "The Battleship March," which became so completely associated with the propaganda that when a stone tablet was erected in Hibiya Park in Tokyo to commemorate this stirring music and Admiral Yamamoto was asked to write the original calligraphy for the carved inscription, he refused to do so.

What he hated most were the exaggerations, for example, the claim that the U.S. carrier *Saratoga* had been sunk, which by now Yamamoto knew was not true. One night in the staff officers' wardroom the officers were listening to Radio Tokyo, which was making some of its big claims about the series of Japanese victories. The admiral became loquacious on the subject:

> All they need do really is quietly let the people know the truth. There's no need to bang the big drum. Official reports should stick to the absolute truth—once you start lying, the war's as good as lost. Information Division's outlook is all wrong. All this talk of guiding public opinion and maintaining the national morale is so much empty puff. . . .

Yamamoto was not privy to Admiral Nimitz's confidence, but this was precisely Nimitz's attitude, and one he would follow scrupulously almost until the end of the Pacific war. Only the enormous damage done by the Kamikazes during and after the invasion of the Philippines caused the U.S. Navy to be less than candid in its reporting, and that was concealment, not braggartry, justified by the need to avoid giving aid and comfort to the enemy.

Steaming across the Pacific, the Combined Fleet was confident, however. At night speed was reduced, but the fleet did not zigzag, as it would have if there had been any nervousness. The problem was that zigzagging increased the danger of collison in fleet movements. In the morning, the zigzagging was resumed. On May 30 the fleet entered a low-pressure zone and the weather roughed up. The destroyers were taking much water, and even the cruisers were wallowing. So the speed was cut to fourteen knots, and at 6 P.M. the fleet formed a single column, again to avoid collisions in the rough weather.

Yamamoto began to worry that the fleet had been discovered after a long, urgent message to Midway was dispatched by an enemy submarine and intercepted by the fleet radio. The message was in U.S. code and could not be read by the Japanese, but its sending was a matter of concern.

In fact, the admiral's hunch was quite correct. Several weeks earlier, the American radio intelligence officer at Pearl Harbor had reported to Nimitz that something was afoot. The Americans had broken the Japanese naval code and could read the fleet messages. Breaking the code did not solve all the problems of cryptography, however. It was true that by reading the Japanese messages, the Americans knew that a major attack was being prepared. They even knew which fleet units were involved, because they had intercepted the message from Admiral Yamamoto to the fleet detailing the order of battle. But they did not know where it was aimed, because the Japanese used the letters ''AF'' to symbolize the point of attack. AF could be anything—Hawaii, Australia, even San Francisco.

A clever young officer on the intelligence staff made a suggestion. Let them trap the Japanese into revealing whether or not AF was Midway, as Admiral Nimitz suspected. So Nimitz sent a message reporting that Midway was short of freshwater. And sure enough, back to Pearl Harbor came an intercept of a fleet message: ''AF is short of freshwater.''

So, as the Japanese fleet headed toward Midway, the Americans knew that they were coming and the Japanese did not know that the Americans knew. This gave the Americans a very big advantage, knowing when to strike and at what. The problem the Americans still had, however, was a paucity of resources. The Japanese carriers outnumbered them six to three, and Admiral Yamamoto's surface fleet, with its giant battleships, was overwhelmingly more powerful than the American surface units, for the original U.S. battle fleet was not yet reconstituted with modern vessels.

On May 31, the rough weather turned worse and a gale began to blow. The weather was so bad that the antisubmarine patrols had to be suspended.

From all the radio activity emanating from the American fleet units, Admiral Yamamoto suspected that the Americans knew they were coming, but it was no more than a suspicion. There was nothing to be done anyway, with the plan already in progress.

Even now, with the greatest attack of his life under way, Admiral Yamamoto had many other things on his mind. A submarine detachment was scheduled to move into Sydney Harbor and attack the battleship *Warspite* and two cruisers. The admiral was hoping that the American ships from the battle of the Coral Sea would be there too, but those ships were sailing out of Hawaii, bound for the Midway battle. The American carriers *Enterprise, Hornet,* and *Yorktown,* with six cruisers and ten destroyers, had sailed on May 28. It was the strongest force the Americans could mount. Yamamoto's fleet had four fleet carriers, one light carrier, four seaplane carriers, seven battleships, and ten cruisers, plus many destroyers and all sorts of transports and special ships.

However, the Japanese material strength was matched by American knowledge. The Americans knew where the Japanese were coming from, of the existence of the four fleet carriers, and when they would begin their attack on Midway. The Japanese had planned to put a screen of submarines between Hawaii and Midway, so they would know when the Americans left Pearl Harbor, but the Americans beat them to the punch. By the time the submarine screen had formed, the American fleet was already past the line, on the way to Midway.

On June 1, the attack on Sydney Harbor went off as planned, and Admiral Yamamoto had a message from Imperial General Headquarters about it. Three Japanese midget submarines had made the attacks. How much damage they had inflicted no one in Tokyo yet knew, but it was known that all three midgets were lost.

On June 3 the Japanese fleet steamed along through heavy fog. In spite of the fog, the Japanese refueled.

On June 4 the Aleutians operations began. Then any hopes that Admiral Yamamoto had about the element of surprise were dashed with a report that the invasion force of twelve transports had been sighted about 600 miles from Midway. In the afternoon, nine B-17s came out from Midway to attack the invaders, but they scored no hits. But then, events tumbled on one another with such speed that Admiral Ugaki, the indefatigable diarist, did not find time to write in his book for four days, and Admiral Yamamoto was beset with problems.

On June 4, Admiral Nagumo prepared to launch his attack. He and his chief of staff, Rear Admiral Ryunosake Kusaka, had some definite ideas about how to make a carrier attack. In the war games around Hashirajima, they had held that it was best to make an all-out strike using all their resources and plastering the enemy. But Admiral Yamamoto, through Admiral Ugaki, had registered some serious objections.

A carrier force is vulnerable when it is concentrating its attack on a target and then is hit in turn by the enemy carrier force. If the force has committed itself completely, then it has nothing but a handful of covering fighters with which to repel the enemy. The attacks on Pearl Harbor, Darwin, and Trincomalee had been made by surprise, with no concomitant counterattack from the enemy. The Coral Sea battle was a case in point: The enemy had reacted and made its own attacks. The result had been the damage to the *Shokaku* and the *Zuikaku*'s loss of planes, which had cut the carrier force at Midway down from six to four.

This had been an answer to Admiral Kusaka's "sword theory," which had been offered at the war games a week or two before the Coral Sea battle. Yamamoto had not liked it at the time, and the Coral Sea battle had confirmed the weakness of the theory. Yamamoto was joined in this feeling by Admiral Tamon Yamaguchi, commander of Carrier Division Two, which included the carriers *Hiryu* and *Soryu*. At the time of the Pearl Harbor attack, Admiral Yamaguchi had favored a strong attack. His Carrier Division Two had not been taken to Hawaii but had been sent to the southern waters instead, much to his disappointment. Yamaguchi was one of the "new breed" of carrier admirals, similar to Jocko Clark and Arthur Radford on the American side—men who had grown up with carriers, understood them, and believed in them implicitly. Yamaguchi suggested a second strike to clean up the job, but he had been ignored. He came away from that encounter convinced that Nagumo and his staff did not understand the basics of carrier warfare: that a commander must be prepared for anything, including an attack on his own fleet while he is attacking another target. And he must be prepared for this move by maintaining enough of his air force in readiness to respond to such an attack. But Yamaguchi knew that neither Nagumo nor his chief of staff would listen. Both were too timid, a timidity born not of cowardice, but of a basic lack of confidence in the carrier's capability of protecting itself. This was a quality shared by several American admirals, notably Frank Jack Fletcher and Raymond Spruance.

During the spring war games, Yamamoto's staff members had asked Admiral Nagumo what he would do if the fleet was attacked by an enemy carrier force while it was making its assault on a land base. Nagumo had passed off the question by saying that he would make sure that no such thing could happen. How he would make sure had never been clarified except by Commander Minoru Genda, the principal architect of the details of the Pearl Harbor attack and Nagumo's most brilliant staff officer. He said the fleet would have several bombers equipped with extra fuel tanks to keep a constant watch out as far as 450 miles in all directions.

Because of the discussions that spring, Nagumo had revised his operational plan to make the Midway attack in two stages. The first attack would be made by planes carrying bombs, and when it returned, a second bomb-laden strike force would be sent off. If the fleet were attacked at the midpoint by the enemy, the second strike could be diverted against the enemy fleet.

The attack on Midway began early on the morning of June 5.* A scout seaplane from the cruiser *Tone* reported that enemy planes were approaching the task force. These were bombers from Midway Island, and so approximately half the planes of the four carriers were sent off to strike the island, while the combat air patrols protected the carriers. After this first attack, however, the pilots of the carrier *Hiryu* returned to announce that destruction of the Midway base had not been complete and that the second strike was needed. The bombers on the decks of the carriers had been loaded with torpedoes, in compliance with the plan worked out at the spring war games. That morning the searches sent out from the Japanese fleet had been less than adequate; Nagumo seemed to have forgotten the essential of protecting his flanks with those long-range search planes. Not knowing of the presence of the enemy carriers, the Japanese then unloaded the torpedoes and began to load bombs on the planes for the second strike.

When Admiral Nagumo did learn of the existence of the American force, he was told that there was only one carrier (because, unlike the Japanese, who concentrated their carriers, the Americans had separated theirs).

The result was an American attack on the Japanese task force at a time when it had just landed its first air strike but had not sent off the second. The decks of the ships were full of planes as the Americans bored in. Because of faulty communications, the American torpedo bombers and fighters got separated. The torpedo bombers attacked first and were mostly shot down. Not one of them put a torpedo into a Japanese ship. But they did force the Japanese fighter cover down near the surface of the sea, so when the dive bombers came in, there were very few Japanese fighters up high to oppose them and their attack was very successful. Soon the *Akagi*, the *Kaga*, and the *Soryu* were all burning, and planes, bombs, and torpedoes were exploding. Only the *Hiryu* was able to carry out an attack on the American fleet, and her planes bombed the carrier *Yorktown*, putting her out of action.

---

*Tokyo time.

Admiral Yamamoto had the stunning news that three of his carriers were lost. Immediately he set about a rescue operation, bringing the flagship and the main elements of the fleet toward the carrier force through thick fog. The Midway landings were postponed while Yamamoto sped up to deal with the American fleet himself. Then Admiral Nagumo decided to break off the attack and withdraw to the north. This was a typical Nagumo tactic: with one carrier still operating, he was leaving the scene.

Late in the afternoon, a float plane from the cruiser *Chikuma* discovered elements of the American fleet retiring to the east at twenty knots. The distance between the Japanese battle fleet and the Americans was then about a hundred miles. Admiral Yamamoto ordered a night attack on the Americans to avenge the loss of the three Japanese carriers.

But then in short order Yamamoto learned that Admiral Nagumo was retiring. Furious, he issued a direct order to reverse course and attack.

Nagumo replied that all four of his carriers were out of action. It was true. The *Hiryu* had been caught late in the day and was afire. He was breaking off just for the night, said Nagumo, and would attack next morning with seaplanes from the seaplane carriers. Furious to the point of tears, reluctant to lose the offensive, Admiral Yamamoto was forced to cancel the night attack ''since no fighting spirit was observed'' from Nagumo. The landing on Midway was called off.

That night the misery was compounded when the cruisers *Mogami* and *Mikuma* collided. The *Mogami* was badly damaged, to the point that she could only make six knots. Now Yamamoto had the new worry of getting the crippled cruisers home. And then came the final blow: The *Hiryu*'s damage control had failed and she was abandoned by all but her captain and Admiral Yamaguchi, who chose to go down with the ship rather than face the disgrace of failure. Once all the crew had been taken off on a destroyer, the destroyer skipper pleaded with Yamaguchi and Captain Tomeo Kaku to leave the stricken carrier, which was burning fiercely. They refused and, donning face masks, climbed up to the bridge, where the flames leapt up around them.

Admiral Ugaki had known Yamaguchi very well, since the days when they were classmates at the naval academy at Eta Jima. ''Judging from his personality and character,'' Ugaki wrote in his diary, ''it is considered certain that he, after having seen that all the remaining crew boarded the rescuing destroyer, composedly killed himself on the bridge amidst shoot-up flame and smoke.''

And so the Japanese navy lost one of its fine carriers, and Admiral Yamamoto lost one of his finest admirals that day.

On June 7 came more trouble. American planes found the *Mikuma* and the *Mogami*, as well as the destroyer *Akashio*, and bombed them repeatedly. The *Mikuma* sank.

That day Admiral Yamamoto developed a new plan borne of desperation. It was to lure the American carriers, which he believed to be at least four in operating condition, toward Wake Island in chase of the Japanese fleet and then use the land-based air force of Wake Island to destroy the American fleet.

The fleet moved on, hoping. Yamamoto developed a serious bellyache, and the fleet physician came to treat him, but was unable to give him any relief. Some relief was given, however, when the staff informed Yamamoto that one American carrier, the *Yorktown*, was adrift north of Midway, and the *I-168* was dispatched to destroy her. She sank the carrier and the destroyer that lay alongside. Even so, it was small recompense for the loss and for the failure of the Midway operation to achieve any of its aims. At least the bellyache was finally diagnosed: roundworms. The doctor gave the admiral some pills, and they cured the ailment.

The effect of the disaster at Midway, however, was not so easy to cure. On the way back to Japan, the Wake Island feint ignored by the Americans, Yamamoto worried over the problem of rehabilitating the carrier strike force. Admiral Nagumo had transferred his flag from the sinking *Akagi* to the cruiser *Nagara*, and she was ordered up to deliver the staff to the flagship for consultations. Admiral Nagumo did not show up, but Admiral Kusaka, the chief of staff, came to the *Yamato* to try to explain. There was not much to say except ''I don't have the words to give my deepest apologies.''

Yamamoto brushed that aside, and Kusaka explained what had happened. The flagship had broken radio silence, which had given the Americans a clue as to the fleet's whereabouts. The radio breach had been in connection with the desperate need for oil for the destroyers and instructions to the tankers. The search planes had failed because they were sent out too late. The carriers had been bunched up, making an easy target for the Americans. And Kusaka and Nagumo had failed to heed the lessons of the spring war games:

> Since my appointment to the present post, the training of the fleet had been based on the principle of one stroke, after sufficient reconnaissance was made, and we had previously always been successful in this. Therefore I couldn't force myself to change the principle.

Admiral Yamamoto might have noted that what Kusaka had done was a breach of discipline, but he did not. Instead, he came to a much more generous conclusion: that all involved were at fault, including himself, particularly for permitting the overconcentration of carriers.

Kusaka was most contrite:

> Admittedly we are not in a position to come back alive after having made such a blunder, but we return only to pay off the old scores some day, so I beg of you from the bottom of my heart to give us a chance in the future.

"All right," said the admiral. And that was that. Nagumo and Kusaka would not have to commit suicide after all.

Yamamoto was taken aback by this defeat, but not prepared to quit. The immediate problem, he reminded them, was to ensure the success of the northern expedition that had landed in the Aleutians and to rebuild the carrier force.

On June 15, the fleet was back at Hashirajima, five ships less in strength than before, but still the most powerful fleet in the Pacific. Officials from the Navy Ministry in Tokyo came down to cheer Yamamoto up, and the Emperor sent a special message, saying he was not in the least concerned about the defeat. "Such things must be expected in a war," said His Majesty, "so don't lower morale, and make further efforts."

The next few days were occupied by a court of inquiry on the sinking of the four carriers and conferences on improving carrier techniques and the carriers. The four carriers sunk—*Hiryu, Soryu, Kaga*, and *Akagi* —were all of the same vintage, and none of them had had adequate damage control compartmentation. This was brought out, and so was Yamamoto's determination to see that any new carriers or conversions would be far more fireproof than the sunken ships.

Admiral Yamamoto was extremely depressed by the American Midway victory, for in reality it dashed his hopes for a short war. His depression was noticed by Admiral Ugaki, who was afraid to approach Yamamoto lest he be rebuffed, for Yamamoto was not the sort of commander you could treat intimately. So Yamamoto continued to be depressed for several days. But on June 27, envoys from Tokyo arrived to report that the Emperor was much concerned about Yamamoto's feelings and had sent a personal message to him. This cheered the admiral up more than a little. But the problem remained. In short order, the Japanese had lost four carriers. Counting the carrier lost at the battle of the Coral Sea, they had now lost five, and they could ill afford it, for as Yamamoto knew very well, Japan's capacity to construct new shipping under wartime conditions was nothing like that of the Americans, and the threat of a war of attrition loomed very high above the fleet that summer.

GUADALCANAL

2 5

As Admiral Yamamoto contemplated the war in the summer of 1942, he continued to feel discouraged about the prospects. July 7 marked the fifth anniversary of the outbreak of the China war. The "China incident," the army continued to call it, with that myopic optimism that allowed them to become ever more deeply mired on the Asiatic mainland.

Yamamoto's real concern was the inability of the Japanese military establishment to produce new weapons and new techniques in a highly technological world. It was axiomatic that nations begin wars with the weapons of the past; the lightning successes of the German war machine in 1939 and 1940 were due to major improvements in technology, but already the Stuka dive bomber, for example, was outmoded. Japan's navy had the finest fighter plane in the world in the Mitsubishi Zero-type fighter. Her Nakajima 97 torpedo bomber and her Aichi dive bomber also were better than their American counterparts. The major reason for the failure of the American torpedo bombers at the battle of Midway was their slowness; the Douglas SBD bomber was twenty years behind the times. But already, Yamamoto knew, the Americans were beginning to catch up.

He was particularly concerned about the ineffectiveness of Japanese antisubmarine warfare techniques. At the outbreak of the European war,

Japan had established a national commission to study techniques and war lessons, but as far as Yamamoto knew, it had produced nothing important yet. He knew that British radar was superior to anything Japan had, so American radar also had to be.

A case illustrating the problem was the attack on the seaplane carrier *Chiyoda*, which was unloading at Kiska in the Aleutian Islands on July 5 when she was attacked by an enemy submarine. One of her destroyer screen was sunk and two others were damaged.

Another matter that concerned Yamamoto was the ineffective Japanese antiaircraft guns. He knew that the Americans had boasted that they were now going to build a superbomber to bomb Japan, and it could be expected that these bombers would be larger and faster and could fly higher than the B-17s. But the effective range of Japanese antiaircraft guns was less than 25,000 feet altitude, and nothing was being done about it.

He was urging the development of an entirely new fighter, the Shiden, and major improvements in dive bombers and torpedo bombers. The British at Taranto had first shown that the aircraft carrier had forever changed the nature of naval warfare, and Admiral Yamamoto had made it even more apparent at Pearl Harbor, Darwin, and Trincomalee. The Americans at Midway had shown themselves superior. Yamamoto guessed the real reason—the breach of the Japanese naval code. But the naval general staff did not believe this. Hampered by traditional thinking and bad intelligence, they still believed the Americans had had half a dozen carriers operating at Midway instead of the three that were actually on the scene.

Now, at last, something seemed to be moving. Following the rapid expansion of empire, the Navy Ministry had taken steps to reorganize the Imperial Navy. The first strike force of the Combined Fleet was disbanded and the Third Fleet was created. Admiral Nagumo was made commander in chief of that fleet. In mid-July, Admiral Yamamoto was told to send his chief of staff up to Tokyo for consultation on several matters, including new inventions in weaponry and an increase in the supply of aircraft for the navy. Moreover, the superbattleship *Musashi* was now completed and ready to join the fleet. Her trials showed that the builders had done a better job than they had with her sister ship, the *Yamato*. There, progress at last!

At the end of July, Admiral Yamamoto had some disquieting information. Through reports published in Buenos Aires, copied from the

American press, he learned that the Americans had known all about the strength and disposition of the Japanese fleet in April. This meant the Americans must have broken the Japanese naval code and would account for several puzzling aspects of the battle of Midway. It did not account for the defeat, which was primarily due to the errors of Admirals Nagumo and Kusaka, but it could account for the failure of the submarine force to discover the sailing of the Americans from Pearl Harbor long before they were expected to leave and the failure of the Combined Fleet to achieve surprise.

The failure at Midway had thrown the Japanese naval plans completely awry. The invasion of Port Moresby by sea was postponed indefinitely. The invasion of Samoa and Fiji also was called off. The army wanted the carriers to make raids on Australia, but Yamamoto would not have the carrier strength for that purpose until new carriers had been completed and other ships had been converted into carriers. Given the fact that the carrier was now recognized as the major fleet weapon, this situation meant that the Combined Fleet was powerless to make a major move at the moment. Also, pushed by the Germans, the army was now talking about an invasion of India, which the navy did not like, and major naval operations in the Indian Ocean.

Another result of the failure at Midway and the loss of those four carriers was the change in strategy in the South Pacific. The army, in a hurry to capture Port Moresby, had now opted to make the attack overland instead of by sea, since no naval air support was forthcoming. The attack was progressing and in July reached Kokoda. To support this and other activities, Admiral Yamamoto had to recommend the building of several new air bases, to take the place of the nonexistent carriers, and one of these was on the island of Guadalcanal, across the strait from Tulagi, the site of the seaplane base.

Then, on August 7, the duty staff officer awoke Chief of Staff Ugaki with startling news: The Americans were attacking Tulagi on a large scale. The attack had begun with naval bombardment and air raids at four o'clock that morning, sunrise at Tulagi. Ugaki awakened the admiral, who called off the day's training operations aboard the *Yamato* and began conferring with the staff about possible countermeasures.

The information came in slowly. By midday it appeared that one carrier, a battleship, three cruisers, and fifteen destroyers were involved, escorting forty transports. So Admiral Yamamoto knew from the first that this was not a raid or a stunt, but a major invasion of Tulagi and

Guadalcanal, where the airstrip had been completed only the day before. Yamamoto ordered the Twenty-Fifth Air Flotilla at Rabaul to launch an air attack with twenty-seven torpedo bombers, eighteen fighters, and nine dive bombers. He also sent the Eighth Fleet, responsible for the Rabaul area, into the battle zone.

From the outset there was no doubt in Yamamoto's mind as to the reason for the invasion or the strength of it. The enemy was launching a major counterattack, whose immediate purpose was to stop the capture of Port Moresby and whose ultimate purpose would be to recapture Rabaul and drive the Japanese from the South Pacific.

So all the talk about the Indian Ocean operation was now scrapped, and the Combined Fleet settled down to its first defensive operation. The initiative had been seized by the Americans for the first time.

On August 8, Admiral Yamamoto decided that this situation was so vital that he must go down and take personal command. The *Yamato* was ordered to sail, and with it the Second and Third Fleets.

That night the Eighth Fleet sent its cruiser force against the enemy. The result was the battle of Savo Island, in which a stunning naval defeat was inflicted on the Allies: Five cruisers were sunk and not one Japanese ship was lost. The attackers' damage was confined to the cruiser *Chokai*, which lost a turret and took a shell in the operations room that killed thirty-four people, and to the cruiser *Aoba*, which suffered damage to one torpedo tube.

The Eighth Fleet and the Eleventh Air Fleet at Rabaul then did Admiral Yamamoto and his staff a very great disservice. They claimed that they had sunk not only the American cruisers, but all the warships in the area and half the transports. If this was true, there should be nothing to worry about, and the American presence on Guadalcanal had been reduced to the point where it ought to be easy to deal with.

By August 13, intelligence indicated that most of the enemy had withdrawn from Guadalcanal. This assumption was based on the withdrawal of Rear Admiral Richmond Kelly Turner's transports and supply ships. The reason for their leaving was that Vice Admiral Frank Jack Fletcher had withdrawn his carrier force from protection of the Guadalcanal operation, which he had opposed in the beginning. This had left some 13,000 Marines on Guadalcanal and Tulagi with very little supply, and it led the Japanese into the erroneous belief that the Americans had all but abandoned the invasion attempt. Although he had had the right answer in the beginning, Admiral Yamamoto allowed himself to be persuaded by his staff that the Guadalcanal invasion was no more than a tempest in a teapot. He prepared to send a small detachment of naval landing troops to Guadalcanal to mop up the remaining few Americans, take control of the airfield, and rescue the Japanese service troops, originally about 3500 on Guadalcanal. Yamamoto now proposed that the amphibious invasion of Port Moresby be rescheduled quickly, as well as the capture of Ocean and Nauru Islands. The sailing of the *Yamato* was canceled for the moment, but Admiral Nagumo's Third Fleet, with its carriers, sailed with Yamamoto's reminder that Nagumo and his staff were eager for revenge for the loss at Midway. The battle of the Solomons, as it was now called in Tokyo, would give them their chance.

The feeling that the Americans had withdrawn from Guadalcanal was intensified on August 16 by a report from the chief of the Naval Operations Bureau in Tokyo. As if to confirm the transient nature of American operations, there also came a report that some two hundred American marines had landed on Makin Island in the Gilberts. Yamamoto wondered what the purpose of this landing really was. Had it been an attempt to divert Japanese minds from the Guadalcanal operations? Or was it an omen that the Americans were planning a landing in the Gilberts? There was no way just then to tell.

So many were the concerns about the Guadalcanal situation and so scarce the real information that Admiral Yamamoto decided he would indeed move fleet headquarters to the big naval base at Truk, at least for the time being.

When Emperor Hirohito heard this news, from the chief of the naval general staff, he was much concerned. He called to the admiral's attention the loss of the cruiser *Kako* to an American submarine a few days earlier and expressed concern over Yamamoto's safety in those waters, all of this an indication of the detailed concern of the Emperor over military matters. Yamamoto's decision to move fleet headquarters south was not taken lightly, but it seemed only sensible in light of changing conditions and his feeling that he must direct personally any operation in which Admiral Nagumo was concerned.

The feeling persisted that the American presence on Guadalcanal was now very slight, and on August 18 a reinforcement unit of only two hundred men was landed, with supplies, to "help" the survivors of the Japanese garrison deal with the American "stragglers." But then reports began to come in indicating that the American force was stronger than expected. The special landing force called the Ichiki detachment was landed. This was a reinforced battalion whose previous assignment had been to land and capture Midway Island and which had thus been idle for some time. Six destroyers landed 800 men of the detachment on Guadalcanal on August 18. Admiral Yamamoto's staff was sure this would be more than enough men to handle the situation, so certain were they that the American marines had evacuated the islands in those transports that had left. On August 21, the Ichiki detachment was ordered to attack and secure the airfield the Americans now called Henderson Field. They did attack that night, and the sound of small arms fire echoed across the valleys of the island in the early morning hours. Yamamoto's staff officers learned that the sound of firing had ended by ten o'clock, and they congratulated themselves on having dealt with the enemy so satisfactorily. But up on top of the mountain, the Japanese lookouts saw what was happening, and a few hours later they reported that the Ichiki detachment had been completely wiped out by the marines. As Admiral Ugaki noted, they obviously had under estimated their enemy and had charged in to face death.

This shocking news was followed by more: Enemy destroyer and minesweeping action around Guadalcanal further indicated that the marines had not evacuated the island. Yamamoto's staff began to appreciate the seriousness of the situation that was developing. They controlled the sea and they controlled the air, but the Americans were still very strong on Guadalcanal and were challenging their control of the air and sea every day, in spite of the herculean efforts of the Eleventh Air Fleet at Rabaul.

Admiral Yamamoto, now aware of the dangers of the situation developing at Guadalcanal, was eager to stop the American counteroffensive, which he now recognized for what it was. The Second Fleet was rushed down to join the Eighth Fleet, which had charge of this area under the reorganized program. From Rabaul, the naval air officers were trying to do too much. Yamamoto became vexed with the commander of the Twenty-Fifth Air Flotilla when he sent a large strike force off on a wild goose chase after an American carrier after it was reported to be 250 miles southeast of Tulagi. That was Admiral Fletcher's carrier force, carefully keeping out of the way of trouble, and the Japanese air strike did not find it. So much effort and so much precious aviation fuel wasted, and this after warning from naval operations that the homeland and the fleet faced a serious fuel shortage within the year.

By the third week in August, the Japanese were getting ready for a long, attenuated battle. The Eleventh Air Fleet had moved its head-quarters from Tinian to Rabaul, taking over command of the air flotillas there. The naval air force operated from half a dozen area airfields. Admiral Nagumo's Third Fleet, the carrier force, was now ordered to search diligently for the enemy aircraft carriers and to attack them, without fail.

But so were the Americans girding for more battle. On August 21, the American transports *Alhena* and *Formalhaut* headed for Guadalcanal to deliver supplies, despite the failure of Admiral Fletcher's carriers to give air support. The number of fighter planes and bombers at Henderson Field was increasing as the Americans and the Australians exerted every effort to get planes in there. The real problem was gasoline, and the Americans would be reduced to ferrying it in by submarine before the surface became safe enough for transport.

The Japanese fleet was coming down. Admiral Yamamoto's flagship was heading for the Harushima anchorage at Truk. Other elements were far ahead, entrusted with delivering supplies and reinforcements to Guadalcanal.

The opposing naval forces began making frequent contacts on August 23. That day Admiral Yamamoto gave several orders:

1. The land-based air forces at Rabaul were to carry out heavy attacks on Guadalcanal.

2. The Third Fleet was to destroy the American carrier force.

3. The Eighth Fleet was to carry out resupply of Guadalcanal and destroy the American supply ships.

A force of destroyers and destroyer transports was nearing Gua-dalcanal to resupply the Japanese. It was covered by the light carrier *Ryujo*, the cruiser *Tone*, and three destroyers. At the same time, Admiral Nagumo, with the big carriers *Zuikaku* and *Shokaku*, was searching for the American fleet with an eye to battle.

The *Ryujo* launched her planes for a strike on Henderson Field, to prevent the Americans from attacking the Tanaka destroyer group. But then the American planes found the *Ryujo* and bombed and dropped torpedoes. One torpedo struck on the starboard side of the engine room, disabling the ship and making her list twenty degrees. Finally, Rear Admiral Chuichi Hara had to give up and order the ship abandoned. She was sunk by a torpedo from a Japanese destroyer.

When the search planes of Nagumo's force did find the American carrier fleet, the results were most satisfactory. Hits were scored on the carrier *Enterprise*, and she had to be sent back to Pearl Harbor for repairs.

The carrier battle was fought sloppily on both sides, and once again Admiral Nagumo, like Admiral Fletcher, showed a distinct reluctance to engage or then to pursue. So although Admiral Yamamoto would have liked to have had a night surface battle with the Americans, it did not happen. The result, as far as carriers was concerned, left the Japanese with their *Shokaku* and *Zuikaku* and the Americans with their *Saratoga* and *Wasp*, very well matched. But from Admiral Yamamoto's point of view, the failure to deal the American fleet a serious blow was not the only problem. The Japanese resupply service was not functioning properly. The transport *Kinryo Maru*, which was bearing much of the reinforcement staff, was damaged, exploded, and had to be sunk with heavy loss of life among the reinforcements.

The problem was what the Americans called the "Cactus Air Force." (Cactus was the American code word for Guadalcanal.) This ragtag assemblage of planes and pilots from army, navy, and marine corps, plus Australians and New Zealanders, was causing a great deal of trouble. Admiral Yamamoto realized that unless he could smash that enemy air power at Guadalcanal, it would be impossible to supply the island by transports. So he ordered the future transport to be carried out in destroyers and minesweepers.

More problems became apparent. The distance from Rabaul to Guadalcanal was a thousand miles, so far that the attacking air forces did not always get through, particularly in foul weather. For this reason, the Eleventh Air Fleet wanted the Japanese carriers to attack the island, but there the rub was in the jockeying between the American and Japanese air task forces, plus the natural caution of Admiral Nagumo, who did not want to risk his carriers.

Yamamoto then ordered the planes that had taken off from the *Ryujo*, come back to find their carrier sunk, and landed on several islands to assemble at Buka, and he sent in ground crews. Buka would become a staging base for attacks on Guadalcanal and would have its own little *Ryujo* air force as well.

On August 25, Admiral Yamamoto assessed the Guadalcanal situation and did not like what he found. He expected the Americans to reinforce Guadalcanal again, and he was having the very devil of a time doing the same.

The worst problem of the Rabaul air force was the dreadful attrition in planes and pilots. It got so bad on August 26 that the commander of the Eleventh Air Fleet sent a message to Yamamoto's staff asking for reinforcements in planes and pilots from the Marshall Islands. The *Kasuga*, a converted carrier that was serving in place of one of the big carriers, was sent to the Marshalls to pick up fighter planes and bring them south. The Eleventh Air Fleet, given the responsibility of sending planes to support the operations in New Guinea on one side and Guadalcanal on the opposite side, was wearing very thin indeed.

By August 28, Admiral Yamamoto had a much clearer picture of the disaster that had befallen his attempts to recapture Guadalcanal with naval troops. The Ichiki detachment had been overwhelmed by the American marines, and only 128 of its members had survived to withdraw to the eastern side of the island. The construction detachment that had originally built the field and had then been attacked was in desperate shape, short of everything, and needed support. But the only communication with Guadalcanal was by messages dropped from planes, and the air forces from Rabaul were having trouble with weather. So on August 28 Yamamoto reluctantly ordered thirty planes from the carriers to land at Buka and begin operations against Guadalcanal from there.

By August 29, the Japanese naval air forces in the South Pacific were feeling the pinch of attrition. On that day in Tokyo the naval general staff decided to transfer the Twenty-First Air Flotilla to Rabaul, leaving the protection of Sumatra and Malaya to the army. They also told the army that until the Guadalcanal problem was settled the Port Moresby invasion would have to wait. Neither army nor navy yet felt that the course of the war had changed; they still planned to expand the empire further.

It did not seem impossible. The Guadalcanal battle surged back and forth. The Americans reinforced their troops on the island, but so did

Admiral Yamamoto's destroyer transports reinforce the Japanese. The first such effort was a failure. The Twentieth Destroyer Division brought troops of the Kawaguchi detachment to Guadalcanal but was attacked by twenty American and Australian planes. One of the three destroyers was sunk, one was dead in the water, and one was damaged. The commander of the division was fatally wounded. This failure made the army very leery of riding in destroyers, and General Kawaguchi, the land commander, flatly refused to do so. On August 30, however, the navy carried out a perfect landing, and a few days later General Kawaguchi relented and rode a destroyer to Guadalcanal. The Japanese still underestimated the number of marines on the island, but Yamamoto believed he could resupply the Japanese troops and bring reinforcements in as they were needed. So as September 1942 began, Yamamoto still had his hopes.

"NO MATTER THE SACRIFICE, SECURE GUADALCANAL"

2 6

September 1942 opened on a growingly desperate struggle for the control of Guadalcanal. Earlier, Admiral Yamamoto had hoped to reduce the American forces on the island by bombing and bombardment, but after three weeks it was apparent that the capture of Guadalcanal must be accomplished by troops on the island. This meant the employment of divisions, not battalions. The problem, given the growing American air presence on the island, was how to get the troops onto the island. The method chosen was a sneak landing by night from destroyer transports stoutly protected by fighting destroyers. On September 2, the last troops of the Ichiki and Kawaguchi detachments were transported from the base at Shortlands to Guadalcanal. That night several field guns also were quietly moved ashore on the Japanese side of the island, giving the troops heavy weapons for the coming attack on Henderson Field.

Rear Admiral Raizo Tanaka, commander of the Second Destroyer Squadron, showed up in Truk on September 2 to explain why he was losing so many ships on the run down "the Slot," as the approach to Guadalcanal was known. The reason was the growing Allied air presence at Henderson Field, but this was not all. Despite the string of defeats meted out to them, the Allied naval forces kept coming back for more, and on the nights of August 29 and August 30, Japanese destroyers landing troops had been attacked by Allied warships as well as by planes.

That day two of Yamamoto's staff officers were dispatched to Rabaul for briefings with the army command of General Imamura and the Eleventh Air Fleet. They took with them Admiral Yamamoto's views on Guadalcanal and New Guinea (where he still had responsibility for naval and air activity):

1. The Guadalcanal battle had to be settled on the land, and this meant the dispatch of many more troops by General Imamura. And only after Henderson Field was secured would the navy be able to safely run task forces to Guadalcanal to make an amphibious landing there and complete the investment of the island.

2. The new landings in New Guinea at Rabi were a complete failure, and the overland campaign along the Kokoda Trail was too difficult to be more than marginally successful. Ultimately, the invasion would have to be amphibious, and Yamamoto was beginning the planning for that right now.

On September 3, a high-ranking delegation came from Imperial General Headquarters to see why things were going so slowly in the South Pacific and why Port Moresby had not yet been captured. Prince Takeda, the vice chief of the army general staff, led the delegation, which included Admiral Ito, the vice chief of the navy general staff. They came in by flying boat from Saipan. Yamamoto entertained them, in lordly fashion. The officers of the *Yamato* always ate very well, with polished rice, fresh fish, beef, and many luxuries. It was the same as with all navies. Soldiers might be starving on Guadalcanal, but life aboard the flagship continued on an almost peacetime level as far as provisions were concerned. The dinner began at five o'clock, accompanied by plenty of sake. Afterwards, the visitors from Tokyo also heard a briefing from the two staff officers who had earlier returned from Rabaul, who told them that General Imamura, the commander of the Eighth Fleet, and the commander of the Eleventh Air Fleet all wanted the attack to be started on September 8. Yamamoto asked Admiral Ito to take this up with Imamura and the others when he went to Rabaul the next day, because the Combined Fleet wanted to wait three more days before launching the attack.

On September 4, the "new" carrier *Taiyo* arrived at Truk. She was not really new, but just the old steamer *Kasuga Maru*, rebuilt with a flight deck. This was the best and quickest answer that Tokyo could give to Yamamoto's demands for more carriers since the losses at Midway. Several such conversions were in the works, including that of the old battleships *Hyuga* and *Ise*, which would have flight decks, too.

The *Taiyo* pulled into Truk, having completed her first major task —transportation of naval aircraft from Tarawa to Rabaul. And in a few hours she was off again, heading for Palau and another load of planes for the South Pacific fighting front.

Since there was so much difficulty in bringing in troops by transport and destroyer transport, Yamamoto turned to bringing them in by landing craft. The whole operation was described as "sneak transportation." But even the landing craft did not get away unscathed. In the first four days of September, some forty landing craft brought troops to the northwest corner of the island, and any that moved during the daylight hours were almost sure to be attacked by the "Cactus Air Force," which was growing in strength every day.

Still the Japanese kept coming in. General Kawaguchi arrived on September 1 to supervise operations. He radioed back to Rabaul that he planned to start land military operations on about September 11. Admiral Yamamoto then set out to coordinate his naval policy with that of the land soldiers. The navy would continue to ferry in supplies and troops by destroyer. It would continue to bombard Henderson Field. And it would continue the search for the American carrier force, with the intention of destroying it. All this demanded endless negotiations with the army, which were carried out by staff officers sent from the flagship at Truk to the army headquarters at Rabaul. But finally, on September 6, the details were hammered out and a sort of combined operation was put down on paper.

On September 7, Admiral Yamamoto assembled his forces aboard the flagship for an important policy meeting. To the *Yamato* came the commanders of the Second, Third, Fourth, and Sixth Fleets and the Eleventh Air Fleet. They went over the plans for the recapture of Guadalcanal.

General Kawaguchi's force would number about 8000 men by September 11. It was to launch the necessary attacks to capture the airfield and to drive the American marines into the sea. No one at the meeting that day had a very clear idea of how many marines were on the island just then—they certainly guessed nowhere near the actual number of 17,000—and all expressed confidence that the land attacks would succeed. After all, the Japanese had done wonders with military forces in Malaya and the Dutch East Indies. It was not the size of the force that counted, but its fighting spirit. Admiral Yamamoto believed fighting spirit was everything.

General Kawaguchi's target date for seizure of the airfield was September 12. On that day, the Eleventh Air Fleet would put up every available plane and concentrate them on Guadalcanal and the Combined Fleet would send its warships down to bombard and to engage any Allied ships.

At Rabaul, General Hyukatake, the commander of the Seventeenth Army, announced that he was prepared to send an entire division to Guadalcanal if it was needed, but he was assured by General Kawaguchi that this would not be necessary. The Kawaguchi detachment could do the job, he said. This assessment was made with unassailable logic: If the Americans really had very many troops on the island, then they would have wiped out the small remnants of the original garrison long since. But that reasoning failed to give account of one important aspect of the American invasion: the dreadful shortage of supply. Because supply was so short, General Vandegrift's marines were conserving food and ammunition, and that meant no more movement than was necessary.

Kawaguchi's troops were just then hacking their way through the jungle, making new trails toward Henderson Field, so they could approach on three sides and rush the Americans.

On September 7, the marines staged a raid on the village of Tasimboko and discovered several brand new thirty-seven millimeter guns that had just been landed from barges.

That day, as the admirals conferred aboard the Japanese flagship in Truk harbor, luncheon was disturbed by Admiral Yamamoto's receipt of a message from the submarine *I-11*, claiming the torpedoing of a carrier of the *Yorktown* type. There were cheers in the wardroom that day, but subsequent days produced no indication of the sinking of a carrier on that day.

The admirals' conference also was interrupted by a message from General Hyukatake announcing the discovery of a large Allied reinforcement unit in the Fiji area. To Hyukatake that meant more troops to be faced on Guadalcanal, and his message to Yamamoto asked that fleet operations be stepped up and the target date for the general attack advanced. This was not easy to do, but Admiral Yamamoto tried to comply.

On September 8, the Allies landed more reinforcements on Guadalcanal, and there also came some bad news from the Japanese on Guadalcanal. The sneak transportation method of using landing craft to move small units of troops had not worked as well as expected. The commander of the naval forces on the island reported that only a third of his men had succeeded in landing. The others had been shot up, many of them killed, by Allied planes flying from Henderson Field. This rate of attrition was almost disastrous, Admiral Yamamoto realized. It was apparent, only three days before the big operation was set to begin, that the Kawaguchi force was in trouble.

On September 10, Admiral Yamamoto sent Chief of Staff Ugaki and several staff officers down to Rabaul to be on hand there as the combined operations began. They passed over Admiral Nagumo's task force, which had left Truk that morning, seeking battle with the American air fleet, and arrived at Rabaul in early afternoon. There Admiral Ugaki learned that because of difficulties, General Kawaguchi had again changed the date for the assault on Henderson Field, back to September 12.

On the night of September 11, the army officers at Rabaul congratulated one another on the coming victory of the Kawaguchi force. So confident were they that the Eleventh Air Fleet sent a reconnaissance plane to Guadalcanal the next afternoon and the pilot tried to land on Henderson Field—only to see about forty Allied fighters parked there and be fired on as he approached. So the field was not taken after all, said the report. And then came an ominous silence from the Kawaguchi detachment, which was supposed to have carried out the land operations of September 12.

On September 15, Admiral Yamamoto had word from Chief of Staff Ugaki that the army assault on Henderson Field had most certainly failed. Communications were so poor that it was hard to get much of a picture, but what did come in showed anything but success.

On September 15, Admiral Yamamoto had official word in a message from the Kawaguchi detachment:

The batteries of the eastern position commenced firing on the evening of September 12 as scheduled, but the main force was delayed by the difficulty of the march in the jungle and was only able to attack on the morning of the 13th. Enemy resistance was unexpectedly strong, so that we suffered a great loss, including battalion commanders. We were forced to withdraw. After regrouping the remaining force on the west side of the river, we are going to plan our move.

(This desperate battle, which stopped the Japanese cold, was known by the Americans as the Battle of Bloody Ridge.)

So the army had failed to take the airfield, the focal position of Guadalcanal. Yamamoto now initiated a series of discussions with the army command, which seemed at a loss to proceed further. What the army must do, said Yamamoto, was bring in enough troops to do the job. He sent Chief of Staff Ugaki to confer with the army high command, to emphasize to them the enormous importance of winning back Guadalcanal.

The emphasis was underlined a day or so later when B-17s put down at Henderson Field.

Admiral Yamamoto was particularly bitter about the failure of the army to complete its part of the task, but the navy continued to look for the American carrier fleet. At this point it consisted of the carriers *Wasp* and *Hornet*. A search plane found part of the task force southeast of Guadalcanal, and so did Commander Takaichi Kinashi in the submarine *I-19*. On September 15 he managed to work his way close to the carriers, and put three torpedoes into the *Wasp*. He also torpedoed the battleship *North Carolina* and the destroyer *O'Brien*, which had to return to base for repairs.

The next day the Combined Fleet sent out its planes to attack the task force, but the weather was so bad that they did not find the American ships. Meanwhile, search planes reported that the Americans had sent two transports to Lunga Point, where they were unloading supplies. More trouble for the Japanese on Guadalcanal. On September 18, the Japanese headquarters there reported worse news: Six transports were unloading in Lunga Roads, guarded by a force of cruisers and destroyers.

The result of Yamamoto's complaints to General Imamura and to Tokyo was the strengthening of the army at Rabaul, but as usual, the army's idea of strengthening was first of all to add eleven members to the Seventeenth Army staff. This was not going to win the battle for Guadalcanal.

Imperial General Headquarters also sent down its prime trouble shooter, Lieutenant Colonel Masanobu Tsuji. This young officer was far more important in the Japanese military scheme than his rank would suggest. He had participated in the Bataan Death March and had counseled a policy of unremitting harshness toward the Allied troops, to show the white man's inferiority. He had also caused the downfall of

Lieutenant General Masaharu Homma, the commander in the Philippines, for being "soft," which is to say humane. Tsuji showed up on the flagship one day asking for more escorts to bring supplies to Guadalcanal.

When Tsuji described the plight of the soldiers on Guadalcanal, already reduced to eating what they could find and grubbing for wild vegetables, Yamamoto's eyes filled with tears. He promised to do anything, including use the *Yamato* as an escort if that were necessary. Of course, that was impossible; a battleship is of no use as an escort and is very vulnerable to submarines if traveling alone. But Yamamoto cared deeply about the plight of the men on Guadalcanal. He was determined to do all he could to strengthen their position and ultimately to save them if that was necessary.

And now a new problem presented itself. The fleet had been consuming fuel at the rate of 10,000 tons per day, and tankers were very short. The fuel stock at Truk was down to 650,000 tons, which was very discouraging. Also, Admiral Ugaki returned from Rabaul to report that the antiaircraft gunners down there were so inept that it was disgraceful. Yamamoto authorized the dispatch of a competent force from the *Yamato* and the battleship *Mutsu* to train the gunners at Rabaul.

The shortage of fuel forced Yamamoto to cancel air operations he had planned to find and defeat the enemy task force on September 20.

It was enough to turn a commander's hair gray, and in fact, it did. Yamamoto had arrived at Truk looking younger than his fifty-six years, but by September his hair had visibly grayed. He was depressed by the army's failures, particularly so because one of the units sent to Guadalcanal was the Sixteenth Infantry Regiment, which included a number of young men from Nagaoka. Yamamoto sometimes spoke angrily of the army's failures and lack of responsibility, such as, for example, when Admiral Ugaki returned from Rabaul and reported that the army high command there stayed up late at night and got up late in the morning, leaving the work to the junior officers.

"Everything is depressing here," he wrote his friend Takeichi Hori in Japan. "The trouble is not the enemy, but our own side."

By the fall of 1942, Admiral Yamamoto had the feeling that he would not survive the South Pacific campaign. "I have resigned myself to spending the whole of my remaining life in the next one hundred days."

THE MEAT GRINDER

27 At the end of September the weather was so bad in the Guadalcanal area that all Japanese naval and naval air operations were hampered. On September 25, Admiral Yamamoto had planned a trial landing on the newly built airfield at Buin, but it had to be canceled because heavy rain had turned the airstrip into a soggy mass. Fighters could not use the field in that sort of weather.

The resupply and reinforcement of Guadalcanal were continuing by barge, but this was not the best way. Too few troops and supplies could be delivered, and on moonlit nights, with the Allied airmen flying from Henderson Field, the barges usually were attacked.

On September 26, a series of B-17 bomber attacks on the Shortlands area prompted the Southeast Area Fleet at Rabaul to ask Admiral Yamamoto to send Admiral Nagumo's carrier force to attack Guadalcanal. The Japanese sensed a major increase in Allied air activity in the whole area. But the trouble was that Admiral Nagumo's carrier force was not ready for action. As Admiral Ugaki observed sourly, it never was ready; Nagumo and his chief of staff paid virtually no attention to anything but direct orders from the commander in chief. On this day the big carrier *Zuikaku* was not ready for action. When queried, Admiral Kusaka lamely claimed that they had been busy training, but, as Ugaki said,

186

although training was important, readiness for action was more important.

Down in the South Pacific the fleet sometimes seemed to threaten to unravel. All those Spartan hours Admiral Yamamoto had spent on training sometimes seemed for nothing, and at times he became very discouraged.

On September 25, the submarine *I-33* had returned to Truk from a Solomons patrol and had tied up alongside the tender *Urakami Maru* for service and some repairs. One of her forward torpedo tubes was damaged. To make the repairs, the crew shifted water in the trim tanks so that the bow of the submarine came out of the water. But the affected torpedo tube was the lower one and the rise in angle was not enough for the repairmen to get at the tube. The torpedo officer got permission from the executive officer to open the cock of the after main tank, which would bring more water into the stern and improve the angle.

In principle this was all very well. But the executive officer was aboard the tender at the moment, and he did not know that all the hatches of the submarine were open because of the heat. As soon as the cock was opened, the stern began to go down, and in a few moments the submarine had sunk so far that the water reached the main hatch and began pouring in. There were seven officers and thirty-seven men aboard at the moment. They rushed to close the hatches and got the conning tower hatch and the forward hatch closed, but it was too late for the after hatch. In two minutes the submarine had gone to the bottom of the anchorage. Divers could not get near because of the air bubbles rushing up from the sunken submarine.

Admiral Yamamoto had been scheduled to go ashore that afternoon for an inspection tour and then to attend a dinner and dancing performance by local natives. Abruptly the recreational trip was canceled and he stood by as rescue operations began.

But there were all sorts of difficulties. The bubbles kept coming up. Knocking sounds were heard from the engine room, which meant survivors, but the rescue buoy had been removed from the submarine to make room for gasmasks. There was no way to help the men down there, except to try to run an air line down and pump air into the boat.

The next morning a staff officer of the submarine force came aboard the flagship to report sadly that the knocking sounds had stopped. The air had not gotten through to the engine room, and there were no survivors.

*   *   *

The weather around Guadalcanal began to improve on September 27.
Finally, the Rabaul air force was able to stage a successful air raid on
the island, bombing Henderson Field.

On September 28, Lieutenant Colonel Tsuji reappeared. As the representative of Imperial General Headquarters, he had taken charge of
army operations on Guadalcanal. He and a staff officer of the Eleventh
Air Fleet and one from the Seventeenth Army came to talk to Admiral
Yamamoto about the need to change military operations on Guadalcanal.

As everyone knew, the Ichiki and Kawaguchi detachments had both
failed to dislodge the Americans from Guadalcanal. It was apparent that
at least a division of troops would have to be sent to the island, but this
meant that at least five high-speed destroyer transports would need to
be added to the support force for the island.

This request created serious problems for Admiral Yamamoto. He
did not have any destroyer transports as such, and by using destroyers
to transport troops, he was depriving the fleet of these valuable ships
—particularly the carrier force. But the need was very great, as everyone
could see, and if he could not provide the transports, then the effort to
recapture Guadalcanal would have to be delayed at least another month.
So Yamamoto promised to provide the transport, as well as to send
down cruisers and battleships to bombard the island.

Yamamoto now began to have an inkling that the claims of the
Eleventh Air Fleet had to be taken with large doses of salt. On September
28, the Eleventh Air Fleet staged another raid on Guadalcanal, and the
pilots came home jubilantly to report that they had engaged thirty-six
Allied fighters and shot down ten of them. They had lost nine planes.
But from the Guadalcanal ground command that day came an entirely
different story. An observer had watched thirty-six enemy planes take
off half an hour before the Japanese attack and thirty-six planes land
half an hour after the Japanese air raid ended. Also, the "Cactus Air
Force" was reinforced that day by eighteen new planes, three of them
B-17s.

The sea war, too, had taken a definite turn for the worse. The
submarine fleet, despite its success in attacking warships, was not per-
forming as well as had been hoped. And at the end of September, the
carrier *Taiyo* was torpedoed by an American submarine. Only thirteen
men were killed, but the carrier was put out of the service for which
she had been most useful: the ferrying of planes from various Central

Pacific points down to Rabaul, where they were being expended with frightening rapidity in the effort to support the war fronts on Guadalcanal and New Guinea at the same time.

All through this Admiral Yamamoto seemed indestructible. Officers who came down from Tokyo on inspection trips remarked that his strength and good health were inspiring to them. He found that hard to believe and told them that he often felt every one of his nearly sixty years. But it was true, perhaps because of the good food aboard the flagship, that Admiral Yamamoto was in good health and, given his underlying pessimism about the future, in good spirits as well.

Many officers came down with tropical diseases. Admiral Ugaki had trouble with his teeth and fever from time to time. Vice Admiral Tsukahara, commander of the Eleventh Air Fleet, fell ill with malaria, complicated with dengue fever, and then contracted a stomach ailment. He had to be relieved of command and sent home to recuperate.

Of course, there was no such "home assignment" for the vast majority of officers and men. If they got sick, they recovered or they died in the South Pacific. It took a remarkable set of circumstances for anyone of lesser rank than an admiral or a general to get sent back to Japan under any conditions. In Admiral Tsukahara's case, it took a telegram from Yamamoto to the Navy Minister. In one of the big early raids on Guadalcanal in August, fighter pilot Saburo Sakai, the leading naval ace of the South Pacific, was badly wounded and barely made it back to friendly territory with his Zero fighter. Because of his reputation, Sakai was sent back to Yokosuka Naval Hospital. But his was a special case, and nearly all the officers and men who came down to fly for the Eleventh Air Fleet died in the South Pacific.

Watching the reports from the Eleventh Air Fleet and noting the disparity between their claims and the reports of the soldiers on the ground at Guadalcanal, Admiral Yamamoto became convinced by the end of September that daylight air raids on Guadalcanal had now become too costly to continue. Some other way of harrying the enemy airfield and keeping the reinforcement under control would have to be found. It would have to be a combination of destroyer and cruiser bombardment at night. These air raids were just costing too many lives.

Admiral Yamamoto was very conscious of the loss of officers and men. He wrote home to a friend that he was the only one left of the senior officers of the fleet, and it made him feel very old. He lamented the loss of so many good people, partly because of the shortage of experienced officers, which was showing itself in many ways. Quietly he discouraged his admirals and captains from the time-honored practice of going down with the ship, for if they did, he told them, then they deprived His Majesty of their services at a time when they were desperately needed.

This issue came to a head with an inquiry from Navy Minister Shimada about Yamamoto's views on the subject of *bushido* as applied to the navy. Imperial General Headquarters was taking the position that a pilot should go down with his plane, a tank commander with his tank, and a captain with his ship. They might as well, because if they lost their equipment or their ship, they had failed, and failure was punishable by death. "Long Live the Imperial Way" was the cry, although, of course, this was not a very old Imperial Way they were invoking.

Yamamoto was quite forthright in his opposition to such policy:

Whatever they did under my command is my responsibility as the commander in chief. If they fail once, use them again and they will surely succeed the next time. . . .

If we do not approve of the skipper surviving when his ship goes down after hard fighting, we shall not be able to get through the war, which cannot be settled soon. There is no reason why we should discourage their survival, while we are encouraging fliers to survive by means of parachute [another Yamamoto policy]. . . .

In a war which must be carried out against tremendous odds, I, as commander in chief, cannot help feeling reluctance in issuing such orders to ask our captains not to return alive when their ships sink. . . .

In this interchange Yamamoto told Tokyo precisely what he thought of Japan's chances of winning the war, and his feelings about the "Imperial Way" of the new *bushido*, which had very little to do with the true *bushido* of the past.

This attitude certainly did not make him popular with the hysterical advocates of the "Imperial Way," who held that to die for the Emperor was the greatest honor. Sometimes Yamamoto wondered why he had not been replaced in command of the fleet before now.

But from Tokyo there was no such stirring, because if Yamamoto were to leave the fleet, who then would take it over, and who could instill the confidence of officers and men the way he had? As everyone in Tokyo knew, if there was one man in the Japanese navy who was irreplaceable, it was Yamamoto.

As the weeks went by and the admiral had irrefutable evidence of America's growing might, his gloomy thoughts persisted. For the most part he kept these to himself, although he occasionally confided bits to his friend Takeichi Hori:

> Things here are hard. I felt from the beginning that America was not likely to relinquish easily positions established at the cost of such sacrifice, and I insisted that a high degree of preparation and willingness to make sacrifices of our own would be necessary, but everybody here always persists in facile optimism. . . .

He was referring here to General Imamura, the commander of the southern armies, and to General Hyukatake, commander of the Seventeenth Army. Their optimism was so great that three times they had sent battalion-sized detachments to Guadalcanal to do a job that required at least two divisions. Spurred by Lieutenant Colonel Tsuji of the Imperial General Headquarters, they were now trying to reinforce Guadalcanal, but it was very late. Admiral Yamamoto could sense the growing might of the American naval and air contingents and knew that the task before him was herculean.

A major problem at this stage of the war was the enormous overconfidence of the Imperial General Staff, created by an unending series of tactical victories in China and then reinforced by the ease with which Japan scored victory after victory over the Western powers at the outset of the war. Hong Kong had fallen after a few days of fighting. General Tomoyuki Yamashita had led 30,000 Japanese troops to a lightning victory over the British in Malaya, where General Percival had surrendered a force of more than 100,000 men to Yamashita. In the Dutch East Indies, the Japanese had moved with equal ease. To be sure, the Americans had holed up in Corregidor Fortress in the Philippines and had to be routed out at great trouble and cost. This was a great irritation to the Japanese General Staff, which had by the spring of 1942 come to regard Japan's lightning victories as the norm and to believe their own propaganda claim that the Japanese army and navy were invincible.

As Yamamoto knew only too well, the word was not "invincible," it was "prepared." In his biography of Yamamoto, Hiroyuki Agawa cites two other officers knowledgeable about the Western world who had experiences similar to Yamamoto's. One was Commander Yuzuru Sanematsu, who had served for several years in Washington. He was appointed to lecture on American affairs at the Navy Staff College, but he found that none of his listeners believed him when he spoke of the enormous industrial might and resilience of America. Another was Lieutenant Commander Michinori Yoshii, who had been stationed in London before the war began. He too tried to tell the truth about the West, but so conditioned was the Japanese military establishment that no one believed him either.

On Guadalcanal, on New Guinea, and at Rabaul, the men who did the fighting knew the facts, but their superiors basked in luxury and continued to believe that what was happening in the South Pacific was merely a temporary setback. The Japanese military oligarchy was still living in the cocoon of its own spinning that had hardened in the 1930s and remained unchanged.

It was very difficult for even the most intelligent of the Japanese field commanders to rid themselves of this feeling of superiority. Admiral Ugaki, for example, in his September 28 diary entry, asked, "Why is it that the attack result reported by our attack forces and the reported number of planes taking off and landing on the island did not coincide?" And on the next day he remarked, "We have to entertain some doubts about our fliers' claims of shooting down so many enemy planes." But on October 2 he had overcome all his doubts and wrote, "It is gratifying that our aerial attacks have been successful lately. . . . In each sortie our fighters are shooting down ten enemy planes in dogfights."

Following Lieutenant Colonel Tsuji's appeal for destroyer transport to Guadalcanal, on the last day of September 1942, Admiral Yamamoto gave orders that beginning the next day destroyers would undertake the delivery of men and supplies to Guadalcanal on all but moonlit nights.

The first attempt was successful, much to Yamamoto's pleasure. Three of the four destroyers sent to Guadalcanal that night managed to unload their men and cargo, although the fourth had to turn back because of mechanical troubles.

Yamamoto also was using the seaplane tender *Nisshin* to carry heavy equipment and supplies to the island. On October 4 the *Nisshin* landed a number of big howitzers to support the Japanese land attacks. She was attacked several times by Allied planes but fought them all off with antiaircraft gunfire.

That day Yamamoto studied the army's plans, and the Eighth Fleet, at Rabaul, sent up its own plan of operations for his approval. Tokyo was obviously getting the message that something had to be done at Guadalcanal, because the next day Yamamoto received Major General Miyazaki, a new chief of staff for the Seventeenth Army, who was coming by Truk on his way to Rabaul. Yamamoto spent more than an hour with the general, trying to apprise him of the realities of the situation in the South Pacific.

A day later, in came Vice Admiral Kusaka, the new commander of the Eleventh Air Fleet. His arrival was another signal of a new approach by Tokyo. But was it too late? The Allied attacks on Guadalcanal and the air attacks on the Japanese forces there were increasing every day, an indication of a buildup by the enemy. And naval intelligence, gathering its information from radio intercepts, reported a buildup of naval forces too.

In view of the increase in American attacks in the Guadalcanal area, Admiral Yamamoto had ordered that more care be taken in coordinating air and sea missions. On October 7, the *Nisshin* was heading for the island again carrying more troops and heavy equipment, but the weather was too bad for the screening fighters to cover her. The seaplane carrier turned back to Shortlands without delivering.

As promised, Yamamoto was planning to send a high-speed convoy to Guadalcanal carrying most of a division and its equipment. But one difficulty seemed to follow another these days, and although the convoy was supposed to go down in the second week of October, the date now had to be delayed until October 15. One reason was the shortage of fighters. At Rabaul, Eleventh Air Fleet had promised to deliver a squadron of fighters to the new Buin Airfield, but they had not yet come. Once the fighters arrived, a great deal of pressure would be taken off the Rabaul bases, and that was the idea, to create a new base much closer to Guadalcanal. But until it could be made operable, it might as well not be there.

So it was with great relief that Admiral Yamamoto welcomed the news that Admiral Kusaka had arrived at Truk by flying boat. The Eleventh Air Fleet had been without a leader for several weeks, and all those delays were the result of the rudderless period of the Eleventh.

At two o'clock in the afternoon, Admiral Yamamoto called a briefing of all the naval elements involved, particularly the Eighth and Eleventh Fleet staff officers and his own Combined Fleet staff. It lasted for two and a half hours, and they hashed over all the plans for the coming assault on Guadalcanal.

Finally, it seemed, Admiral Yamamoto's warnings to the army about the nature of the enemy they faced were beginning to get through. On October 8, Yamamoto's chief of staff conferred with army staff officers from Tokyo and Rabaul, and after that for the first time Yamamoto had the feeling that the army was taking notice of reality. The army team said that they were planning to send five or six divisions and at least twenty-five battalions of engineers and special troops to the South Pacific. They no longer believed that a few battalions and a grand exhibition of fighting spirit could handle the job.

But, of course, this was going to take some time, until the middle of 1943. In the interim, Guadalcanal had to be recaptured.

The army men still seemed to believe that this was going to be an easy task. Indeed, the inspection party from Tokyo stopped off at Truk and said they were going to Kwajalein and then to Timor. They planned to go down to Rabaul around October 25, which was plenty of time for them to inspect Guadalcanal "after the capture" and return to Tokyo by the first of November.

This was army dreaming. The reality was something else. That day, October 8, the *Nisshin* again failed to deliver its goods and troops to Guadalcanal because she was attacked by a dozen planes, including torpedo bombers. The *Nisshin*'s seaplanes drove off the attackers, but two planes were lost, although their crews were rescued.

Yes, the transport of men, equipment, and supplies to Guadalcanal was very difficult. And as if this were not enough, the ground crew that had been sent down to Buin to straighten out the mess at the airfield there reported back that the field was really unusable because it was so wet after rain. The crew predicted that if it was used, half the planes would be lost in ground loops and crashes because of the bad surface.

This was the sort of nagging problem that helped make Admiral Yamamoto's temper a bit short these days. He could be very friendly with the staff—one evening he spent in Admiral Ugaki's cabin, gossiping like a school boy. But the next day he was short-tempered about a dozen details.

Ugaki knew why: The Guadalcanal operation was approaching fast, and it was critical that the island be captured. The army was far too confident for the admiral's liking; the army always was.

This was the most important operation since Midway. Admiral Yamamoto was prepared to commit all the major elements of the Combined Fleet, for, as he put it, "it cannot be unsuccessful." If the plan failed, then the Combined Fleet would be rendered useless for all practical purposes. The army at Rabaul might not know it and the Imperial General Headquarters in Tokyo might not admit it (although by the number of inspectors and other officials they were sending down to the South Pacific it seemed that they had a good idea), but here was the turning point of the war in the Pacific. The loss of the four carriers and the cruiser *Mogami* at Midway had been serious, cutting down the carrier force. But since Guadalcanal began, the attrition to the Japanese Combined Fleet had been steady, and although none of the major carriers had been lost in this struggle, hundreds of planes and skilled pilots had been sacrificed. And the new nagging matter of fuel would not go away.

As Yamamoto had said so many times, the problems would not come in the beginning, nor for the first six months or a year after the beginning of the war. Now the war was approaching its first anniversary, and every week became more dangerous to Japan, as the American production juggernaut gained strength. But still there was no point in talking about such matters to the army high command; they had closed their minds to the outside world.

Even now at Rabaul the main effort was devoted to rationalization of the Japanese position. The sense of urgency that Yamamoto felt was not shared by the army, not even by Lieutenant Colonel Tsuji, the most aggressive of the lot.

Knowing all this, and with a growing sense of despair for the future, Admiral Yamamoto prepared for what he thought would be the decisive land-sea-air battle of October.

TOWARD DEADLY BATTLE

28

In the second week of October 1942, nobody in the South Pacific could miss the signs of coming battle. General Hyukatake, belatedly, was sending 15,000 men to join the 10,000 already on Guadalcanal. They were staging down from the Shortlands, by destroyer and by barge, careful to travel only at night, since anything Japanese that moved within a 250-mile radius of Guadalcanal during the daylight hours was likely to be worked over by the growing force of Allied fighters and bombers from Henderson Field. Besides, General Kenney's Fifth U.S. Air Force was mounting as many missions as it could in this direction, and from Espiritu Santo, Admiral Halsey's land-based air bombers also were coming forth to scour the Guadalcanal waters.

The Japanese plan had been put into effect on October 4. In this second week, the air attacks on Guadalcanal were increased enormously. Admiral Yamamoto had told Eleventh Air Fleet not to count the cost, and Admiral Kusaka was obeying his orders. Fifty, sixty planes in a sweep coursed over Guadalcanal, engaging the American fighters that came up, and bombing the airfield and any other likely installations they could find. They never failed to take a good look at Lunga Roads for transports that might be worth attacking.

General Hyukatake landed on Guadalcanal on October 10—and was appalled at what he found there. The troops were actually starving, a fact that had not been communicated to the general before. It was a measure of how distant the relationship was between the army commander and his army that he did not know; his subordinates were afraid to tell him. Now he had seen for himself what he should have known for many weeks. What was needed was more: more guns and more soldiers. But first he sent a message back to Shortlands: Before any more troops were landed, food and medicines must be brought in for the remnants of the Kawaguchi and Ichiki detachments.

Nearly every night now the "Tokyo Express" was driving down on Guadalcanal, landing men and equipment. The *Nisshin* made several successful voyages, bringing in the howitzers that were to be trained on Henderson Field.

Not recognizing the Japanese buildup for what it was, General Vandegrift's marines made several attacks. But the fighting was so brisk that Vandegrift contented himself with tightening his defenses around the Matanikau River and the airfield and waiting for the Japanese to act.

On October 8, the weather had cleared and the Japanese high command was not feeling quite so desperate about the condition of Buin Airfield. That day the Eleventh Air Fleet sent thirty planes, a combination of fighter planes, to Buin to begin operations against Guadalcanal.

Two days later the fleet was preparing for action. Admiral Ugaki, despite having a tooth pulled that day, had all the orders ready. And already the forces were moving fast. General Hyukatake had embarked the last of the Japanese Second Division troops with tanks and heavy guns. From Noumea, Admiral Turner of the American amphibious force had sailed with 3000 more American troops to assist General Vandegrift.

To protect this convoy, the Americans had sent out the task force built around the carrier *Hornet*, another built around the modern battleship *Washington*, and a third force of cruisers and destroyers under Rear Admiral Norman Scott that was to patrol "the Slot" and watch for enemy attempts to send ships down that would either bombard the airfield or land troops. Admiral Scott's cruiser force consisted of the *San Francisco*, the *Salt Lake City*, the *Helena*, and the *Boise*, plus five destroyers.

At Rabaul, Vice Admiral Gunichi Mikawa, commander of the Eighth Fleet, had sent out a special force on October 10 to protect the landing of the last Japanese troops scheduled to arrive on Guadalcanal. It consisted of the cruisers *Aoba, Furutaka*, and *Kinugasa* and two destroyers, all under the command of Rear Admiral Aritomo Goto.

X Day was to be October 15. That day the Japanese army would advance on Guadalcanal and retake Henderson Field under the helpful wings of the Eleventh Air Fleet and guarded at sea by the ships of the Combined Fleet. Meanwhile, Admiral Nagumo's task force would set out to find and destroy the American carrier or carriers that Admiral Yamamoto knew to be out there somewhere.

On Sunday, October 11, the Japanese Second Fleet left Truk, and so did the Second Carrier Division and the Third Fleet. They were all moving into preselected positions to play their roles in the great recapture campaign. To buck up the army to its responsibilities, Admiral Yamamoto sent a telegram to General Hyukatake announcing the sailing of the fleet. Yamamoto still feared that the army would take any pretext to try to delay the land operations.

That day, the Eleventh Air Fleet was scheduled to make two major attacks on Henderson Field, but the fighters found no Allied fighters on the ground or in the air, and the bombers did not arrive because of bad weather. So the air attacks of October 11 were a waste of time and fuel.

At Rabaul, the men of the Eleventh Air Fleet were under enormous tension, and it was beginning to show. The night of October 11, a dozen Allied planes bombed Rabaul for the first time at night. Their bombs were devastating, killing a hundred and ten men of the Eleventh Air Fleet. Admiral Kusaka was so upset that he radioed Admiral Yamamoto and asked for reinforcement of the Rabaul air fleet by more planes from the carriers.

Obviously this was impossible: Yamamoto could not sacrifice his carrier planes to protect Rabaul, whose air defenses should have been built up a long time ago. The problem here in the South Pacific, as Yamamoto had noted several times, seemed to be always too little too late. It was an indication of the change in the war that he had expected since before the beginning.

The night of October 11, the Sixth Cruiser Division of the Japanese fleet was supposed to break through down "the Slot" and bombard the airfield from Lunga Point, but instead, the two forces met off Cape Esperance and mauled each other. The Americans had the best of it. The cruiser *Furutaka* and the destroyer *Fubuki* were sunk, and the cruiser *Aoba* had to be sent back to Japan for repairs. The Americans lost the destroyer *Duncan*, the cruiser *Boise* needed major repairs, and the cruiser *Salt Lake City* needed minor repairs.

But neither side had stopped the other from landing troops. The men of the Americal division landed at Lunga Roads, and the last of the Japanese Second Division landed on the Japanese side of the island. The seaplane tenders *Nisshin* and *Chitose* managed to unload their heavy equipment once again. They started back for the Shortlands base after unloading, but were caught by an American air raid that disabled the destroyer *Murakumo* and sank the destroyer *Natsugumo*.

This was bad news, but to Yamamoto the most important news was that the planes carrying out the attacks were carrier planes, which meant that the American carrier force was somewhere in the area. He gave orders that it was to be found and called for a search by the land-based air forces. He also ordered the Nagumo carrier force to speed south to engage the enemy. So the preparations for the great Japanese attack continued.

On Monday, October 12, Admiral Yamamoto knew that the X-Day operation was ragged and threatened to come unraveled. Inadequate searches could be blamed for the encounter between the Japanese cruiser force and that American cruiser force led by Admiral Scott. The problem the next day was much the same: The Eleventh Air Fleet planes that set out to attack the enemy task force did not find it, and the planes assigned to hit Henderson Field for the most part did not bomb. It is true that the weather over Guadalcanal that day was not good, but the real problem with the Eleventh Air Fleet by October of 1942 was the attrition of r· ›t leaders. So many of the experienced men had been lost that some ..ghts were led by relatively inexperienced men. And what could be done about that?

The night of October 12, four transports left Rabaul and two left Shortlands, bound for Guadalcanal with the last of the supplies. The navy promised a major air attack on October 13 and night bombardment of the airfield and Lunga Roads by major fleet elements on the night of October 14.

These orders had already been issued when Colonel Miyazaki, chief of staff of the Seventeenth Army, and Captain Ohmae and Commander Genda of the Eleventh Air Fleet showed up at the flagship to argue for a major ship bombardment and a reinforced convoy to go to Guadalcanal. Admiral Ugaki was able to tell them that the admiral was one step ahead of them.

On October 13, as promised, Admiral Kusaka's Eleventh Air Fleet planes plastered Guadalcanal and particularly the air field with bombs. They cratered the runway repeatedly and wrecked much of the metal netting that allowed the Americans and Australians to use the runway in muddy weather. They burned up one of the few fuel dumps at the airfield. The first raid was followed by a second, just as damaging, and at the end of the day the Allied fliers were to all effects grounded.

They scarcely had time to relax before the next act began. The howitzers that the Japanese had transported with such difficulty aboard the seaplane carriers now began to speak, shelling the airfield. They did so until the Americans called up three destroyers from the Lunga area to return fire. As the better part of valor, the howitzers ceased firing.

"I think the chance of turning the tables has been grasped at last. It has been a long struggle," wrote Admiral Ugaki that night in his diary. But there was more to come.

Earlier in the day Admiral Yamamoto had prepared it. He sent messages to the Third Battleship Division—Admiral Takeo Kurita and the battleships *Kongo* and *Haruna*—telling them not to fail in this night's bombardment of Henderson Field. And they did not. They came down on Guadalcanal on the night of October 13, with a load of a thousand shells for the fourteen-inch guns, and they shelled the airfield for an hour and a half. At the end of the bombardment, fuel dumps were blazing, more than half the aircraft in the area were destroyed, and the field was unusable. As they moved off at nineteen knots at 1 A.M., Admiral Kurita reported back to Admiral Yamamoto: 920 shells fired, guided by three lights set up by the troops ashore; effects good.

"The whole area of the airfield was turned into a mass conflagration of gigantic size with numerous flames shooting up. Explosions continued until dawn." This was the report that came to Admiral Yamamoto that night.

Admiral Yamamoto was very pleased. All that training at Hashi-rajima had not been in vain. Two battleships coming into confined waters in the dead of night and bombarding an airfield with fourteen-inch guns was an unprecedented action. Audacity had its purposes.

Admiral Yamamoto was up late that night. At 3 A.M., having assessed the bombardment of the airfield as a complete success, he ordered the Nagumo carrier force to advance south and find and attack the Allied carrier fleet. But lest Henderson Field come alive again, Nagumo was not to come within 200 miles of the island until he found the enemy task force. Yamamoto was audacious, but he also had the caution of common sense.

On Guadalcanal the next morning, October 14, the howitzers began firing again, putting more holes in the runways and keeping the engineers from working on the field. At noon Japanese bombers attacked again.

The navy and the navy airmen had certainly done their part of the job, and for the army, so had the howitzers. The promise that Henderson Field would be neutralized had been kept. The Americans had built a short, rough runway next to the matted field, usable only in dry weather. This remained usable, but it was very small and very primitive. As for aircraft, only a handful of planes remained, and only four were dive bombers. There were no torpedo bombers left intact at Henderson. So, really, the Japanese navy had carried out the first step in Yamamoto's plan to capture Guadalcanal.

The next step was to reinforce the army. With some 20,000 troops on Guadalcanal, they were expecting reinforcements this night that would swell the number to more than 22,500.

Starting on the morning of October 14, Admiral Kusaka began all over again on Admiral Yamamoto's orders. At 9:30 A.M. the bombers from Rabaul began to arrive. The noon raid was the big one: Twenty-six bombers made more holes in the runway, but they did not see the "cow pasture" field nearby. An hour later another raid came by. This time the Americans managed to scramble more than twenty fighters into the air. These attacked the Japanese bombers, shooting down nine of them as well as three Japanese fighters.

But the waters around Guadalcanal that day were Japanese waters. The Americans had no bombers, and the six transports bearing the Japanese reinforcements were on their way, spotted by American search planes that could do nothing as they watched them come heading down "the Slot." Also down came the cruisers *Kinugasa* and *Chokai* and two destroyers.

By midafternoon on October 14, the Americans managed to cannibalize enough wrecked planes to put together four SBD dive bombers and seven army planes. They drained gasoline out of wrecked planes and got enough for one mission. The planes took off and bombed the ships they saw, but they made only one glancing blow on the destroyer *Samidare*.

Late that afternoon, the mechanics managed the miracle of putting nine more bombers in the air, along with the remaining army planes and some of the F4Fs. They attacked the six Japanese transports, but the Zero fighters of the Eleventh Air Fleet were there in force and drove the Americans away. This was the end of American operations at Henderson Field that day. The field was down.

Offshore, the Japanese and American fleet units were milling around, not quite sure of themselves, neither quite figuring out what the enemy was trying to do. The American force was split into three task forces. The Japanese fleet also was split into three task forces: the First Carrier Division, under Admiral Nagumo, with the *Shokaku* and *Zuikaku*; the Second Carrier Division, with its light carriers; and the main element of the fleet, battleships and cruisers. The Japanese also were making excellent use, as they always did, of their float planes from the seaplane carriers *Nisshin* and *Chitose*. The major task for these planes, when not in defense, was scouting. They scouted diligently, sometimes catching glimpses of American ships through the overcast, but not knowing exactly what they were seeing.

One of *Chitose*'s float plane pilots, off Indispensable Shoal, sighted what seemed to be a carrier through the clouds. But then in a moment the clouds closed in, and the next time the pilot looked there was nothing.

So the Japanese carrier forces looked and looked and found nothing that day.

The high-speed transport convoy steamed steadily south, under the escort of the Japanese Fourth Destroyer Squadron, with the *Akizuki* flying the command flag. All went well until 2 P.M., when the convoy was attacked by enemy planes, but the ships fought the planes off, and since the weather was good, planes from Buin and Buka came to help. Another raid hit the convoy but was repelled again, as once more the Japanese fought back. As darkness closed in, the convoy reported to Yamamoto's flagship that it would reach Savo Island at about 8 P.M.

That evening Admiral Yamamoto issued his orders for the next day to the fleet: The carrier force was to attack the enemy south of the Solomons, where the American carriers must be. The task force from the east was to hit the force southeast of the Solomons.

The seaplane carrier *Chiyoda* had aboard a half dozen midget submarines, and her skipper was eager to try them out. Wouldn't it be a fine idea to let them loose between Guadalcanal and Russell Island to harry the enemy while the Japanese convoy unloaded?

But Yamamoto vetoed the plan. Too risky. The midgets might make a mistake, and even if they did not, why risk them on a gamble of this sort? Superweapons were all very well, said the admiral, but they had limitations. There was no point in throwing away lives uselessly. There were situations in which a midget submarine might be useful—Sydney Harbor had been a case in point—but Lunga Point was certainly not Sydney Harbor. To Yamamoto and his chief of staff this seemed a fool's mission.

That night of October 14, all went very well for Admiral Yamamoto. The fast convoy came south without being discovered and moved into the Guadalcanal anchorage at 11 P.M. The cruisers *Kinugasa* and *Chokai* approached the Lunga Point area and began the bombardment once more of the air field. They each fired 400 rounds of eight-inch ammunition. The effect was not so spectacular as that caused by the battleships the night before, but the bombardment provided cover for the unloading of the 4000 troops, guns, and supplies of the fast convoy.

All night long the Japanese unloading was covered by the float planes. Then, as dawn came, fighters from the Second Carrier Division and then land-based fighters came in to circle and repel possible Allied invaders. But Henderson Field was silent this morning.

There was nothing the Americans could do, for even the "cow pasture," that little runway alongside the main runway of Henderson Field, had been battered. In fact, the Americans managed to get two planes ready to take off, but both groundlooped in shellholes in the runway of the little strip. So it appeared that Admiral Kusaka's Eleventh Air Fleet really controlled the skies over Guadalcanal once again.

Surprisingly, the Americans managed to get one plane into the air later that morning and then another. It was surprising because virtually everything that could be combined to fly had already been used. The two planes set fire to two of the transports on the beach, and a flight of B-17s from Espiritu Santo set fire to another. This did not worry Rear Admiral Raizo Tanaka unduly. He had been instructed to land those transports, and he had. They had all been off-loaded of their troops, and most of the supplies from the undamaged transports also were unloaded. Admiral Tanaka estimated that the ships were eighty percent cleared.

This eventuality had been considered and so had the plan; they were grounded. They were expendable, although their supplies must be gotten ashore for the troops. So Tanaka decided to leave the damaged transports *Sasako Maru*, *Azumasan Maru*, and *Kyushu Maru* on the beach and take the undamaged ones away before the Americans could launch another air attack from outside. After night fell, he would return with his convoy and complete the unloading of the damaged ships.

Tanaka did not confide in Admiral Yamamoto, who would most undoubtedly have ordered the job finished while it could be. For the Americans were not totally without resources. More gasoline was being brought to Henderson Field by transport plane. Ammunition and supplies came in too. The heroic mechanics of the "Cactus Air Force" put together still another dozen airplanes under the noses of the Japanese. Admiral Tanaka did not know it, but by steaming away late that morning of October 15, he had endangered Admiral Yamamoto's plans.

That day, an American tugboat was towing a big gasoline barge to Guadalcanal, guarded by a destroyer. The little convoy was spotted by planes from the Japanese task force, which identified the destroyer as cruiser and the barge as a "floating dock." Admiral Yamamoto thought this was some new idea for strengthening the American forces at Guadalcanal, so he ordered an attack on the convoy. An attack was made, and the barge was abandoned and floated down into Sealark Channel. There went the big hope of getting gasoline for Henderson Field; Admiral Yamamoto had had the right hunch.

Yamamoto's fleet elements were searching diligently for the Allied carriers and other warships, but they did not find them. They decided the enemy must have run off to the south, and they did not chase. The task lay around Guadalcanal.

On that night of October 15, the cruisers *Myoko* and *Maya* bombarded Henderson Field again, adding to the damage. Yamamoto was now waiting a little impatiently for the next step. The cruiser *Aoba* came into Truk, having limped up after the battle of October 11 off Cape Esperance, and Yamamoto went aboard her to pay homage to the souls of Rear Admiral Goto and the others killed in that action. He did not say much about it, but he blamed Goto for throwing a monkey wrench into the works by allowing himself to be surprised that night. It had caused the change in plans that was giving the Americans more precious time.

In fact, a dud shell had struck on the bridge of the *Aoba*, killing Admiral Goto and the executive officer of the ship, and a half dozen others. The *Aoba* was not sunk, but the heavy cruiser *Furutaka* was. And here Admiral Yamamoto had a delicate problem. After an American shell hit in the engine room, the *Furutaka* began to go down. The ensign was pulled down, and all hands were told to give three cheers for the Emperor and then abandon ship. The Emperor's portrait was removed from the sheltered bridge, but unluckily the bearer was drowned and the portrait lost.

The captain of the *Furutaka*, his ship sinking, tried to commit suicide in his cabin, but members of his staff had secreted his revolver and his short samurai sword. He went up to the bridge to tie himself to the compass so he would go down with the vessel, but the ship sank beneath him. He was left floundering in the water and was finally rescued.

By the time the captain got to Truk, he was wishing he were dead, and he said so on the flagship. But Yamamoto and his staff comforted the captain and told him it was right that he had been saved to fight again for Japan.

After talking to the crew of the *Aoba*, Admiral Yamamoto went back to the flagship with a new confidence about Japanese fighting ships as compared to American. For the crew had told him that they had been hit by a large number of dud shells.

"I now have confidence that we can't lose this battle," said Yamamoto. And he waited.

That afternoon came more reports of Allied ships, but nothing could be pinpointed. A submarine had a report, and air search planes had reports, but the enemy fleet was not found that day.

Later in the afternoon, the transports still not quite unloaded were supposed to turn back to Guadalcanal and then help unload the ships that had been grounded and were still afire. But Admiral Tanaka decided to send them into Shortlands because it was not worth the effort. This was a mistake, Yamamoto knew.

But just now he had something far more important on his mind. The continuing reports of battleships and carriers meant there was something out there in the waters south of Guadalcanal, and he wished his people would find it.

The enemy was maneuvering very shrewdly, just keeping his distance from the Japanese force, ready to strike if an opportunity presented itself. Yamamoto could not tell how many carriers there were, but he was sure there were more than one. From what he could ascertain, the force gathered south of his battle fleet was the only Allied force in the area. This enemy had to be destroyed before Guadalcanal could be considered safe.

Yamamoto had great respect for this enemy. He also knew that he had to outwit the enemy somehow and draw him into battle, and that it must be done within the next ten days. So he told Admiral Ugaki to get on with the planning: how to bring the enemy to battle.

DECISION AT GUADALCANAL

2
9

On October 16, Admiral Yamamoto felt a new sense of urgency. He told Chief of Staff Ugaki that unless the Guadalcanal issue was joined within ten days that he had no confidence in victory. Everything he saw showed that time was on the side of his enemies.

The fleet's consumption of fuel was alarming in this game of hide and seek with the American carriers. The attrition among the aircraft and pilots of the Eleventh Air Fleet was alarming too, and every day the soldiers on Guadalcanal ate more food and consumed more ammunition and other supplies. The rate of consumption was overreaching the capacity of the Japanese naval forces to support the troops ashore.

The reports that reached Yamamoto indicated that the Americans did not share the Japanese supply problem. The American effort was becoming easier while his own became harder.

Saturday, October 17, dawned with rain and wind, the sort of weather typical of this typhoon season, and not at all welcome to Admiral Yamamoto. The search planes were out early, but they identified only a single cruiser and two destroyers off Lunga Point. The enemy ships bombarded the Japanese landing area at Tassafaronga and set fire to an ammunition dump on the shore, causing it to blow up and burn. The loss of ammunition was a serious blow to the hopes of General Hyukatake and proof of Admiral Yamamoto's contention that time was running out.

Yamamoto did not know it, but his despair was shared by the enemy commander, Rear Admiral Robert Ghormley, representative of Admiral Nimitz's Pacific Ocean Areas Command in the South Pacific. On October 15, Ghormley had sent a situation report to Admiral Nimitz describing the plight of the Americans.

Guadalcanal was virtually out of aviation gas. Japanese warships attacked every night with impunity, and their bombardment wrecked the airport installations, destroyed aircraft, killed men, and played hob with troop morale. The shore-based aircraft of the "Cactus Air Force" had been virtually wiped out in spite of the efforts of the ground crews to keep the planes flying. What seemed to be an enormous Japanese striking force was forming south of Truk. Thousands of enemy troops were infiltrating into Guadalcanal, with tanks and big guns. With the forces available to him, Admiral Ghormley said, he could not stop the Japanese.

With this message, Admiral Ghormley wrote finis to his own career, but what he had to say was true. As badly off as Admiral Yamamoto considered himself to be, the American plight was more desperate because at least the Japanese had an aggressive commander.

But now the Americans would have one too, however, because Ghormley's call for help was answered by his relief from command and the appointment of Admiral William F. Halsey, an old acquaintance of Yamamoto's from the day when America's Great White Fleet had visited Japan, and the most aggressive of the American task force commanders.

On Guadalcanal, General Hyukatake was doing his best, but he could not mount the assault, now delayed until October 20, the new date selected for the all-out attack by sea, air, and land. The Japanese fleet was at sea, milling about, waiting, and consuming fuel at a depressing rate. The Eleventh Air Fleet was flying more than its usual quota of missions each day and suffering more than the usual rate of attrition from enemy action, weather, and tired aircraft.

General Hyukatake had requested a naval bombardment for the morning of October 20, but he called off the request. The big battle had to be delayed once again.

On October 18, the Eleventh Air Fleet planes attacked Henderson Field in force. The destroyers brought down a thousand more troops that night, and the fleet milled about. Yamamoto had asked his staff to come up with some plan to force the enemy fleet into swift action, but the staff could not produce a workable idea.

The fuel situation at Truk grew more troublesome daily. On October 18, the tanker *Kenyo Maru* arrived there, her belly empty after having drained off the last drops to refuel Admiral Nagumo's strike force that had nothing to strike. The fuel supply ashore was perilous, so she took 4500 tons of oil each from the flagship *Yamato*, the battleship *Mutsu*, and the oiler *Nissho Maru* and headed back toward the Nagumo fleet.

Two other ships came up that day to fuel from the *Yamato*. Yamamoto noted ruefully that his flagship had become a tanker! And it worried him that the fuel consumption of the fleet down south was so great, with nothing happening, that the fleet's oilers could not keep the ships supplied.

This situation could not last much longer. He had news from Tokyo that home consumption in Japan was so great that fuel was short there too. Imperial General Headquarters and the Ministry of Production had sent orders to the Borneo oil fields to step up fuel output and use raw fuel because there was no time to refine it.

On October 19 there was still no definite word from General Hyukatake about the time of his attack on Henderson Field that would trigger the fleet and air actions. Hyukatake's troops had threaded their way through raw jungle to reach a point less than a kilometer from the airfield, but there they waited for the artillery and equipment to come up. The general had most recently announced a postponement of the attack date to October 22:

> The time is now ripe for us to engage with the enemy once and for all, and this Army is ordered this morning to commence a general offensive on October 22. We will fight gallantly and expect to respond to His Majesty's wish by annihilating the enemy with one stroke.

This sort of change was very disconcerting to Yamamoto, whose little faith in the army was not helped by bombast. But he issued new orders setting the date for Y Day as October 22. The battleships and cruisers would attack the airfield with a long bombardment to cover the troop movement.

But October 22 came and still the army was not ready. Another false start was declared, and wearily the Yamamoto staff adjusted the orders to the fleet and to the Eleventh Air Fleet at Rabaul.

Yamamoto had five carriers down there, searching for the Americans. They were separated into two forces (a lesson learned from Midway). Admiral Nagumo's First Carrier Division, including the supercarriers *Shokaku* and *Zuikaku*, made up one section. Admiral Kakuji Kakuta commanded the other section, with three carriers: the *Hiyo, Junyo*, and *Zuiho*. On October 22, however, the flagship *Hiyo* developed engine troubles, because as a converted tanker her engines had never been changed to compensate for the extra demands of carrier work. She had to be sent back to Truk for a survey, and the admiral transferred command to the carrier *Junyo*.

Admiral Yamamoto was now receiving a great deal of bad intelligence. On October 21, search planes reported on three battleships, a heavy cruiser, and a number of destroyers at a point 255 miles off Guadalcanal, bearing 145 degrees, and a submarine also reported seeing something like that. But there weren't so many American battleships in the South Pacific operating together. So what had the Japanese seen? They saw a lot of destroyers and small ships, as they usually did, and blew up the proportions. This was not a matter of braggartry, but of misinformation. Ship identification from a periscope or a point 10,000 feet in the air is not easy, but the Japanese were worse at it by far than the Americans. Throughout the war, they consistently overstated the size of Allied warships they encountered. This sort of reporting made it difficult for a fleet commander to make adequate plans in a hurry.

Even more misleading was a report that day from the submarine *I-176*, which claimed to have sighted two battleships, two cruisers, and several destroyers 120 miles east of St. Cristobel Island. After putting two torpedoes into one battleship, the captain said, the I-boat was forced down by destroyers. When she surfaced later, the sea was empty.

"The enemy may have escaped with big damage," said the report. But in fact the "enemy" had no damage at all from submarines that day. This was the sort of report that by now Admiral Yamamoto took with many grains of salt.

Even so, the reports brought confusion. The next day, October 21, reconnaissance planes reportedly sighted three battleships, three cruisers, and many destroyers in two groups, most of this illusory in terms of ship sizes. If one added all the sightings together, it gave the Americans a fleet that included seven or eight battleships and at least five carriers.

What was certain, however, was that the Allied fleet was out, some-where south of Guadalcanal, and this was the important fact to Admiral Yamamoto.

On October 21 came another of the incessant delays. The army postponed the land attack on Guadalcanal still another day, to October 23. Yamamoto's chief of staff, Admiral Ugaki—Vice Admiral Ugaki now—adjusted the orders to the fleet. But Yamamoto also warned the army that he could not guarantee the diversionary bombardment even one more day past that, because of the necessity of coming to grips with the Allied fleet.

In fact, Yamamoto was becoming more than a little disturbed by the army's constant dillying and dallying. It showed the army's complete failure to understand the necessities of joint operations and made the fleet's job extremely difficult.

On the morning of October 23, the naval battle seemed at hand. Elements of the American fleet were sighted southeast of the Solomons in the Santa Cruz Island area. The Americans had apparently put bait in the form of large surface ships in that area, for the carriers were still unseen and unheard from. So Yamamoto figured that the Americans were setting a trap for him. He sent warnings to all his forces to watch out for the carriers.

From the army on Guadalcanal came the usual discouraging news. The general attack scheduled for that morning had not materialized. The jungle was too thick, said the army. So nothing happened until afternoon, and then came another telegram that postponed the assault until October 24! Yamamoto had come to the conclusion by this time that the army simply did not know what it was doing on Guadalcanal.

His contention was borne out on the night of October 23, when the army was to make an assault on the right bank of the Matanikau River. The assault failed. "The Oka regiment [which had earlier failed to take the position] doubled its disgrace," wrote Chief of Staff Ugaki in his diary that day.

But when Ugaki talked the matter over with Yamamoto as they stood on the bridge of the flagship, he got the impression that Yamamoto was somewhat heartened by the appearance of action on the part of the army. If the army could pull itself together, it seemed certain that the attack could succeed, because the enemy was most certainly unaware of what was happening. Indeed, the report from Guadalcanal that day said that the marines were playing tennis on the south end of the airfield! Such inattention should mean victory for the Japanese.

was no indication of the readiness of General Vandegrift's marines. They knew the Japanese would be mounting a major attack at any moment, and they were waiting for it. But the Japanese army, grown so contemptuous of its opponents by many victories in the recent past, knew virtually nothing about the strength or character of the marines on Guadalcanal. They were confident of victory, even though they could not seem to get organized.

At least the army seemed determined to start its offensive against Mt. Austin and the airfield on the following night. And this time Yamamoto believed they had to go on with it, because, as he told Admiral Ugaki that day, he had learned that the army chief of staff in Tokyo had promised the Emperor personally that the attack would be carried out.

Meanwhile, down south, at an enormous cost of fuel, the Combined Fleet Task Force was supposed to be moving against the enemy. But Admiral Nagumo again showed his essential timidity. He was worried because the Japanese force had been shadowed all day by an American flying boat. So at dusk he changed course and moved back up to the north, out of range of trouble. Yamamoto was furious, but what could he do? Admiral Nagumo had been entrusted with coming to grips with the enemy. How he accomplished it had to be his responsibility. What Yamamoto feared was that Nagumo would avoid the action altogether, and while that would save Nagumo, it would destroy Yamamoto's chance of winning the battle of Guadalcanal. Nagumo's action might make it impossible to coordinate the air, land, and sea attacks, as Yamamoto wanted to do, and that might mean defeat.

The more Yamamoto thought it over, the more apprehensive he became about Nagumo's behavior. And so that night he sent an urgent message telling Nagumo to turn south again immediately and seek action with the enemy in conformation with the plan for the tripronged attack. "Do not hesitate or waver," he said.

Admiral Nagumo threatened to throw a monkey wrench into the whole battle plan by disobeying orders. The Second Air Division, with its smaller carriers, was well to the south, and the idea was to catch the Americans in a vise, with a task force on each side of them, pouring in the attack from two directions. With Nagumo lurking up north to stay out of trouble, the plan would fail. And for once the army seemed about to do its job properly.

That night Yamamoto stood by, waiting and reading every dispatch from Guadalcanal. Just before dusk a torrential rain storm struck the island, the army command reported. What would that do? Yamamoto could only wait, apprehensively, for it was his experience that almost any little thing seemed to throw the army off balance. But in this case the rain ought to have been salutary, for the advance column had reached a point less than a mile from the airfield by noon without arousing the enemy. And so Yamamoto waited, more content, hoping that the heavy rain had worked to the advantage of his army comrades, as it had in the battle of Okehazama in 1560, when General Nobunaga Oda defeated Yoshomoto Imagawa under just such conditions.

Then at about 2 A.M. Admiral Yamamoto had a welcome message that he had been awaiting, half fearful that it would never come:

> 2100 BANZAI. THE KAWAGUCHI DETACHMENT CAP-
> TURED THE AIRFIELD AND THE WESTERN FORCE
> IS FIGHTING TO THE WEST OF THE FIELD.

It was the signal that the Guadalcanal airfield had at last been captured!

Relieved, Admiral Yamamoto issued new orders. The Eighth Fleet was to move immediately to a point 150 miles southwest of Guadalcanal, and the Second Fleet was to move to a point 150 miles northeast of the island. Rear Admiral Tamotsu Takama's Destroyer Squadron Four would advance down "the Slot" to Guadalcanal and support the Japanese troops with gunfire.

Having read the good news and issued the orders, Yamamoto went to bed. But at dawn he was awakened with the news that the airfield had not been captured. And then there was silence from Guadalcanal. At midmorning a reconnaissance plane flying over the island reported that fighting was going on on the airfield itself.

Midafternoon brought an explanation:

> Control was difficult because of the complicated terrain. Only one enemy position protruding from the south end of the airfield was actually taken, but the airfield itself has not been taken. We regrouped this morning, and the force on the right bank of the Lunga River reached a point five kilometers southwest of Lunga Point. Four enemy planes took off, and two of them landed soon afterward.

The last sentence was the important one. So the airfield was still entirely and safely in enemy hands after all! The army had failed again.

What had actually happened was this: On the night of October 24, the Japanese had reached the south end of the field at a place the Americans called "Coffin Corner." Major General Yumio Nasu was to attack from the east, and General Kawaguchi was to attack from the west. But General Nasu had arrived first and had waited for General Kawaguchi to come up. When Kawaguchi's troops had not arrived by 9:30 P.M., General Nasu got nervous and sent his troops out anyhow to meet the strictures of the Y-Day orders. He attacked in a driving rainstorm, just as Admiral Yamamoto had hoped he would.

The Japanese stormed around "Coffin Corner," and one contingent, led by a colonel, managed to get behind the line, to the edge of the airfield. The colonel, eager for victory, jumped the gun and radioed a triumphant message: "The airfield is captured."

After that the Japanese continued the attack. Six times that night General Nasu's troops hit the marine line, but it held. Finally, overcome with disappointment, General Nasu led his troops himself and fell under the American fire. The American line held. In the morning the marines counted 1000 bodies in front of their positions, and in the morning the troops of that one colonel, behind the line, were hunted down.

The marines still held Henderson Field. General Kawaguchi arrived, and of course the army promised a new attack on the coming night. And, of course, Admiral Yamamoto had to hope (against hope) that it would succeed. For if it did not succeed, and if Nagumo did not come to grips with the enemy at sea, then all Yamamoto had planned would have failed, and it would have to be started all over again.

If the attack failed this time, whether or not it could be repeated ever again seemed now most questionable. Not only the army, but the navy was suffering from new difficulties. The carrier *Hiyo*, the flagship of the Second Air Division, was back at Truk, and her propulsion mechanism was seen to be in dreadful shape. She would not be ready for action in the near future. She really needed a new engine system. So the Second Air Division was deprived of one of its carriers. The fuel shortage was growing more serious every day. Really, this golden opportunity of the moment might be the last chance.

At sea, having received Yamamoto's direct order, Admiral Nagumo still hesitated. The order had come when he was fueling. He could not move just then, could he? And as he stopped fueling and got ready, reluctantly, to move south, a staff officer rushed in to report that they had shot down an American carrier scout plane.

"Stop refueling," said the admiral. "Turn the carriers and head north!" So for twelve more hours Admiral Nagumo steamed directly away from the American task force, which, spurred by Admiral Halsey, was now actually seeking battle. Nagumo sent out scout planes and was very much relieved to discover that they found no American planes or ships. At the end of the twelve hours, he stopped, completed the fueling, and headed south again at high speed to expend some more of the fuel he had just put into the ship's tanks.

So Admiral Nagumo was at last headed south at high speed, looking for the enemy. But the weather took a hand, and Nagumo's search planes did not find the enemy task force.

The Second Carrier Division, down south, was sighted by a B-17 bomber, and so Admiral Kakuta also headed north so as not to be surprised by the enemy without the presence of his counterpart task force on the other side.

Admiral Yamamoto approved of this action, but he did advise Kakuta to send as many planes as possible over Guadalcanal on the way up to attack and support the army operations there.

At 11:15 on October 25, a Japanese patrol plane sighted part of the American task force thirty miles east of Rennel Island. But because the Second Air Division was heading north, it was too late for them to try an attack, and it was too far from the Japanese bases for land-based aircraft to strike.

By this time, Admiral Yamamoto was aware of all the aspects of the battle for Guadalcanal, except what was going on at Rabaul. Communications there and between Rabaul and the flagship were less than adequate, and what happened on October 25 was the result of this failure.

On the morning of October 25, Admiral Kurita also had the army message that Henderson Field had been captured, and he acted accordingly. He sent a reconnaissance plane to inspect the field, accompanied by eight Zero fighters. Sure enough, the plane found the field pock-marked and silent, with many wrecked aircraft on the edges. No Allied planes rose up to meet them, which seemed to be proof that the field was indeed in Japanese hands. (The reason was that the runway was soaked from that torrential rain of the previous afternoon, and it would be noon before it was dry enough to use.) So the Japanese zoomed over unaware, and not very careful. The reconnaissance plane caught an antiaircraft burst from one of the American guns, nosed over, and crashed into the ground, a fact that Admiral Yamamoto never learned. The Zeros kept buzzing around until American fighters began to take off and engage them.

Admiral Takama hastened south. So did three destroyers of the Sixth Division, stopping at Lunga Point to destroy the U.S. tug *Seminole* and a patrol boat. The Japanese reported that they were both destroyers. The Japanese ships also saw a cruiser. Actually, the tug and the patrol boat were there, and so were two old four-stack destroyer transports, carrying supplies to Lunga Point. The Japanese attacked them, but the destroyers escaped when several fighters from Henderson Field attacked the Takama force and bombed the Takama flagship, the cruiser *Yura*. Another bomber damaged the destroyer *Akizuki*. The Japanese then retired to the north, but the *Yura* was hit again by two waves of American bombers, and she began to burn. She was abandoned and sunk.

All during the day of October 25, at Rabaul, Admiral Kusaka's Eleventh Air Fleet basked in the warm knowledge that the airfield on Guadalcanal was in Japanese hands. Wave after wave of fighters was sent north, with orders to land at Guadalcanal. Not being able to land, they obeyed orders and stayed over the field circling, waiting, and fighting the American planes when they took off. At last, seventeen of them were shot down, and the rest limped back north, losing more planes to attrition on the way.

That night of October 25 Admiral Yamamoto issued a new order to all his fleet forces:

ATTACK!

And the admiral went to bed hoping, even now, that the army would come through and capture Henderson Field.

But before dawn he was awakened with bad news. The report had come in from the navy liaison staff on Guadalcanal: The army had started its new attack at 10 P.M., but because the Nasu force had been decimated, there was no two-pronged attack. The Kawaguchi detachment now attacked frontally, and the result was once again failure.

What now? asked Admiral Yamamoto through his liaison man at Rabaul, but the army had no answer. They had depended on the night attack and on that solely. They had operated on the principle that their forces were superior to those of the enemy, in fire power and in numbers, and they had learned the opposite. Now, quite frankly, they did not know what to do.

At sea the Japanese and American forces were moving closer to one another finally, because of Admiral Yamamoto's direct order to Admiral Nagumo. The Japanese fighting fleet consisted of three units: Admiral Nagumo's strike force, with the carriers *Zuikaku* and the flagship *Shokaku*; Admiral Mikawa's destroyers and cruisers; and Admiral Kondo's Second Fleet, with two battleships, five cruisers, destroyers, and the Second Air Division, which now consisted only of the carrier *Junyo*, since the *Hiyo* was out of service. The light carrier *Zuiho* was operating separately.

Even so, the Japanese outnumbered the Americans in ships, as well as planes, with 212 to the American 172 aboard the *Enterprise* and the *Hornet*. Furthermore, the Japanese pilots of the *Shokaku* and *Zuikaku* were the best in the Japanese air navy, their experience going back to the Pearl Harbor attack.

Early in the morning the Japanese search planes located the American fleet, about 400 miles to the southeast and about 600 miles from the American base at Espiritu Santo, with a second unit about 30 miles west of Rennel Island.

Admiral Yamamoto stayed close to the situation room this day, following the progress of the battle he had sought for so long, the battle that should decide the fate of Guadalcanal in spite of the army's failure.

The task force sent off its first planes at 5:10 A.M. on October 26, with the second wave going fifty minutes later and the third wave of torpedo bombers an hour after that. The outgoing planes met the incoming American planes in midcourse. *Junyo* also reported that she was launching ten fighters and nineteen bombers to attack.

In this attack, the Japanese planes reported that they set one carrier afire, which was quite correct; they had grievously hurt the *Hornet*. They also reported that there were three carriers, which was not true—there were only two—and they reported damaging the *Enterprise* until she was dead in the water, which was not true, and sinking two battleships, which was not true either. They did torpedo the destroyer *Porter*, which later had to be sunk, and the battleship *South Dakota* was damaged and the cruiser *San Juan* badly damaged. They hit the *Enterprise*, but did not stop her operations. It was the *Hornet* that took the blows this day, and ultimately she was abandoned by Admiral Kinkaid, the commander of the American force, as he fled the battle scene to protect the last remaining American carrier in the South Pacific.

At the end of the day, Admiral Yamamoto counted up: The carrier *Zuiho* had a huge hole in her flight deck and was on her way back to Truk for repair. The *Shokaku* also was damaged. But the key message was from the chief of staff of the Seventeenth Army on Guadalcanal, and it told Admiral Yamamoto what he knew but hated to hear:

> In spite of the whole-hearted cooperation of your fleet, our attempt to capture the enemy position at Guadalcanal airfield has failed, for which I am ashamed of myself. Under the present situation, we think we are forced to make a new offensive with more strength on a much larger scale. . . .

A staff officer from Imperial General Headquarters dropped in at Truk from Tokyo on his way to Rabaul. The army was going to strengthen the whole area, bring in an area army command, and add at least seven divisions to the fight for Port Moresby and Guadalcanal. It all sounded very promising, but in his heart Admiral Yamamoto knew the battle was now lost. To be sure, he had sunk another American carrier, but Nagumo's force had picked up an American flier and he had told them about the future. They had asked about American carriers, and he had named them: *Langley, Lexington, Saratoga, Ranger, Yorktown, Enterprise, Wasp, Hornet, Essex*, and *Bonhomme Richard*. Admiral Yamamoto had never heard of most of these.

As Admiral Ugaki said in despair: "The enemy builds and christens second- and third-generation carriers as quickly as we destroy them."

So already, even before that first year of war was ended, Admiral Yamamoto's gloomy prediction had come true. "For the first six months or a year, I can run rings around the enemy, but after that. . ."

The moment of truth had arrived. The assault on Guadalcanal had failed, and so had the opportunity to win the war.

THE BITTER END

30

Emperor Hirohito had already congratulated Admiral Yamamoto with an Imperial Rescript issued in honor of the victory at the Battle of Santa Cruz, but on October 29, the Emperor indicated his strong feelings about the events on Guadalcanal so that they would be known to the sailors and soldiers of Japan:

> The Combined Fleet did great damage to the enemy fleet in the South Pacific. I commend this deeply. However, the situation in that area is still grave, so you shall make double efforts.
>
> What I would like to add on this occasion concerns the latter part of the Imperial Rescript. As Guadalcanal is the place of bitter struggle and is also an important base for the Navy, I wish you would make efforts to recapture it swiftly without being satisfied with the success at this time.

The words were honeyed, but the meaning was unmistakable; the Emperor was very much displeased with the army's performance, and the Imperial displeasure was enough to make a cabinet minister commit ritual suicide. Yamamoto and the other commanders in the South Pacific blanched at these words of chastisement and pledged themselves to retrieve the situation.

"We are deeply impressed with Your Majesty's gracious words," was the message Yamamoto sent back to Tokyo. "In view of the current grave situation, we, officers and men, will make further efforts and pledge ourselves to meet Your Majesty's wishes."

On October 30, the entire Combined Fleet assembled in Truk Harbor —a magnificent sight to behold, with the huge carriers and big battleships flanked by the cruisers and destroyers. Admiral Nagumo came aboard the flagship to report, and said he had sunk three carriers and a battleship. Yamamoto knew this was not true, but he said nothing.

The meeting with Nagumo and his staff was very painful. There had never been any love lost between Yamamoto and Nagumo, and this was apparent to their staffs. Nagumo's chief of staff was quite rude in his dealings with Admiral Ugaki. The Third Fleet Commander was bursting with pride at his accomplishments, and his staff let it be known to Admiral Ugaki that they blamed Yamamoto for the failure of the army to capture Guadalcanal. Why this should be so was obscure, except for one reason: Nagumo was boiling with anger at the direct orders received from the commander in chief to get in there and fight, and he knew that all the fleet knew about it. Of course, the whole matter went back to the old days, when the "fleet faction," and the "treaty faction" quarreled over naval policy. The "fleet faction" had had its way ultimately, and Yamamoto's survival was a matter of chagrin to Nagumo. In recent times he seemed to have taken every suggestion from Yamamoto amiss.

The day was spent carrying out ceremonial duties. Yamamoto went aboard all the vessels damaged in the fight down south, paid his respects to the souls of the dead, inspected the damage, and then attended a memorial service for all those of the Third Fleet who had been lost in battle.

Late in the morning, all the unit commanders who participated in the battle of Santa Cruz were assembled aboard the flagship for a critique. Admiral Yamamoto gave a speech, lauding them for their efforts and urging them on to greater glory in the future, when they would have to finish the job of taking Guadalcanal and destroying the enemy fleet. He said nothing about Nagumo's new failure.

Lunch was served aboard the flagship to all the senior officers of the fleet, and they made small talk about the "victory." Again nothing was said. Nagumo knew how Yamamoto felt about what had happened, but the commander in chief glossed it over for the rest, in the interest of building fleet morale. It was apparent that Nagumo would have to be dealt with, but this was not the time.

That day word came from Tokyo that there would be no further land action against Guadalcanal until the end of the year. The army had to have some time to regroup and bring in a force sufficient to do the job.

That same day Admiral Inouye, commander of the Fourth Fleet, was relieved and replaced by Vice Admiral Baron Samejima Tomoshige, and Inouye came aboard the flagship to pay his respects. He brought a macaw as a present for Admiral Ugaki, and Ugaki noted in his diary that he would probably have a lot of time to play with the bird that fall, since nothing could be expected to happen about Guadalcanal.

Yamamoto's feeling of need to take Guadalcanal very quickly was reinforced that day when a search plane found what appeared to be a new enemy airfield under construction not far from Cape Taibo. This development was one of Yamamoto's nightmares. The importance of Guadalcanal could not be overestimated.

The next few days were spent reviewing the recent battles, with an eye to improving performance. The damaged ships—*Shokaku, Zuiho*, and *Chikuma*—were all sent back to Japan for repairs. On November 4, Admiral Nagumo sailed for home on the *Zuikaku*, with orders to rebuild the carrier air group and spend some time in training the new men.

Yamamoto had a portent of things to come. Starting on November 1 the Americans stepped up their naval activity around Guadalcanal. Destroyers and cruisers appeared, bringing in transports, and then they stopped to bombard the Japanese positions on the island. This was a turnabout from a month before, and there was not much that Yamamoto could do about it, with the army having failed and his own forces somewhat in disarray. He ordered torpedo bombers to come and attack from Rabaul, but the weather in the first week of November was difficult and the bombers failed to make contact with the enemy.

Meanwhile Yamamoto still had the responsibility of supplying the forces on Guadalcanal while they waited for the new buildup. On November 6, a successful landing was made by the destroyer fleet, bringing in food and ammunition. This would be the system of the future. And Yamamoto began the construction of new airfields around Guadalcanal, the closest at Balale Island, twenty miles east of Shortlands.

By November 8, the army's plans had been revealed. The Second

Division on Guadalcanal would be withdrawn to the west, but the four mountain guns would be left south of Henderson Field with their crews, ammunition, and supplies. They would harry the enemy. The force that remained south of Koli Point would stay in the area, carrying out guerrilla warfare as long as supplies lasted.

The left bank of the Matanikau River, which had fallen to the marines, would be recaptured. Several convoys would be sent to Guadalcanal, carrying troops and supplies. The plan was to put 60,000 men on the island with supplies for twenty days and then to recapture the island in December.

On November 9, Admiral Yamamoto sent the new strike force he had assembled at Truk off to the Rabaul area. This force would support the convoys that were to move into Guadalcanal, bringing new troops and provisions for the Second Division and the survivors of all those other units dispatched to Guadalcanal in the past. The carrier *Junyo*—the only Japanese carrier left in the South Pacific—was the centerpiece of the force, which included three cruisers and a dozen destroyers.

Colonel Hashimoto, the chief of the operations section of the Imperial Army General Staff, stopped off to confer with Admiral Yamamoto on his way home to Tokyo from an inspection far down south. He reported that the situation on Guadalcanal had been much worse than anybody thought and still was. The fighting force was down to about a quarter of its potential, owing largely to disease and hunger. This was indeed bad news. And equally bad was the colonel's estimation, which agreed entirely with Yamamoto's, that nothing could be done until that airfield was captured. The American air presence on the island created an enormous roadblock to all Japan's plans in the area. And the army indicated it would not really be ready to move until about January 20.

This was most unsatisfactory. Yamamoto ordered a liaison mission sent back to Tokyo to tell Imperial General Headquarters his views on the seriousness of the Guadalcanal situation. The outcome of the war might depend on it. As if to underline Yamamoto's views, Rear Admiral Yoshitomi of the Seventh Submarine Squadron arrived at Truk on November 11 from Rabaul to report that the Allied air raids were now so often and so effective that ships had to change anchorage every day. He had given up trying to base submarines in that harbor.

On November 12, the navy liaison team on Guadalcanal reported that half a dozen cruisers and many destroyers had escorted a strong force of Allied transports to Lunga Point and supervised their unloading.

The Eleventh Air Fleet had launched a torpedo attack, but the Allied ships had shot down most of the attackers, and the enemy had then gone back to Lunga Point and resumed the unloading. This report was in sharp contrast to one received from the Eleventh Air Fleet, which depended on fliers' debriefing. The Eleventh Air Fleet report indicated that the air fleet had sunk one cruiser and set four ships on fire. It was almost as if the air fleet were reporting on an entirely different action. Given this sort of misrepresentation by the pilots, who seemed to be growing younger and less experienced every day, the future at Guadalcanal looked dimmer and dimmer.

There was one bright spot in mid-November. Yamamoto finally got rid of Admiral Nagumo. There was no way he could do this directly. The Naval Personnel Office in Tokyo had complete control of appointments below Yamamoto's own level, but there were ways. One of them was to explain to friends in Tokyo, through the liaison officers sent up to report on the South Pacific campaign, just what had happened at Santa Cruz and what had been happening since the first failure to take advantage of opportunity at Pearl Harbor. The result was that Admiral Nagumo was relieved of operational command and sent back to Japan to take command of the Sasebo Naval Base. There he could do no further harm to the war effort. Much to Yamamoto's relief, Vice Admiral Jisaburo Ozawa, a man he could trust, was appointed to command the Third Fleet.

The problem in mid-November, as Yamamoto saw it, was to hasten the construction of air bases near Guadalcanal, so that the American fleet could be attacked as it came down to deliver and protect supply missions. If this could not be done, then Guadalcanal could never be retaken, and the necessary buildup of troops and supplies could never be delivered.

How greatly the situation at sea and on land in Guadalcanal had changed was now brought home to the Japanese in an unmistakable manner. For during this period of waiting for the army to bring in sufficient force, the navy was to keep the Americans occupied and protect the Japanese troops still waiting on Guadalcanal for reinforcement and resupply.

On November 12, Rear Admiral Koki Abe was sent by the Eighth Fleet down to Guadalcanal to bombard Henderson Field and keep the number of aircraft used by the Allies down to a minimum. He had the cruiser *Nagara* and eleven destroyers out in front and the battleships *Hiei* and *Kirishima* behind. They ran down on Guadalcanal that night at eighteen knots. In recent days, the Americans had gained strength and fighting spirit from Admiral Halsey, and a large force of warships had brought a large force of transports to Lunga Point to reinforce the marines. Off Guadalcanal that night were eight destroyers and five cruisers, protecting the transports and waiting for a fight.

That evening, Admiral Abe was running in a squall, and finally he got sick of it. He was too close to land for comfort, so he made a 180-degree turn to get away and into clear water. Then he turned again 180 degrees and resumed course, having let the squall run by. But the turns separated the admiral's fighting force into two distinct units.

Then fate took a hand. It was just after 1 A.M. on Friday the 13th, traditionally an unlucky day for somebody. This day the unlucky one was Admiral Abe.

Rear Admiral Daniel Callaghan was the commander of the American force. His radar picked up the two columns of Japanese ships not far from Savo Island, the scene of that earlier cruiser disaster for the Allies. The two forces virtually ran into each other as they steamed swiftly to the confrontation. The battleship *Hiei* opened fire on the American cruiser *Atlanta* and in a few moments had killed Rear Admiral Norman Scott and all but one man on the ship's bridge. Soon the *Atlanta* was blazing and sinking. But the Americans fought back, and their destroyers came up alongside the *Hiei* so close that their small guns raked the bridge, killing Captain Suzuki and wounding Admiral Abe.

Generally speaking, the Americans were not as skillful as the Japanese at the use of torpedoes from surface craft, but this night the U.S. destroyer *Sterett* put two torpedoes into the *Hiei*.

The fight was bloody, bloody, bloody. The Japanese destroyer *Yudachi* was sunk, so was the *Akatsuki*, and the destroyer *Murasame* was badly damaged. The Americans lost the cruiser *Atlanta*, the destroyer *Barton* blew up, the *Monssen* was burned, the cruiser *Juneau* was damaged, and so was the *San Francisco*. Half a dozen American destroyers also were damaged. And after the battle the American cruiser *Juneau* blew up and sank, or so the Americans thought. Actually she was torpedoed by the submarine *I-26*.

But the terrible loss, for Japanese morale and prestige, was the loss of the battleship *Hiei* in this fight. The damage from shells and torpedoes had caused the *Hiei*'s engine room to flood, and she went dead in the water. Some of her boilers were started again, but she had lost her steering. Then she was hit by American bombers, which caused more damage. The battleship *Kirishima* was sent to tow her to Shortlands, but her skipper decided that the only way to save her was to run her aground.

Admiral Yamamoto sent a message to the captain: It might be useful to put a destroyer alongside to act as *Hiei*'s lost rudder. But more planes came over, and she was torpedoed two more times. The battleship division commander lost confidence in his ability to save her. He said he was going to sink her with torpedoes. What he did not say at the moment was that his fleet was in terrible shape; every one of his destroyers had suffered some damage in the recent fight, some of them very serious damage.

Yamamoto wanted to save the battleship and ordered her left as she was, with a submarine to stand by until dark, and then they would see what to do. He dropped in at Admiral Ugaki's cabin to talk it over. They would have to decide soon, he said, because otherwise the Americans might send photo planes over and take pictures of the battered battleship, her 1600 men all taken off, sitting in the water like a target. The propaganda value to the enemy would be enormous, he said. And so, before the day was out, the *Hiei* was sunk and her secrets were saved from the Americans. Thus Japan lost one of her most valuable capital ships.

Yamamoto's attempts to save her had been prompted by two motives. First was the propaganda value, as noted. But second was a nagging feeling, growing stronger all the time, that the Japanese navy was being whittled down constantly by attrition, without any hope of rebuilding fast enough to affect the outcome of the war. The supply of fuel in Japan had fallen to a million tons of oil, and Imperial General Headquarters had made permanent its instructions to the fleet to use the Borneo resources and keep the fleet in southern waters, close to the source of supply. Steel, aluminum, copper, and the hundred other materials that went to build a battleship were likewise in desperately short supply in the homeland. All this while, every time Yamamoto turned around, he encountered the names of new vessels launched by the Americans. As he had foreseen, the American productive capacity was getting into high gear.

The good news on November 14 was that the cruisers *Suzuya* and *Maya* had joined the light cruiser *Tenryu* and a destroyer to bombard Guadalcanal again and had apparently been successful, according to reports from observers ashore there. Many fires on the airfield were noted, and the ships suffered no losses. But the bad news was that the support force for this action ran into serious trouble. The cruisers *Chokai, Kinugasa,* and *Isuzu* were caught by carrier bombers off New Georgia Island. The *Kinugasa*'s captain and executive officer were killed, and the torpedo officer had to take command. Then she flooded and sank. The *Chokai* was set afire and so was the *Isuzu,* but both managed to make Shortlands, protected by destroyers.

Then came more bad news for Admiral Yamamoto: The second big convoy bound for Guadalcanal since the failure of the attack against the airfield had left Shortlands on the afternoon of November 14, but it was picked up and shadowed by a B-17 bomber that afternoon. More bombers attacked. Two big transports were sunk, the *Nagara Maru* and the *Canberra Maru,* and three were damaged. Rear Admiral Raizo Tanaka, commander of the destroyer squadron entrusted with the resupply program, decided to withdraw back toward Shortlands, but Admiral Yamamoto ordered him to turn around and resume the voyage. Guadalcanal must be resupplied that night.

All right, said Tanaka, he would run the convoy down to Guadalcanal and ground the transports. He had to take such desperate measures because the sea was now alive with American ships and the air filled with Allied planes. All that Yamamoto had feared was coming to pass; he was being outnumbered by the forces of an enemy that he could have defeated just a year earlier.

That afternoon, the flagship was numbed by more bad news: Search planes had found one group of four cruisers and destroyers eighty miles south of Guadalcanal, another group that included a carrier and two battleships to its northwest, and a third group that was said to include two battleships to the east. Of course, some of this was misidentification of ships by the search planes, but the fact was that the Allied fleet was growing very fast, and Admiral Yamamoto's power to stop them was decreasing. The carriers *Shokaku* and *Zuikaku,* sent home for repair, would not be back down before the end of the year. The Eleventh Air Fleet at Rabaul was so badly decimated by too many missions and too many losses, at Guadalcanal and over New Guinea, that it could not even launch an attack on these Allied ships because it had sent its only effective strike force to New Guinea a few hours earlier.

Yamamoto had already told Tokyo that they would have to rebuild the Eleventh Air Fleet, but again this was going to take time, and he had no time.

* * *

Admiral Tanaka's convoy continued south. It was whittled down to four transports now and only five protecting destroyers. Tanaka reported to Yamamoto that they would reach Guadalcanal at 11 P.M. and could run the transports aground there. Yamamoto said nothing, but the commander of the Eighth Fleet told Tanaka not to run aground but to stand offshore, not anchoring, and then in the morning, if the enemy attacked them, to run aground.

Separately that night the battleship *Kirishima*, the cruisers *Atago* and *Takao*, a light cruiser, and six destroyers were going down to bombard the airfield again. And so there was another naval and air engagement. The Americans called it the end of the Battle of Guadalcanal, but the Japanese thought of it as a separate struggle. The result was that the supply convoy was beached, the battleship *Kirishima* was sunk, and so was the destroyer *Ayanami*. The Japanese claimed two cruisers and two destroyers sunk and three battleships, one destroyer, and one cruiser damaged. But no matter the claims, the losses were far too heavy on the Japanese side. All four of the grounded supply ships were set afire, and many of the supplies were lost. And equally serious for the future, eleven big transports loaded with supplies had been sent out, and only four of them had arrived, burning, and with much of their loads lost. The effort to supply Guadalcanal had to be regarded as essentially a failure. Admiral Yamamoto apologized to General Hayukatake. For the first time, the navy had not been able to complete its task.

Of a total of 20,000 men, only 2000 got ashore, along with 360 cases of ammunition and 1500 bales of rice. It was not enough to supply the Seventeenth Army forces for more than two or three days. There had been 30,000 men on Guadalcanal, 5000 of them sick and needing evacuation. Now there were 32,000 men and no supplies. The convoy, by bringing in another 2000 men to feed and taking none off, had simply added to the army's problems.

Now there were no more transports, and even if there had been, it was obviously suicidal to send them to Guadalcanal, where the air and the sea were both controlled by the Americans. Yamamoto had to devise some other method to carry out the resupply. He put his staff to work, and they began experimenting with such devices as half filling gasoline drums with rice, which would then be dropped off a destroyer and picked up on the shore. Desperate measures indeed!

On November 16, Yamamoto ordered that half the two army battalions scheduled to leave Rabaul the next day be transported by destroyers. As if Yamamoto did not have enough troubles, the news came this day that the Allies were advancing rapidly on Buna. If Buna and Salamaua fell into Allied hands, the Port Moresby invasion was finished, and the South Seas Detachment fighting in New Guinea would be lost. Already the Seventeenth Army staff was talking about abandoning Buna, which would mean that Rabaul would become untenable all too soon. Now attention turned to New Guinea.

Yamamoto stopped to assess his situation. Just three months earlier he had taken the *Yamato* and the other ships of the Combined Fleet out of the Hashirajima anchorage and headed south. And what had been accomplished? Really nothing. The war was going worse and more quickly than he had expected.

At this point, Admiral Yamamoto had to watch as the Americans resupplied Guadalcanal; his efforts had to be directed at trying to stop the disaster building at Buna in New Guinea, where the Allies had surrounded Buna village in the past three days.

He rushed the Tenth Destroyer Division to Buna, carrying 800 troops. That day, November 21, observers saw five Allied destroyers and two transports enter the Lunga Roads and begin unloading. There was absolutely nothing Admiral Yamamoto could do to stop it.

The situation was so serious that the admiral called a conference. Lieutenant General Imamura, the new area army chief, and Lieutenant Colonel Tsuji, the representative of Imperial General Headquarters, came from Rabaul to meet aboard the *Yamato*. Tsuji said he was going to ask Tokyo to send down the Twenty-First Mixed Brigade and a regiment from the Philippines to throw into Buna.

General Imamura had obviously already given up Buna in his own mind and spoke of defending the Lae Salamaua line. But Yamamoto, the airman, reminded the army that the Allies were building several airstrips around Buna, and if these were completed and the area was in Allied hands, then the air attacks on Rabaul would increase and the situation there would become ever more difficult. But Imamura said he simply could not fight the war on all those fronts and that Buna was going to have to be sacrificed.

At the end of the conference everyone knew the situation was desperate in the South Pacific.

* * *

So as November moved to its close, Yamamoto had hard lines to study. His chief of staff, Admiral Ugaki, summed it all up starkly in his diary: "The situation there offers no optimism at all."

Admiral Yamamoto felt very much personally involved in the fate of Guadalcanal. Lieutenant General H. Adachi visited the flagship on his way to Rabaul, where he would take over the Eighteenth Army to fight a new battle in New Guinea. He and the staff he brought down had come from North China, and they knew nothing about the area or about fighting Americans. Yamamoto and his staff had to correct the usual army misunderstanding, a result of the army's own propaganda. The Americans, the navy told the army, were neither effete nor cowardly, but were very powerful fighters with "fervent fighting spirit."

At dinner the conversation turned to the conduct of the Second Division on Guadalcanal, and particularly of the Sixteenth Regiment, which had collapsed under pressure. Yamamoto observed that unless the Sixteenth did better, he was not going to be able to go home to Nagaoka. This Nagaoka Regiment had failed because of the incompetence of its regimental and battalion commanders, and he had already sent messages encouraging them to clear up the past dishonor. Probably, he said, they would not come back alive. In fact, he said, he, too, would not be able to go back home again unless Guadalcanal was recaptured. Gone now from the table was any talk of getting home. Yamamoto had earlier told Admiral Ugaki that they would plan to take the flagship back to Kure in the spring, but no longer. The naval disasters around Guadalcanal, and the supply disaster in particular, had changed everything. All this was said in a bantering way, but everyone at the table recognized Admiral Yamamoto's pain.

Meanwhile, the desperate attempts to supply Guadalcanal continued. On November 25, the submarine *I-19* tried, but arrived in the Tassafaronga area and found it heavily defended by the Americans, so she gave up the attempt. The *I-17* surfaced, sighted an enemy PT boat near the shore, and submerged. She came back again off the Japanese-held coast and surfaced again, but the landing craft she expected did not show up. Her captain saw blinking lights ashore but did not understand them, so he drew off and submerged again. Another failure.

And the chief of staff of the Seventeenth Army was clamoring for help.

On November 26, the *I-17* finally did manage to get inshore and unloaded eleven tons of supplies.

And what was this? The staff reports told Admiral Yamamoto that the Allies were bringing in at least two transports a day to supply their forces. All of them were protected by cruisers and destroyers, as well as by many aircraft.

Yes, the balance had changed completely. The sea and air around Guadalcanal, day and night, were Allied sea and air now, and the Japanese risked everything when they came up to the island.

By the end of November, Admiral Yamamoto's feelings about Guadalcanal were beginning to change. The American radio had announced that the island was "secured," and although this was premature, Yamamoto knew the Japanese were at the point of no return in terms of reconquest of the island. The army was now talking senselessly about the coming offensive against Guadalcanal, when Yamamoto knew that he would not have the seapower to undertake that offensive. New Guinea was strategically more important than Guadalcanal, but he did not have the resources to undertake the resupply of New Guinea either.

On November 27 another submarine succeeded in landing twenty tons of supply to the Japanese at Camimbo. The chief of staff of the Seventeenth Army was effusive in his thanks, an indication of the desperate plight of the army on Guadalcanal.

On November 30 the destroyers began the attempt to resupply Guadalcanal by loading drums with supplies and casting them offshore in the hope they would drift ashore. But from the Seventeenth Army came this forlorn report:

Supplies received, for 32,000 men, between November 25 and 28:

Rice	2850 bags
Biscuits	704 cases
Canned fish	246 cases
Soy sauce	156 cases
Salt fish	80 cases
Salt	8 cases
Sugar	4 cases
Powdered soy paste (miso)	106 cases

As Admiral Ugaki put it, this was just chicken feed.

As Admiral Yamamoto considered the deteriorating military situation, he grew snappish and sometimes unloaded his frustrations on poor Chief of Staff Ugaki, but Ugaki rolled with the punches. He knew his commander. Yamamoto's temper might flare, but he would forget the irritation very quickly, and not the issues.

In the next few days, more battles were fought: the battle called Tassafaronga, at which the Americans took a beating again at sea but recovered immediately, and the affair in which the destroyer *Takanami* was sunk. But, as always these days, the Japanese emerged from these fights poorer than the enemy, even if they "won." For the supply missions were simply not being filled, and the Seventeenth Army was pleading now for resumption of some sort of supply system by any means at all.

Enemy transports came into Lunga roads regularly to unload supplies. Yamamoto permitted the use of a midget submarine here, and it attacked three transports on the night of December 3, shot two torpedoes, and submerged. The submarine was attacked and sank, but the crew was saved.

Ten destroyers ran down to Guadalcanal on December 3, jettisoning 1500 drums of supplies. But only a third of the supplies got ashore, the people on Guadalcanal indicated.

By December, the hopelessness of the Guadalcanal situation was beyond further concealment. Only half the men on the island were capable of fighting. The rest were suffering from beriberi or malaria, and men were dropping at the rate of about 5000 a month. Supplies came in by trickle, and many units had none at all. The commanders and staffs of Eleventh Air Fleet, Eighth Fleet, Second Fleet, and Fourth Fleet all agreed with Admiral Yamamoto and his staff that it was time to do something drastic. Yamamoto sent two staff officers to Tokyo to recommend most strongly that the Guadalcanal position be evacuated as quickly as possible and the whole operation in the South Pacific be turned to defense for the moment. Now all they could do was wait for the orders to come to try to rescue what was left of the more than 32,000 men who had been landed on Guadalcanal.

"A GREAT LOSS SUSTAINED . . ."

31

The miscalculations of the Imperial Japanese Army in the autumn of 1942 cost Japan its chance to recover Guadalcanal. By early December it was apparent that the American air forces had grown so strong that the Japanese troops on the island could not be successfully resupplied.

The Americans were sending two or three transports every day to supply the marines, and new fresh American army troops were coming to Guadalcanal. A Japanese fleet pilot flying over the island reported that there were now six airstrips on Guadalcanal. No wonder, then, that the resupply missions ran into constant trouble. They were harried on the high sea by B-17s, whose crews had learned how to hit ship targets in the past few months. They were harried in the Solomons by planes from the "Cactus Air Force" of Guadalcanal and planes of the land-based air forces operating out of Noumea. At night they were harried by PBY bombers. On moonlit nights it was virtually impossible for the destroyers to operate without being attacked.

Yet Admiral Yamamoto did not try to alibi the navy's responsibility for the failures. On December 8, he sent a staff officer to Rabaul to try to work out details of future planning with General Imamura's people. Yamamoto told the staff officer to tell the army that the navy took the responsibility for its own unpreparedness at Guadalcanal.

That said, then what was to be done? The real problem was troop supply. For example, on December 7, the anniversary of the beginning of the Pacific war, Admiral Ugaki noted in his diary that so many Allied transports were landing supplies at Guadalcanal "that it was rather too much trouble to make notes about them." As for the Japanese, a flotilla of eleven destroyers under the Fifteenth Destroyer Division set out for Guadalcanal that day but was attacked by fourteen bombers and forty fighters. The destroyer *Nowacke* was hit so badly she became unnavigable. The destroyer *Arashi* was damaged badly in the boiler room. The flotilla turned back, taking the damaged ships in tow.

Now the Japanese subcommanders began to become fretful. Admiral Mikawa of the Eighth Fleet and Admiral Kusaka of the Eleventh Air Fleet questioned the advisability of continuing operations against Guadalcanal. It was too costly, they said. But Admiral Yamamoto was pledged to support the army and the thousands of troops undergoing so much hardship on the island. That the hardship was real, there was no doubt. Captain Monzen Kanae, the navy garrison commander on Guadalcanal, sent a visiting card back to Admiral Ugaki with a scribbled note:

Hardships and shortages have reached beyond the limit this time. We have had no wine, no smoking, reduced rations, no tea, no salt. But fortunately I am fine and burning with the spirit of revenge. . . .

This was all very well, but the spirit of revenge did not recover Guadalcanal and did not feed the troops.

The problem was the same at Buna in New Guinea. On December 11, the garrison there reported that it had only 150 rounds of ammunition left for its two antiaircraft guns. And Allied air power was interdicting resupply here too. Two hundred Japanese soldiers tried to move overland from Basabua to Buna. Only nine of them made it.

On December 11, another attempt was made to resupply Guadalcanal. The destroyers reached the island, but there they were attacked by American PT boats, and the destroyer *Terutsuki* was torpedoed. Half the crew were rescued, and the rest swam ashore, but the ship was sunk by the Japanese because she was unnavigable. The first report indicated that the destroyers landed 1200 cases of provisions, but later it was discovered that they actually landed only 200 cases.

The same difficulty now existed at Buna. On December 13, five destroyers left the Admiraltes for Buna. They were shadowed by B-17s all the way. On December 14 they reached Manbale, north of Buna, and unloaded there. The 800 men and supplies would have to be taken to Buna by landing craft.

By December 19 the attacking Australians in the Buna area had taken part of the airfield. But the Japanese were still holding out.

On Guadalcanal the situation grew more desperate by the day. The Japanese soldiers were sick with dengue, malaria, and dysentery. They suffered from beriberi and starvation. Only one man in five was capable of fighting. The Eighth Army still insisted that destroyers must be used to bring in supplies and troops, but Yamamoto was running out of destroyers. In the past three weeks, *Nowacke, Arashi, Asashio, Isonami, Terutsuki,* and *Sawakaze* were either sunk or put out of action. The light cruiser *Tenryu* was also sunk. So how could Admiral Yamamoto continue to supply Guadalcanal?

Desperate attempts were made with submarines and air drops. But the submarines were too often detected by PT boats, and the air drops too often fell wide of target.

Admiral Yamamoto and the army were agreed that at least five divisions had to be brought down to Guadalcanal to recapture the island. At the moment they were waiting for decisions from Tokyo as to the future. Until Tokyo took some action, there was very little to be done.

In Tokyo heads were rolling. Colonel Hattori, the army staff chief of operations, was dismissed because of the failure on Guadalcanal, and his boss, Major General Tanaka, chief of the operations bureau, was transferred out as well. These changes were welcomed by Admiral Yamamoto, who for four or five years had nursed a feeling of intense dislike for all things and all people army. He felt they were responsible for the plight in which Japan now found itself, the war definitely turning around and Japan going on the defensive. Lieutenant Colonel Tsuji of the General Staff had not impressed him very well; he did not trust Lieutenant Colonel Tsuji. He did not trust any of them.

At this point, Admiral Yamamoto wanted Admiral Fukudome to come down to the Solomons and New Guinea to see for himself what the problems were and what had to be done. But the days went by and no one came.

On Guadalcanal the troops cried out for orders to attack. They would rather charge into the face of the enemy, even hopelessly, than sit there and starve to death. From Tokyo came word that the resupply of Guadalcanal was to be continued no matter the losses.

The new chief of the army operations section, Colonel Sanada, came down to Rabaul and on his way home to Tokyo stopped off at Truk to confer with Admirals Yamamoto and Ugaki. The situation on Guadalcanal, he admitted, was far more serious than anyone in Tokyo had believed. He spoke of sending 10,000 men, and then of sending another two divisions. But he was talking about January and February.

All very well, said the admirals, but did he realize that, the way things were going, only about half those troops would ever arrive and only about a third would be equipped and capable of fighting? What was needed was control of the air, and that meant a lot more planes than either the army or the navy was providing. The navy did not have the planes or the pilots. Typical was a new fighter group that arrived to join the Eleventh Air Fleet at Rabaul. Of sixty pilots, forty-four had no experience in Zero fighters. They all had to be trained. The army simply would not use their planes and pilots, saving them for land offensives. The protection of the island areas was a naval responsibility, said the generals. On December 24, the Buna garrison reported that the end was very near. It came four days later.

Colonel Sanada went back to Tokyo to recommend the abandonment of Guadalcanal and concentration on New Guinea by the army. The desperate situation on Guadalcanal was underlined by the chief of staff of the Seventeenth Army, who reported to Yamamoto that the men were keeping alive by eating coconuts, tree buds, and seaweed. They were so weak they could not even send out a patrol.

On December 30 it became apparent aboard the flagship that the situation on Guadalcanal was hopeless. The army simply had stalled too long, and Tokyo was not supplying the extra ships and planes that would be necessary to reinforce the island.

Finally, on January 3, Admiral Fukudome, the chief of the operations bureau of the Naval General Staff, and his newly appointed army counterpart arrived at Truk. General Imamura's people arrived from Rabaul. And there on the flagship the decision was made: Guadalcanal was to be evacuated and the major effort of army and navy was to be first the capture of Port Moresby and second the recapture of Guadalcanal. No timetable was set for the latter.

Admiral Yamamoto assembled his destroyers, and on February 1, 1943, the evacuation of the troops from Guadalcanal began. It was the most successful destroyer operation in months, carried out in the dark of the moon. A cruiser led twenty destroyers down to the island night after night, and they came back carrying the half-dead troops. Yamamoto had expected they might lose half the destroyers, but they were very skillful and very lucky. One destroyer was lost, the *Makigumo*, but no more, largely due to the herculean efforts of Admiral Kusaka's Eleventh Air Fleet, which put all its fighters in the air above Guadalcanal these nights.

By February 8 the evacuation was complete. They had taken off 13,000 men, and they had left about 24,000 dead behind them, most of them victims of starvation and disease. Guadalcanal was now irrevocably in Allied hands.

ASSASSINATION OF AN ADMIRAL

3
2

Although Guadalcanal was lost, and so was Buna on the New Guinea coast, the Japanese High Command in Tokyo did not think of giving up the battle for the South Pacific. Instead, with the approval of General Tojo, who had now assumed the mantles of war minister and chief of the Imperial General Staff as well as Prime Minister, the Japanese created a new plan.

They would concentrate on the attack on New Guinea, and once that battle was won, they would come back and take Guadalcanal. This decision had been made on December 31 in an Imperial Conference, at which the Emperor had issued a Rescript outlining the future:

Today the finest of the Japanese Empire's army, navy, and air units are gathered. Sooner or later they will head toward the Solomon Islands, where a decisive battle is being fought between Japan and America.

So at the beginning of 1943, forces were shifted from Manchuria and China to the South Pacific, and more planes and ships were brought into the South Pacific.

Although Admiral Yamamoto had been distressed at the loss of two battleships in the last days of the Guadalcanal campaign, he still had a strong fighting force, and it would be stronger as soon as the carriers returned from repairs in Japan. He still felt it was possible to achieve the "decisive sea battle" if it could be done swiftly. He knew that the Americans were building carriers furiously, but they still did not have them in the South Pacific.

Admiral Yamamoto moved his advance air bases back to Kolombangara and New Georgia Islands. And as of February the navy undertook the delivery of supplies to both navy and army troops in the Solomon Islands. The first supply mission was carried out without incident by three destroyers, which went to Kolombangara on February 13, 1943.

The new plans devised in Tokyo called for a major military operation, supported by the Combined Fleet, to begin from Lae, the Japanese base in Papua. It was to start in March. The Imperial High Command did not know that the Allies were going to start a two-pronged campaign in February, first to move up the Solomon Island chain and isolate Rabaul and second to move up New Guinea to the Vogelkap and prepare to jump off to the Philippines. No, despite the definite defeats at Buna and Guadalcanal, the Japanese were still thinking offensively, not defensively. But in the new army-navy agreement drawn at the end of 1941, it was agreed that all troops would be evacuated from the Solomons south of New Georgia Island. This meant pulling out the garrisons of the Russells and several other smaller groups of islands, and it was done. Consequently, when the Americans began their drive on the Russells in February, they found no enemy there to oppose them.

January was devoted by the Japanese to buildup. The Eleventh Air Fleet at Rabaul was reinvigorated with pilots and new planes. Plans were laid for resumption of the air attack on Guadalcanal. Admiral Yamamoto knew very well that he must somehow achieve control of the skies before he could achieve control of the sea. Guadalcanal had been a great lesson to him.

And here was the plan: From the four big air bases in and around Rabaul, Japanese navy planes would stage down to Buka base on the northern tip of Bougainville. Another base they would use was at Buin, on the southern end of Bougainville. There were three other major air bases at Ballale, and Vila, and Munda on New Georgia, which was the closest to the Americans in the south.

But as the resupply missions for the southern Solomons began in

February, Admiral Yamamoto immediately noticed a difference. Now it was even more difficult to run ships to New Georgia and Kolombangara than it had been in the Guadalcanal campaign, because the Americans, Australians, and New Zealanders were building up their air forces very rapidly. Vice Admiral Aubrey W. Fitch, the very experienced air task force commander (*Lexington* in the Battle of the Coral Sea), had taken over as director of land-based air forces, and he operated out of Espiritu Santo Island. The center of all this activity as far as the Solomons was concerned was Guadalcanal, which now housed two fighter airstrips and two bomber airstrips. By February, the Allies had 300 planes on Guadalcanal.

Admiral Yamamoto's second supply mission to the southern Solomons was carried out on February 19. The Japanese ships were attacked from the air, but they made the trip all right, unloaded their supplies, and returned to Rabaul.

The successful American landings in the Russell Islands brought new problems for Admiral Yamamoto, however. On all moonlit nights of the future, he could expect night air attacks on his convoys. There was only one way to escape them, and that was to limit the resupply missions to the ten nights of the dark of the moon each month.

So, as March approached, Admiral Yamamoto told the army they would have to reinforce their garrisons on New Georgia and Kolombangara against American assault, and they did so. The second phase of the Solomons battle was approaching.

On February 27, Yamamoto's ships again successfully ran a supply mission down to Kolombangara, although they lost the *Kirikazwa Maru* to American bombers on the return voyage.

On the night of March 5, however, the destroyers *Murasame* and *Minegumo* set out from the Shortlands base with provisions for the garrison of the airfield at Vila on Kolombangara, and both ships were sunk by an American task force. Admiral Yamamoto did not know it, but the Americans now had four task forces operating in the South Pacific, and his job was going to become more difficult every week.

At the end of February, Admiral Yamamoto had the right idea, but very little information. The idea was that he had to destroy Allied air power in the South Pacific before much else could be done. His intelligence was extremely faulty, and he had no idea of the enormous buildup then being undertaken by the Fifth U.S. Army Air Force to support General MacArthur's campaign in New Guinea. The Americans were still short of ships and troops to send to the South Pacific, but they were getting caught up with their airplane building program and their very efficient pilot training program and so had plenty of planes to send. Heavy B-17 and B-24 bombers, medium B-25, B-26, and A-20 attack bombers, and new fighters, including the very fast P-38 twin-engined fighter interceptor planes, were arriving in Australia week after week.

The next move planned in the South Pacific was the capture of Wau Airfield on Papua, which controlled the Huon Gulf. Troops of the Japanese Fifty-first Division were to do this job, and they were to be taken to New Guinea from Rabaul by the navy. Eight transports and cargo ships set out, guarded by eight destroyers. But on March 2 this convoy was beset by an enormous Allied air armada, which represented the buildup of the Fifth U.S. Army Air Force. In two days of air attacks, despite heavy cover of fighters provided by the Japanese air forces at Rabaul, the Allied planes decimated the New Guinea convoy. At one point a lookout aboard a Japanese ship counted more than a hundred Allied planes overhead. The transports were sunk, and so were most of the destroyers. It was the worst single day in the history of the Japanese forces in the South Pacific. The few troops that did get ashore straggled in at the wrong places and the wrong times. The supplies mostly went down to the bottom of the sea. On the night of March 3, American PT boats appeared around Dampier Strait to finish off the convoy.

At Rabaul, on March 10, the army and navy commands assessed the situation. Seven thousand men had set out, and three thousand of them had not made it to Lae. The naval reinforcement had been a failure, and the army decided thereafter that all reinforcement and supply would have to be by barge. So the tables were turned, and Yamamoto's fleet was defeated in this battle, not by sea forces, but by air forces, as Yamamoto had feared.

The first part of March was equally disastrous for the Combined Fleet in the Solomons. The resupply missions to New Georgia and Kolombangara ran into constant trouble. But Yamamoto persevered, and at Rabaul he supervised the rebuilding of the Eleventh Air Fleet.

In March, a new argument raged at Imperial General Headquarters in Tokyo. The army claimed that Yamamoto was not giving sufficient support to the campaign to capture New Guinea. Yamamoto's representatives claimed that it was necessary to knock out the big American air base at Guadalcanal before he could undertake any significant operations. Since the army dominated Imperial General Headquarters, the army won, but they did agree to let Yamamoto make a major effort against Guadalcanal in the air, without committing any land forces.

And so was born Operation I, a campaign to knock out Allied air power in the Solomons and New Guinea. Admiral Yamamoto ordered down the carriers *Shokaku, Zuikaku, Zuiho, Junyo*, and *Hiyo* to help with this operation.

The Eleventh Air Fleet brought in scores of new planes and pilots. The carrier planes were taken ashore at Rabaul to operate with the Eleventh Air Fleet. Together the force was the largest yet used by the Japanese in the South Pacific. On April 1 they sent sixty fighters over Guadalcanal. The Americans put up forty planes. In the fighting, the Japanese lost eighteen planes and the Americans six. Six months earlier the loss ratios would probably have been the reverse, but in those six months the Americans had matured, the Japanese had lost most of their best pilots, and the American aircraft coming off the production lines were found to be superior to the Japanese planes.

Operation I was scheduled to begin on April 7. It was in two parts, one to hit Guadalcanal and the second to hit New Guinea. Just after 7 A.M. on April 3, Admiral Yamamoto participated in a ceremony aboard the flagship in Truk harbor honoring the birthday of the Emperor Jimmu, the first Japanese ruler. Then at 7:15 he and members of his staff left the ship and traveled by flying boat to Rabaul and broke out Yamamoto's flag at the Southeast Area Fleet office there. That evening Yamamoto dined with Admiral Kusaka, commander of the Eleventh Air Fleet, Admiral Ozawa, commander of the Southeast Area Fleet, and Admiral Mikawa, commander of the Eighth Fleet. Yamamoto was suffering from beriberi and tension and was very tired, so he went up the hill to the quarters of the Eighth Fleet and to bed at 7:30 that night. But he was jolly enough. He discussed his habit of writing down significant poetry from Emperor Meiji's hand in a little diary he kept in his pocket, and at Admiral Ugaki's request (Ugaki was something of a scholar), he lent the chief of staff the diary for the night.

The day after Yamamoto's arrival was April 4, his sixtieth birthday. He went down to the Rabaul Field, where the 204th Air Group was located. This was the major field of operations for the Zero fighters of the Eleventh Air Fleet. Captain Yochiro Miyano, the commander, assembled the men, and Admiral Yamamoto in his snow white uniform mounted the platform, paid obeisance to the picture of the Emperor, and then told the men about Operation I and the need for absolute success:

> Now we are approaching the difficult battle, a sequel to the last one. However difficult a time we are having, the enemy also has to be suffering. Now we must attack his precious carriers with Rabaul's great air strength, and cut them down so they cannot escape. Our hopes go with you. Do your best.

The planes could not take off that day. The weather was too bad. The next day, and the next, and the next, the rain came down in buckets. But April 7 dawned bright and sunny, and there also came to Rabaul the electrifying news that the Americans had massed a large task force around Guadalcanal—five heavy cruisers, ten destroyers, and ten transports. So the young men took off.

Admiral Yamamoto came down to the field in his white uniform and stood on the sidelines quietly, watching them go. The planes revved up and roared off, and the last sight they saw behind them was the figure of the admiral on the field, waving his cap.

They came back reporting great victories over the Allied air forces and the sinking of a number of Allied warships off Guadalcanal. On April 9, Emperor Hirohito sent Yamamoto a telegram of congratulations.

For four days, the Japanese made massive raids. Each time a flight took off, Admiral Yamamoto was there on the field, in his white uniform with the gold braid, waving his cap and smiling. The effect was magical, the morale of the Eleventh Air Fleet had never been higher. More than six hundred Japanese planes took part in this series of attacks. The importance of it was attested to by the commander in chief's presence on the field at every takeoff.

Between flights, Yamamoto would climb back up the hill to Kusaka's house. There he played shogi with members of the staff or talked quietly to Admiral Kusaka about air affairs or to Admiral Ugaki about fleet business.

Day after day the pilots returned to report on successes. By April 16 they were reporting that they saw no Allied planes on the airfields and that the Japanese planes had mastery of the air. The Emperor sent more congratulations, and Imperial General Headquarters called off Operation I, declaring it a great success. Here was the Japanese assessment of the operation:

Results and Losses of Operation I

Operations (Dates of Execution)	Planes Participated	Vessels	Airfields	Planes Shot Down	Losses
X 7 April	157 fighters 67 bombers	2 large, 6 medium, 2 small transports, 1 cruiser, 1 DD sunk; 1 medium, 1 small transport seriously damaged; 1 large trans- port slightly damaged		41 (31)	12 fighters 9 bombers
Y-2 11 April	71 fighters 21 bombers	2 medium, 1 small 1 DD sunk		21 (9)	2 fighters 4 bombers
Y 12 April	131 fighters 43 medium bombers	1 large trans- port sunk	11 places afire at Port Moresby (3 big explo- sions included)	28 (7)	2 fighters 6 medium bombers
Y-1 14 April	52 fighters 37 medium bombers	1 large, 1 medium transport sunk; 2 to 3 small transports damaged	5 places afire at Rabi	27 (6)	5 medium bombers

Continued

Results and Losses of Operation I *(Continued)*

Operations (Dates of Execution)	Planes Participated	Vessels	Airfields	Planes Shot Down	Losses
Y-2 14 April	75 fighters 23 bombers	2 large, 1 medium transport sunk; 2 large, 3 medium, 1 small transport seriously damaged; several other ships damaged		17 (3)	2 fighters 3 bombers

Condition of Planes Expended

Classifications	Planes Prepared	Planes Lost	Percentage
Carrier fighters	206	25	12
Carrier bombers	81	21	26
Land medium bombers	83	15	18

These were the results reported to Admiral Yamamoto, and they were very welcome to him. (Unfortunately, they were very inaccurate and most misleading, for the Americans had really suffered relatively little damage, especially in comparison to the enormous buildup of forces that was underway.)

So Operation I came to an end.

When they had first arrived at Rabaul, Admiral Yamamoto and Admiral Ugaki had suggested that they go down to the front line to visit the pilots and ground crews at the fighting air bases. Both men knew there was danger involved, but Yamamoto wanted to impress on his airmen the absolute necessity of maintaining control in the air. If they did not, he said, there was no hope of winning in the South Pacific. He had the feeling that Admiral Kusaka and his subordinates had been remiss in not going to the front bases before to encourage the men there.

Just after the Operation I's success was announced, General Imamura of the Eighteenth Area Army went down to New Guinea himself. He came back to report that if another battalion or two could be sent there, the Japanese should be able to hold on.

But Imamura also reported that he had had a very narrow escape on the flight. While they were in the air, on their way from Buin to New Guinea, they had been jumped by about thirty American fighters. Only because the pilot was very skillful and ducked into cloud cover did they escape being attacked. The word about that trip redoubled Admiral Yamamoto's determination to visit his own front-line bases in the Shortlands, at Buin and Buka, to urge his people onward.

They would fly down in two "Betty" bombers, Yamamoto in one and Ugaki in the other, since it was Yamamoto's rule never to have the commander and the chief of staff in the same aircraft.

All this information was given to the communications section, and for some reason they sent a long, detailed message about Admiral Yamamoto's itinerary to all places concerned. Down at the Shortlands, Rear Admiral Joshima, the commander there, told his staff that this was indeed a very foolish thing to do. For he was not at all sure that the Americans were not monitoring Japanese communications, and he was worried, because of some recent events, that the Americans had somehow managed to break the Japanese naval code. On April 17, Joshima felt so strongly about the dangers that he flew up to Rabaul to warn Admiral Yamamoto.

But Yamamoto would not agree to cancel the trip. "I've let them know, and they have got things ready. I'll leave tomorrow morning and be back by dark. Why don't we have dinner together?"

On the night before leaving, Yamamoto and Ugaki discussed the sort of uniforms they should wear. Yamamoto was thinking of wearing a white open-necked shirt, but Ugaki persuaded him that they should wear the new formal dark green field uniform instead, so Yamamoto put it on that morning. He was to have his picture taken in that uniform, but for some reason the photographer did not show up.

As Admiral Yamamoto dressed early that morning, in his own room in Admiral Kusaka's house, he absently stuffed a wad of clean white toilet paper into a pocket and a clean white handkerchief into another.

He put the pocket diary in his left-hand breast pocket and buttoned it. He put on the black airmen's boots that slipped off so easily and attached the medal ribbons to his left breast. He put on his sword belt and short samurai formal sword, one made by the famous swordsmith Sadayoshi Amada of Niigata, his home prefecture, a sword given him years ago by his older brother Yihachi.

The others—Paymaster Kitamura, staff officers Imanaka and Muroi, and Weather Officer Unno—met Yamamoto in the dining room. Then they all went out and waited in front of the house for the cars that would take them to the airport.

Admiral Yamamoto took the pilot's seat in his aircraft, and Admiral Ugaki took the pilot's seat in his. But the copilots actually did the takeoffs, since they were familiar with the area.

The planes taxied down the runway and were off, circling above the twin volcanoes of the mouth of the bay and then heading southeast. They flew at about 5000 feet, with nine fighters in V formations of three to the right, the left, and behind them. Ugaki looked over at the command plane and saw Admiral Yamamoto in the pilot's seat and the others moving around in the plane.

They reached the west side of Bougainville and headed over the jungle at about 2000 feet. In Admiral Ugaki's plane, the pilot handed the admiral a piece of paper. "Expect to arrive Ballale at 7:45," it said. Ugaki looked at his wristwatch. It was just 7:30.

Suddenly, the plane went into a steep dive, and Admiral Ugaki looked out. They were following Admiral Yamamoto's plane. In a moment they knew the reason: One of the protective fighters had spotted a group of twenty-four enemy planes and had jinked down to warn the lead "Betty." The pilot—whether it was Yamamoto at the controls or not no one will ever know, but he was still sitting in the left-hand seat—suddenly dropped down just over the jungle to try to escape the enemy.

Aboard the two bombers the crewmen opened the gun ports and got ready to fire. The Zero fighters were already engaging the enemy planes, which were P-38 twin-engined twin-nacelle fighters.

As Admiral Ugaki described the events in his diary,

By the time we dropped to the tree level, air combat was already in progress between our escorting fighters and the enemy. There were four times as many enemy planes as Japanese, and they bore down mercilessly, seeking the two bombers. We made a quick turn of over ninety degrees to evade them. Watching the sky above and noticing an enemy plane charging in, the skipper tapped on the shoulder of the chief pilot and directed him to turn left or right.

The first plane turned to the right and the second to the left. The distance between us was increased.

After we had evaded the enemy fighters twice, I turned to the right side of the plane to see how the first plane was doing. What I saw was astounding! The first plane was staggering southward, just brushing the jungle top at reduced speed, emitting black smoke and flames. It was about 400 yards from us. I said to myself "My God." I could not think of anything else. I grabbed the shoulder of Staff Officer Muroi, pointed to the first plane, and said "Look at the Commander in Chief's plane!"

That was the last time I saw it. All this happened in about twenty seconds. Then our plane turned sharply again to avoid another enemy fighter, and we lost sight of the admiral's plane. But all we saw was a plume of black smoke rising up from the jungle, and we knew. Everything was over.

At that point Admiral Ugaki's plane emerged from the jungle and crossed the beach line toward the sea. Then a P-38 was after them, and Admiral Ugaki could feel the bullets hitting the bomber. Although his life was at risk, he could not help but feel admiration for the speed and agility of the enemy plane and the skill of its pilot. "His gunfire caught us splendidly, and bullets could be seen on both sides of the plane. He made many hits. Several of the people aboard had already been killed, including Staff Officer Muroi, whom I saw leaning on a table with his face down and arms outstretched."

The pilot tried to set the plane down on the water gently, but it was no use. It ditched at full speed, rolled over to the left, and cartwheeled. That was all Admiral Ugaki could remember. He was thrown from the pilot's seat and blacked out.

When he came to, he was floating on the surface. The fuselage of the plane had already gone down, and the right wing was standing up and burning. He could not see anyone at all. The admiral discovered that his right wrist was broken, but he found a wooden box, grabbed it for support, and swam toward shore. A crewman passed him, swimming rapidly, and would not stop. Ugaki saw four soldiers on the shore, and one of them came into the water and rescued him. In a little while he was taken to an army aid station and then later to a hospital.

That day a search plane confirmed the location of Yamamoto's plane, and search parties were sent into the jungle overland. The army team recovered the bodies. Admiral Yamamoto was found sitting in the pilot's seat, which had been wrenched loose and thrown out of the plane. He was strapped in, gripping his short samurai sword by the handle, his face composed, and, to the rescue team, looking almost alive and very dignified in death. A postmortem examination found two bullets, one in the lower jaw and one in the back, and the doctors concluded that he was killed instantly by gunfire.

Later, Ugaki learned that the enemy had been employing fighter formations of this type in that area for several days—a departure from their previous techniques. But no one had warned the party of the change. He believed they had suffered from bad luck, but he was wrong. Luck did not enter the matter at all.

The fact was that several days earlier, when the details of Admiral Yamamoto's planned morale-building trip were announced by radio, the long message had been picked up by an American radio station in the Aleutian Islands and sent to Pearl Harbor. There it was decoded by Admiral Nimitz's code experts, who had broken the Japanese naval code months earlier.

The news was taken to Admiral Nimitz, and he was asked what should be done. He conferred by message with Admiral Halsey, who suggested that Yamamoto be ambushed. But this was not the sort of decision that Admiral Nimitz felt able to make. He sent the word to Admiral King, who consulted with naval intelligence and got the same answer Nimitz had gotten from Halsey. But again, King did not feel it was his place to order the murder of an enemy commander, even in wartime, so he passed the buck to Secretary of the Navy Frank Knox. The secretary felt that this was indeed a matter of high policy and passed the buck to President Roosevelt. And so it was from President Roosevelt himself that Admiral Yamamoto received his death warrant.

A flight of P-38 fighters equipped with long-range gas tanks was laid on from Henderson Field. They flew to Ballale, intercepted the Japanese just as they were preparing to land, and shot them down in spite of the covering Japanese fighters. Thus was Admiral Yamamoto killed, the only commander on any side in World War II to be assassinated by the direct order of the chief of government of the enemy.

The body was burned there in the heat of the South Pacific, and the ashes were sent back to Japan in state aboard the destroyer *Yugumo*. In

Tokyo, the Emperor awarded Admiral Yamamoto the Grand Order of the Chrysanthemum, first class, and promoted him posthumously to the rank of fleet admiral.

The ashes were taken up to Tokyo by special train from Yokosuka, where it was met at the station by Yamamoto's widow and many dignitaries, including the Emperor's military aide. Then came a state funeral, after which the ashes were divided in two parts. One part was placed in the Tama cemetery in Tokyo and the other taken home to Nagaoka, where it was placed in the Yamamoto section of a small cemetery in the middle of the city with a marker two feet high.

The death of Admiral Yamamoto was a terrible shock to the people of Japan. To many, particularly in the navy, it marked the beginning of the end of the war. Some said that somehow, if Yamamoto had lived, he would have pulled the rabbit out of the hat and prevented Japan's ignominious defeat. Perhaps the Americans thought so too; Admiral Nimitz had often said that Yamamoto was the biggest danger he faced. In the end, events had conspired to put Yamamoto into the hands of his enemies, and they had reacted as men do in war. Thus went to his death a friend of America, a firm advocate of Japanese-American friendship, and a thoroughgoing opponent of the Pacific war who, by a quirk of fate, had ended up becoming Japan's chief instrument of battle.

No one will ever know what impelled all these American leaders to order Yamamoto's assassination. Later they had second thoughts, because they had revealed the fact that they had broken the Japanese naval code, a fact invaluable particularly to the American submarine commands, which used information regularly to find Japanese shipping. Halsey virtually panicked, ordered all correspondents to keep quiet, and shipped all the pilots involved out of the Pacific.

Even so, Halsey failed. An Australian newsreel man got home from Guadalcanal, broke his word, and broke the story. It appeared in the neutral press and was picked up by the Japanese in Argentina. The Americans were very lucky, however. The Imperial General Staff had the answer, but they found it impossible to believe. Even Admiral Ugaki, when it was suggested to him that the codes might have been broken, said it was patently impossible. Thus the Americans were saved from the consequences of their own rash actions, and no harm was done to their cause.

But why did the Americans make so dangerous and foolish a move to "get" one man? It may be that they feared him, but there is another possible explanation. At the beginning of the war, it was revealed that Admiral Yamamoto had written a letter to a right winger who had been complaining about his "pro-Americanism." Employing the sarcasm of which he was a master, he had said that the only way the Japanese were going to win a war with America was to go to the White House and dictate the terms of the peace. The right wing press had gotten hold of this letter and had perverted it to indicate that Yamamoto intended to dictate the terms of peace from the White House, and this had infuriated many Americans.

The Japanese have still another explanation for the assassination: Many of them believed it was "revenge" for the Japanese attack on Pearl Harbor, and still do. The secret died with President Roosevelt, and so the speculation may go on and on. But one thing was certain, and all the world knew it when it happened: In killing Admiral Yamamoto, the Americans had rid themselves of their single most effective enemy in Japan.

ACKNOWLEDGMENTS

I am much indebted to Seiichi Soeda, media coordinator of the Japan Foreign Press Center in Tokyo, for arranging parts of my 1987 trip around Japan to see the haunts of Admiral Yamamoto. Through his help I visited Kagoshima, the old fleet base where the Pearl Harbor attack was planned, and Nagaoka City, in Niigata Prefecture, where Admiral Yamamoto grew up. Previously I had visited the Eta Jima Naval Academy and gone through its museum, which has much memorabilia relating to Admiral Yamamoto. I also visited the naval museum at Sasebo and the museum at the Yasukuni Shrine, which also has materials pertaining to Admiral Yamamoto.

For translation and interpretation I am indebted to Yoko Asakawa, Hiroko Hattori, and Itsuko Sakai, as well as to Mr. Soeda, who filled in once or twice.

Admiral Zenjiro Hoshima, now in his mid-nineties, told me a good deal about Admiral Yamamoto, under whom he had served during the war and earlier in the Navy Ministry. The Buddhist priest Zengan Hashimoto of Nagaoka told me many stories about Yamamoto's visits to his old home town and his affection for everything pertaining to Niigata. Atsuo Ohnishi, principal of Nagaoka High School, and half a dozen members of his staff showed me around the school and their museum, and Principal Ohnishi gave me some prepared materials which he had kindly translated into English for me. He also told me about the school spirit and the origins of

251

the system under which it operates, unique in Japan as an example of student-teacher cooperation and respect. Mr. Ohnishi also went far beyond the call of duty, giving up part of his Kyoto holiday to greet me in Nagaoka.

Seizaburo Hiura, the mayor of Nagaoka City, and his staff were extremely helpful in many ways, including a tour of Yamamoto Park and several museums dedicated to the admiral's memory. I am particularly indebted to Akio Inagawa, who spent three days driving me and my interpreter around Nagaoka. We were taken everywhere that had any connection with the admiral, including his favorite restaurant on a hilltop outside town, where he loved to go and eat a certain smoked fish dish.

Masataka Chihaya, a former Imperial Navy officer, kindly supplied me with the annotated secret diary of Vice Admiral Matome Ugahi, Yamamoto's chief of staff. Captain Shin Itonaga of the National Institute for Defense Studies spent part of a day informing me about several matters. Kenji Koyama, specialist in World War II history at the National Institute for Defense Studies prepared much information for me. I am also indebted to several librarians at the Japanese Defense Agency library and the National (Diet) Library in Tokyo.

In Sasebo I wanted to interview Masako Tsurushima, one of the geisha who was extremely close to Yamamoto, but I discovered that she had moved way to the south and was living in seclusion. The new proprietors of the Togo restaurant were very kind to show me around what had been one of Yamamoto's favorite haunts and to point out an example of his calligraphy that hangs above the front doorway.

In the beginning, perhaps impelled by instinct from my journalistic youth, I was very much interested in Yamamoto's love life. Several years ago Masako Tsurishima published a number of Yamamoto's love letters, which created an enormous stir in Japan. But as I went along and read Hiroyuki Agawa's biography of Yamamoto (published in the United States under the title *The Reluctant Admiral*), I realized that it was possible to fall into a trap that would lead me to emphasizing Yamamoto's loves, inevitably at the expense of his importance as a military man and political personality. I was also aware of the Yamamoto family's deep antipathy to any of that sort of publicity. Therefore, ultimately, I did not deal with the women in Yamamoto's life except peripherally.

I am, as always, totally indebted to my wife, Olga, for her unswerving loyalty and patience during my absences in Japan, as well as for research work and editing of my manuscript.

NOTES

1. Crossroads

Part of the material for this chapter came from my long interview with Vice Admiral Zenshiro Hoshima in Tokyo in the summer of 1987. He had served under Admiral Yamamoto in the period 1936–1939, when Yamamoto was vice minister of the navy.

The tale of Yamamoto and the military policemen is from Eichi Sorimachi's biography. Sorimachi was a navy man and a friend of Admiral Yamamoto's. Virtually all the tales he has to tell are completely documented by the source and are usually written in first person by the source. Sorimachi was obviously an indefatigable interviewer. Biographer Agawa faults Sorimachi for painting too rosy a picture of Yamamoto. In his biography he adopted the "warts and all" approach, with a good deal of emphasis on the "warts" and enormous emphasis on the admiral's affairs with a number of geisha over the years. But the fact is that the geisha had nothing to do with the affairs of the Imperial Navy, except to provide recreation and meeting places, and that is easy to forget in the contemplation of these lovely women.

The story of Yamamoto's trip to join the fleet is from Agawa and Sorimachi. Sorimachi has published a number of Yamamoto's poems, most of which do not improve with translation. The political information about Japan's naval and military affairs comes from research done for my *Japan's War*. The account of the meeting in the Naval Ministry to discuss the Rome-Berlin-Tokyo alliance is from Sorimachi. Yamamoto's comments about death and the future come from a letter to his friend Hori.

2. The Boy from Nagaoka

The material about Nagaoka comes from interviews with various city officials and from an official book *Furusato Nagaoka no Ayumi*, which tells of the history and development of the city. The story of the Takano family is from various biographies of Yamamoto. The material about Yamamoto's native home comes from my observation. I visited the house, which has been preserved and turned into a city shrine, located in a little park that used to be the playground of young Yamamoto. The story of Torasaburo Kobayashi came to me from Mr. Ohnishi, the principal of Nagaoka High School.

I tried to trace the first name and life of Mr. Newall, the Christian missionary teacher who gave Yamamoto his start in the English language, but the American Bible Society was unable to find anything about him, which suggests that he was not a regular missionary but an independent teacher in Japan.

The stories of Isoroku's life in Nagaoka come from the school people and from the Sorimachi biography for the most part.

The material about Admiral Togo is from Georges Blond's biography.

3. Eta Jima

Much of the story of Yamamoto at Eta Jima comes from the Kamata book on Yamamoto's Naval Academy days. The story of his problems with his lineage comes from Sorimachi.

4. The Young Warrior

The material about the Russo-Japanese War is from *Japan's War* and from the Blond biography. The story of the battle of Tsushima is from Blond, and the story of Yamamoto's part comes largely from Sorimachi.

5. Young Officer

The material about Japan and the treaty of Portsmouth is from *Japan's War* and *Pacific Destiny*. The material about American racism is from *Asians in the West*.

Yamamoto's activities in that period are detailed in Sorimachi.

6. Moving Ahead

The material about Japan's conquests comes from *Nimitz and His Admirals* and *Japan's War*. The material about Yamamoto is from Sorimachi.

The material about my search for Yamamoto is from my own experience in Japan.

7. American Year

The story about Admiral McCollum came to me from my friend Dean W. Allard of the Navy Historical Center in Washington. The story of Yamamoto's adventures in the Western Hemisphere is from Sorimachi.

8. Kato vs. Kato

The material about the naval factions in Japan is from the Agawa biography. The material about the Washington Conference is from *The American Attitude*. The material about the Zaibatsu is from *Japan's War*.

9. Air Power

The story of Yamamoto at Kasumigaura is from Sorimachi.

10. Attaché

The story of Yamamoto's work in America is from the various biographies. All the tales in Sorimachi are told in the words of the participants. All the biographers make much of Yamamoto's recommendation to young men to read Sandburg's biography of Lincoln. The material about American restrictions on Orientals is from *Asians in the West*.

11. Ship Captain

Sorimachi tells the stories of Yamamoto in the wardroom and of the loss of the entire strike force of the *Akagi* on that stormy day at sea.

12. The London Naval Conference of 1930

The material about Japan's economy is from *Japan's War*. The material about Hirohito is from *Fifty Years of Light and Dark*. The stories of the London Conference are from Sorimachi and Agawa.

13. Politics or Aeronautics?

The stories of Tokyo after the London Conference are from Sorimachi and *Fifty Years of Light and Dark*. The material about the political situation in

Japan is from *Japan's War*, as is the tale of the shooting of Prime Minister Hamaguchi. The story of Admiral Yamashita is from Sorimachi.

14. The Compleat Admiral

The stories about Yamamoto and the *Akagi* come from various sources. Yoshitake Miwa was interviewed by Sorimachi and told the story of the attack group leader's sake party. He was also the source for the story about the stubborn flight leader who nearly burned up. The material about the seizure of Manchuria is from *Japan's War*.

15. London Failure

The material about the Japanese navy buildup comes from the research I did for *Japan's War*. The study of the "fleet faction's" rise is from Sorimachi. Agawa tells the story of Yamamoto's departure from Tokyo. The story of the London meetings is from all these sources and from *Japan's War*. The quotation from Yamamoto regarding Japan's rise is from Agawa.

16. Yamamoto and the Air Force

Most of the material collected for the discussion of Japanese naval techniques comes from research done for *Nimitz and His Admirals*. The material about the army and politics is from *Japan's War*, including the story of the "2–26 incident," as it was called in Japan. I also used *Fifty Years of Light and Dark* here. The story of Admiral Yonai's activities and his alliance with Admiral Inouye is from Sorimachi.

17. Target of the Right

The statistics about Japan's raw materials are from the *Encyclopaedia Britannica*. The discussion of the *tosei ha*'s rise to power is from *Japan's War*. The material about Koki Hirota is from *War Criminal*, Saburo Shiroyama's biography of Koki Hirota, published by Kodansha International in 1977.

It is hard to recall those days in the 1930s when Americans had so little regard for Japan's industrial ability and so much contempt for the Japanese ability to imitate others. Because of cottage industries at home and the demand abroad, the Japanese produced large quantities of cheap toys and other goods. It was true that they did name a town USA—but only in response to a jingoist American attitude calling on people to "Buy American—Buy Only Goods Made in USA."

As for Japanese "copying," the West gave Japan no credit for originality at a time when the Japanese were already producing some of the best optics in the world and excellent motorcars, planes, and tanks. The contempt of the West for things Oriental was blinding. I encountered it as a boy in Portland, Oregon.

The material about the "China incident" comes from *Japan's War*. The story using Yamamoto's earthy language is from Agawa. The story of the "Panay incident" is from research I did for the book *The Lonely Ships*, the story of the U.S. Asiatic Fleet, published by David McKay of New York in 1976. Shigeharu Enemoto's story is from Sorimachi.

18. Planning for Pearl Harbor

Much of this material comes from research done for *Japan's War* and from *Fifty Years of Light and Dark*, pages 91–93.

19. Year of Decision

Much of this material comes from *Sensoroku*, the secret diary kept by Admiral Matome Ugaki during the war. Admiral Ugaki was Yamamoto's chief of staff from 1941 until the latter's death in April of 1943. Imperial Japanese Naval Order Number One is from the Japanese Defense Agency's history of the Pacific War.

20. Waves of War

The early part of this chapter depends on the Ugaki diary. The story of Yamamoto's trip to Tokyo is from Sorimachi. The account of the meeting with Emperor Hirohito is from the Defense Agency history. The note about Admiral Yamamoto's unexpected trip home is from Agawa. The agony of the waiting is from Ugaki's diary.

21. War on Three Fronts

The account of the Pearl Harbor attack is from the Defense Agency volume on Hawaii operations and from Gordon Prange's *At Dawn We Slept*, the account of the Pearl Harbor attack published by McGraw-Hill in 1981.

22. Success upon Success

Admiral Ugaki's diary was important for this chapter. The discussion of submarines is based on my studies for five books on the subject. The material about the Pacific raids is from *Nimitz and His Admirals* and the Ugaki diary. The material about Admiral Ohnishi is from my book *The Kamikazes*, published by Arbor House in 1983.

23. Early Warning

The material in the early part of the chapter is from the Ugaki diary and the Defense Agency volume on Guadalcanal. The material about the Doolittle raid is from *Nimitz and His Admirals* and the Ugaki diary. The material about the Battle of the Coral Sea comes from my own *Blue Skies and Blood*, published by Paul Eriksson in 1965.

24. Midway

The material about Midway is from the Japanese history of that battle, my Nimitz book, and the Ugaki diary. The story of Yamamoto's antipathy to "horn blowing" is from Agawa. The discussion of the intelligence operations concerning Midway is from the Holmes book. The discussion of Admiral Nagumo's failure to separate his ships is from the Ugaki diary.

25. Guadalcanal

The Japanese Defense Agency history volume on Guadalcanal was vital to this chapter. So was Ugaki's diary. The material about the attack on Guadalcanal and Tulagi comes from my *Guadalcanal*.

26. "No Matter the Sacrifice, Secure Guadalcanal"

Much of this material comes from research done for my own study of Guadalcanal, and from *Japan's War*. Admiral Ugaki's diary was very useful. So was the Guadalcanal volume of the Defense Agency history.

27. The Meat Grinder

The story of the resupply effort comes from the Defense Agency Guadalcanal volume for the most part, with an assist from Ugaki. The story of the sinking of the *I-33* is from Ugaki and the Defense Agency volume on the submarine war. The material about Admiral Yamamoto's health in this period is from Sorimachi. The quotations from Yamamoto about devotion to duty are from the Ugaki diary. The letter to Takeichi Hori is from the Agawa biography.

28. Toward Deadly Battle

This chapter depended largely on the Japanese Defense Agency history of the Guadalcanal battle and the Ugaki diary. The account of the marines' activity is from *Guadalcanal*. The tribulations of the Japanese fleet have not previously been appreciated in the West. Admiral Yamamoto won all the battles, as the Americans knew, but it was not enough; the Ugaki diary shows how control of the air, which passed gradually into the hands of the Allies, made all the difference at Guadalcanal and that the real reason for the Japanese defeat was the failure of the army leaders to appreciate the nature of the struggle and the nature of the American enemy in time to act with decision. It is true, as the Ugaki diary indicates and the Defense Agency history hints, that Admiral Nagumo's failure to obey his orders in spirit cost the Japanese dear, but this was not the key point.

29. Decision at Guadalcanal

The Ugaki diary was central to this chapter. The Defense Agency history gives all the statistics of Japanese fuel and ammunition consumption for the period. The American side of the story is from the marine records, as used in the book *Guadalcanal*. The story of the premature Japanese army announcement of victory and the subsequent failure is from the Ugaki diary. The battle of Santa Cruz, in which the carrier *Hornet* was sunk, was undeniably a Japanese victory. Admiral Kinkaid was very wise to retreat, even though the disgrace of leaving the *Hornet* to the enemy was considerable. If Admiral Nagumo had been a little more aggressive, as the Ugaki diary shows, the Japanese also would have sunk the carrier *Enterprise*.

30. The Bitter End

The Ugaki diary indicates the degree to which Emperor Hirohito really controlled the war effort of the Japanese. He was truly the Supreme Commander, as it shows, exerting his influence to make the army come to grips with its problem. The burning quarrel between Admiral Yamamoto and Admiral Nagumo is indicated by all the Japanese sources—the Ugaki diary, the Agawa biography, and the Sorimachi biography in particular—but is hard to find in the Defense Agency history. The outcome of the Battle of Guadalcanal (naval), which the Americans won, did not seriously affect the outcome at Guadalcanal. What did affect the outcome was the failure of the navy to resupply the army forces on Guadalcanal, and that was partly because of the loss of the battleships at the Battle of Guadalcanal, as the Ugaki diary indicates. It was the problem of attrition. The Defense Agency history shows how the Eleventh Air Fleet was whittled down by constant attrition, the necessity of covering the Guadalcanal front and the New Guinea front at the same time. The account of supplies received in one shipment to Guadalcanal is from the Ugaki diary.

31. *"A Great Loss Sustained . . ."*

The account of Admiral Yamamoto's dealings with the army at Rabaul is from the Ugaki diary. The account of the Japanese on New Guinea is from my studies for *The Jungles of New Guinea*, to be published by Avon Books in 1989. The material about the Eleventh Air Fleet is from the Defense Agency history.

32. *Assassination of an Admiral*

Whenever I mention "assassination" in terms of the killing of Admiral Yamamoto, I run into a storm of criticism from gung ho American military people. But murder in war needs no justification, does it? The whole process is murder. On publication of *Japan's War*, in which I made the statement that Admiral Yamamoto was assassinated, I had several letters from angry American naval officers. I have not changed my views. When the Japanese translated Burke Davis's Book *Get Yamamoto*, they called it *Murder by Espionage*, the meaning being that the Americans used radio espionage to murder the admiral.

Here is the Japanese publisher's promotion blurb from the jacket of the book:

"1943, April 13. In the Pacific War battleground an American radio receiving station intercepted a Japanese radio message. Deciphering it with difficulty, they discovered important news: the commander in chief of the Japanese Combined Fleet Admiral Yamamoto's itinerary for an inspection tour.

"The Americans had already decided that Admiral Yamamoto was a unique person. The Japanese nation idolized him. Moreover he had sent out the Pearl Harbor attack. So, execute Yamamoto.

"Yamamoto was coming to a place not far from the American bases.

"Yamamoto's itinerary would take him around bases encircling Guadalcanal . . . so they sent the P-38s. . . ."

The material about the Japanese plans for 1943 in the South Pacific comes from the Defense Agency history. Admiral Ugaki's diary adds some sidelights on the I Go Operation that seemed so successful to the Japanese but was hardly noticed by the Americans.

The story of Yamamoto's last mission comes from Ugaki, the Defense Agency history, my own *Guadalcanal*, the Davis book, Sorimachi, and Agawa. Most important is a handwritten report made by one of the survivors, which is in the files of the Japanese naval history division in Tokyo. The story of Admiral Yamamoto's funeral is from the pages of *Asahi*, the *Japan Times*, and the Sorimachi biography.

BIBLIOGRAPHY

Published Works

Agawa, Hiroyuki. *Yamamoto Isoroku*. Tokyo: Shinzensha, 1969 (translated and published in English by Kodansha International in 1980).

Blond, Georges. *Admiral Togo*. New York: Macmillan, 1960.

Boei Senshishitsu (The Japanese Self-Defense Agency's 101-Volume History of the Pacific War).

―――. *Southeast Area Naval Operations, Guadalcanal, until Withdrawal. Guadalcanal, after Withdrawal.*

―――. *Hawaii Sakusen* (Hawaii Naval Operations).

―――. *Midowai Sakusen* (Midway Operations).

Davis, Burke. *Chosatsu* (Murder by Espionage), Admiral Yamamoto's Death, translated from Burke Davis, *Get Yamamoto*. Tokyo: Genshobo, 1969.

Holmes, W. J. *Double Edged Secrets*. Annapolis, Md.: Naval Institute Press, 1979.

Hoshina, Zenshiro, et al. *Dai Hei Yo Senso Hishi* (The Secret History of the Pacific War). Tokyo: Nihon Koku Bokyo Sha, 1987.

Hoyt, Edwin P. *Japan's War*. New York: McGraw-Hill, 1986.

―――. *Guadalcanal*. New York: Stein and Day, 1982.

―――. *The Glory of the Solomons*. New York: Stein and Day, 1981.

―――. *Nimitz and His Admirals*. New York: Weybright and Talley, 1968.

―――. *Pacific Destiny*. New York: W. W. Norton, 1980.

―――. *Asians in the West*. New York: Thomas Nelson, 1970.

―――. *The American Attitude*. New York: Abelard Schuman, 1968.

Kamata, Yoshiro. *Yamamoto Isoroku no Eta Jima Seikatsu* (Yamamoto's Life at Eta Jima, The Japanese Naval Academy). Tokyo: Genshobo, 1981.

Lehmann, Jean-Pierre. *The Image of Japan*. London: Allen & Unwin, 1978.

Mainichi Newspaper Staff. *Fifty Years of Light and Dark*. Tokyo: Mainichi Newspapers, 1975.

Matsushima, Keizo. *Yamamoto Isoroku*. Tokyo: Tonaji Shuppansha, 1953.

Nomura, Jitsu. *Rekishi no naka no nihon kaigun* (Inside History of the Japanese Navy). Tokyo: Hara Shobo, 1980.

Okamoto, Shumpei. *The Japanese Oligarchy and the Russo-Japanese War*. New York: Columbia University Press, 1970.

Sorimachi, Eiichi. *Ningen, Yamamoto Isoroku, Gensai no shogai*. Tokyo: Hikawado, 1970.

Togawa Yukio. *Yamamoto*. Tokyo: Kojinsha, 1973.

Ugaki, Matome. *Sensoroku*. Tokyo: Genshobo, 1960.

Watanabe, Ukuchirau. *Denshi, Yamamoto Gensui* (Biography of Admiral Yamamoto). Tokyo: Chikura Shobo, 1945.

Papers

Yamamoto letters, from the library of the Nagaoka High School, Nagaoka, Japan.

Account of the death of Admiral Yamamoto, from the Japanese Defense Agency library, Tokyo.

Biographies and notes on Yamamoto's life from the files of the Defense Agency Library, Tokyo.

Newspapers

Asahi Shimbun

Mainichi Shimbun (Nichi Nichi Shimbun)

The Japan Times

INDEX

263